Audible Difference

Languages for Intercultural Communication and Education
Editors: Michael Byram, *University of Durham, UK* and Alison Phipps, *University of Glasgow, UK*

The overall aim of this series is to publish books which will ultimately inform learning and teaching, but whose primary focus is on the analysis of intercultural relationships, whether in textual form or in people's experience. There will also be books which deal directly with pedagogy, with the relationships between language learning and cultural learning, between processes inside the classroom and beyond. They will all have in common a concern with the relationship between language and culture, and the development of intercultural communicative competence.

Other Books in the Series
Context and Culture in Language Teaching and Learning
  Michael Byram and Peter Grundy (eds)
Critical Citizens for an Intercultural World: Foreign Language Education as Cultural Politics
  Manuela Guilherme
Developing Intercultural Competence in Practice
  Michael Byram, Adam Nichols and David Stevens (eds)
How Different Are We? Spoken Discourse in Intercultural Communication
  Helen Fitzgerald
Intercultural Experience and Education
  Geof Alred, Michael Byram and Mike Fleming (eds)

Other Books of Interest
Effective Language Learning
  Suzanne Graham
Fluency and its Teaching
  Marie-Noelle Guillot
Foreign Language and Culture Learning from a Dialogic Perspective
  Carol Morgan and Albane Cain
The Good Language Learner
  N. Naiman, M. Fröhlich, H.H. Stern and A. Todesco
Identity and the English Language Learner
  Elaine Mellen Day
Language, Culture and Communication in Contemporary Europe
  Charlotte Hoffman (ed.)
Language Learners as Ethnographers
  Celia Roberts, Michael Byram, Ana Barro, Shirley Jordan and Brian Street
Language Teachers, Politics and Cultures
  Michael Byram and Karen Risager
Motivating Language Learners
  Gary N. Chambers
New Perspectives on Teaching and Learning Modern Languages
  Simon Green (ed.)
Target Language, Collaborative Learning and Autonomy
  Ernesto Macaro

Please contact us for the latest book information:
Multilingual Matters, Frankfurt Lodge, Clevedon Hall,
Victoria Road, Clevedon BS21 7HH, England
http://www.multilingual-matters.com

**LANGUAGES FOR INTERCULTURAL COMMUNICATION
AND EDUCATION 5**
Series Editors: Michael Byram and Alison Phipps

Audible Difference
ESL and Social Identity in Schools

Jennifer Miller

MULTILINGUAL MATTERS LTD
Clevedon • Buffalo • Toronto • Sydney

Library of Congress Cataloging in Publication Data
Miller, Jennifer
Audible Difference: ESL and Social Identity in Schools/Jennifer Miller.
Languages for Intercultural Communication and Education: 5
Includes bibliographical references and index.
1. English language–Study and teaching (Secondary)–Foreign speakers. 2. English
language–Study and teaching (Secondary)–Social aspects. 3. English language–
Spoken English–Study and teaching (Secondary) 4. English language–Study and
teaching (Secondary)–Australia. 5. Teenage immigrants–Australia–Social conditions.
6. Immigrants–Australia–Education (Secondary) 7. Identity (Psychology)–Australia.
8. Group identity–Australia. I. Title. II. Series.
PE1128.A2 M553 2003
428'.0071'2–dc21   2002015943

British Library Cataloguing in Publication Data
A catalogue entry for this book is available from the British Library.

ISBN 1-85359-642-6 (hbk)
ISBN 1-85359-641-8 (pbk)

Multilingual Matters Ltd
UK: Frankfurt Lodge, Clevedon Hall, Victoria Road, Clevedon BS21 7HH.
USA: UTP, 2250 Military Road, Tonawanda, NY 14150, USA.
Canada: UTP, 5201 Dufferin Street, North York, Ontario M3H 5T8, Canada.
Australia: Footprint Books, PO Box 418, Church Point, NSW 2103, Australia.

Typeset by Archetype-IT Ltd (http://www.archetype-it.com).
Printed and bound in Great Britain by the Cromwell Press Ltd.

Contents

Foreword

ALLAN LUKE
University of Queensland

The young women and men who speak about their lives, their languages and their education in *Audible Difference* are part of the large community of migrant second-language speakers in the schools of Brisbane, where Jenny Miller and I both live. Jenny Miller is a teacher, long-time colleague, and one of Queensland's most experienced, dedicated English as a Second Language teachers and teacher-educators. The story here is about their struggles and dilemmas, their pathways and their successes as they try to make their way through Australian schools and communities whose local economies and cultures are, like so many, in transition. That transition is in response not just to unprecedented linguistic and cultural diversity – if it were just that, it might be a much simpler issue, one which educational systems and governments have been working on throughout the postwar period. It has become more complex in the face of globalisation and its discontents, including a loss of historical White privilege in what have become communities of difference. Not only do these new contexts surround and inundate traditional 'deficit' thinking about educational achievement, but they also call into question many of the axioms of 'multiculturalism' and 'multilingualism' that have guided schools for the past decades.

I write this in the aftermath of September 11; Australia's 'Tampa Incident', where refugees were turned away from the northern Australian coast; and, only a few weeks ago, the tragic events in Bali. It is a moment where 'learning to live together' in difference is back on the table for educators everywhere. It is a moment where the neo-liberal educational models of the last two decades suddenly look much more suspect – along with claims that schools were principally about the production of human capital, that deregulated markets would solve educational inequality, and that concerns over racism and anti-racism, intercultural capital and communication, social justice and the ethics of community and citizenship had become subordinate issues in an inexorable crunching of numbers and measuring of system, teacher and student performance.

No doubt the responses of some systems will be a defensive nationalism, official monolingualism, a new educational fundamentalism around 'the basics', and calls for a core curricular monoculture. Yet if education systems in the North and West learn one thing from the events of the past year, it should be that we need to do a much better job of educating for, about, against, within and around globalised flows of capital, information/discourse and bodies; and that we and our students need to engage in a critical dialogue and debate about the causes, concomitants and consequences of these flows in our everyday lives and those of Others. Diversity in new conditions will require new vocabularies for talking about ourselves, our new found heterogeneity, blended identities, and hybrid practices.

It is also an opportunity for us to reconsider how we think about and frame issues of racial, cultural, and linguistic diversity. There are limits to the sensibility that Bob Dylan once described as 'pitying the poor immigrant', where we see our responsibility to second-language learners as ameliorative and compensatory. One of the clear lessons of *Audible Difference* is about the political and practical limitations of the assumption that equity and discrimination are principally matters of 'race' or 'language'. Working with and through these kids, Jenny Miller here shows us the complexity of their identity papers, the kinds of difference within difference that they use to engage with Australian schooling, workplaces and community lives. This work takes up key principles of second language acquisition from a critical ethnographic and sociological perspective.

I moved to Queensland from Canada in 1984, to live and work in the provincial city of Townsville. At the time, nobody would have associated this state with issues of multiculturalism and multilingualism. It was then dominated by rural and primary industries, and until the last ten years had a modern history of right wing, White triumphalist governments. Yet it is a place of Aboriginal and Torres Strait Islander lands and cultures, with the largest Indigenous population of any Australian state. Many indigenous children are second-language and dialect speakers. It has longstanding Chinese, Sikh, Italian, Greek, Vietnamese and Pacific Islander populations, those who provided rural industries with over a century of labour, technical expertise and community. In the time I have lived here, the old Queensland and the old Australia have changed. Though less than the national average of almost 30%, about 18% of Queensland school age children are second-language speakers. Though they vary from recent waves of refugees from Eastern Europe, the Middle East and the Horn of Africa,

Vietnamese migrants from the 1970s and 80s, to middle-class children from the Chinese Diasporas of Southeast Asia – their overall achievement is a decile plus behind mainstream achievement in English language literacy and numeracy. Where poverty intersects with second language and recent migration, achievement levels dip even further.

As elsewhere, a key element of the overall social problem is systematic discrimination against difference. Racism is an ensemble of social practices and technologies by which dominant classes and groups assert economic, social and interpersonal power against subordinate groups, often on the basis of phenotypical appearance. It takes many practical forms: as a form of exclusionary material, physical partitioning of space; as discourse practice, and as a form of social imaginary and shared cognition. In the past decade, critical discourse analyses published in journals like *Discourse and Society* have documented the discourse strategies and practices of racialisation and racism – from particular namings and social categorisations, to media reports, to instances of face-to-face symbolic violence.

Yet the experience of discrimination isn't solely on the basis of race or appearance, as Jenny Miller demonstrates. And this work moves towards a broader sociological template for explaining how the 'cards' of race, gender, and social class are played out – via linguistic competence, accent and 'audibility' – but also through the bodily performance that language always entails. Pierre Bourdieu (1991) puts it this way: 'the practical evaluation of the symbolic relation of power that determines the criteria of evaluation prevailing in the market concerned takes into account the specifically linguistic properties of discourse only in so far as they express the social authority and social consequence of those who utter them' (p. 71). In this explanation, the 'character of the voice ... a durable disposition of the vocal apparatus ... is one of the most powerful of all social markets', working to constitute authority in relation to 'overtly social qualities such as aristocratic and academic titles; clothing ... institutional attributes' and so forth. Beyond its locutionary content, speech is a bodily performance of identity, a production of the self as 'object' – as Miller argues, as 'audible' and observable entity. In the same way as the (racialised) body produces speech – accented speech racialises its own production and produces its speakers.

The claim that Jenny Miller makes so clearly here is that sound/speech/audible code is a marker that, for many of these students, may 'trump' the card of race, or at least be played in tandem with that card and those of gender, generation, and other forms of identity. We see instance after instance, in classrooms, in accounts of everyday service transactions and schoolyard conversations, where accent and audibility is taken as a marker of 'distinction' and 'class', authority and power. But the question of how recognition and marginalisation gets enacted is always a question of value, value which is played out in linguistic markets. This question is rigorously addressed in this study. Given the extensive work on the spread of English as cultural capital and commodity, its branded, prestige and now commercial varieties, we can begin to speak of a political economy of speech and speakers, where accent, audibility and bodily performance constitute both value and risk.

In *Audible Difference* Jenny Miller offers no simple solution, but a powerful message for language teachers and teacher-educators: to work in ways that enable these students to traverse new and risky life pathways through the social fields of these new economies and cultures, requires something more than the standard-issue disciplinary toolkit of ESL qualifications – an understanding of linguistic structures; psychological, psycholinguistic and sociolinguistic theories of language acquisition and use; and a fair dose of humanist commitment. This just won't do any longer. To work with these kids we need a much stronger sociological analysis of the complexities of power and capital in the everyday institutions and communities where they live and work – an analysis of the dynamics of who gets counted in, on what grounds and sounds and signs of difference, and with what consequences. Indeed, isn't this precisely what they'll need as critical citizens?

References

Bourdieu, P. (1991) *Language and Symbolic Power*. Cambridge: Polity Press.

Author's Preface

I have always attached importance to the sound of people's voices, to the act of speaking and to the ability to speak in a way that is acknowledged by others. *Voice* as a unique and identifying feature can be used reliably by forensic science to determine a person's identity, but the 'knowability' of voice is also part of everyday life. One word on the phone, one 'hello' – and even after long periods of silence we know who is speaking. Students enact merciless parodies of their teachers' voices and language; public figures must be mindful that their voices command attention; and while there are film stars who are not fashionably beautiful, there are precious few outside of comedy genres who have a grating and unpleasant voice. Why is the way we sound so important, whether there is an audience of one, or of thousands?

Since adolescence, I have felt intuitively that the way people speak had a lot to do with who they are recognised to be and how they are treated. In the past, I was not thinking in terms of self-representation, but in my mind, identity and speaking were inextricable. This is not to imply that someone physically unable to speak has no recognisable identity – for they find a voice by other means, just as writers articulate identities with words on the page. Yet for people in social situations, speaking is the way to express not just what they have to say but who they are, whom they are with, what they are doing, and how they wish to be heard. Speaking provides a vital means of participation, involving others, and requiring the collaboration of others, our hearers and coparticipants in conversation or activity. It is through language that we represent and negotiate our identities to others. We also recognise others as members of 'our group', through hearing them speak, and possibly identifying with what we are hearing. The process involves far more than literally speaking the same language (although that helps). We must also share the discourse in use, what Gee (1996: 127) has called 'ways of being in the world, or forms of life'. Without this, there can be no collaboration or negotiation. The great travel writer Paul Theroux recounts the agonising and silencing experience of being trapped in a tourist group with whom he shared the English language, but nothing else. They did not recognise him. When he had a chance meeting with a sympathetic woman at the theatre on a stopover in Paris, he poured out the story of the painful tour group. He writes,

> It did me a lot of good to tell her these things, because I had been so secretive on the tour it was like being invisible. It certainly wasn't much fun to be the dim, dull fellow in the mackintosh, keeping out of every conversation. Keeping quiet gave me chest pains. I longed to lecture them about the Middle East, and if they gave me half a chance on the subject of travel I could seize their wrists like the Ancient Mariner and a tale unfold. (Theroux, 1989: 18)

Not only was his identity unknown and unavailable to the group, he felt invisible, and suffered viscerally from his (self-imposed) silencing. The relief at being able to represent himself as himself to the woman was palpable. So what happens when someone has even less choice and opportunity to speak than Theroux on this trip? What happens when you do not even share the language of those around you?

In conceptualising the study, I began by questioning how one represents identity when suddenly cut off from the primary communicative and sense-making resource, one's first language. To explain this point further, consider the following scenario.

> You are a fifteen year old female student named Kate, a high achiever at school, an aspiring singer and talented pianist. You have a heavy schedule of school assignments, music lessons and performance rehearsals, and you are also a keen writer, debater and voracious reader of both pulp fiction and the works of Jane Austen and the Brontës. In addition to these activities, you maintain a complex social network of girlfriends from several schools. School dances, city markets, hanging out in the mall, teen magazines, phone calls, movies, pop music, one or two TV soaps, junk food and a particular style of grunge-related fashion are vital to your existence. Family networks are also important, though complex, due to distance and divorce. You are insightful about people, and interested in psychology, often maintaining a cool analytical approach to problems and relationships. At only 15, you have a great deal of knowledge and considerable understandings about people, the world and yourself. This is communicated to all who have dealings with you through the medium of language, in which your many competencies, and some insecurities, are expressed. You are aware, without knowing the academic terms, of a range of discourses and genres appropriate to different situations – as shown in

your talk with parents, brother, teachers, close friends and cooler acquaintances.

Through some serious personal or political upheaval, you find yourself in a new country. You do not speak the language. What of the above are you able to represent to others? Who are you, if you are unable to meaningfully communicate your sense of self to others?

I want to look at the implications of the phrase, 'You do not speak the language' in this book. For many linguistic minority students in anglophone Australia, speaking English and being heard to be doing so is an ongoing challenge, requiring continuous risk-taking and uneven success. As one Japanese student confided to me about her Australian peers, 'It is difficult to talk to them – children speak without mercy.' It will be suggested in the study presented here that being audible to others is critical if one is to belong, as social identity hinges so firmly on our use of language that the self seems obliterated when we are unable to voice it. A simple experiment to validate this claim is to remain silent in a group social interaction where you would normally be highly verbal, particularly if strangers are present. Or stand in the midst of a chattering group who are not speaking your language. To what extent can you be represented, heard and known, if you cannot represent yourself by speaking? The situation is also familiar to travellers in foreign countries, although there are important differences between tourism and immigration. Where good will exists, we may be left smiling and shrugging. Where there is no good will, we may be assumed somehow deficient, or worse. In fact there is much at stake, and the recent literature on identity and language use from a sociocultural perspective has shown that different values are attached to varieties of language and indeed to the hybridised identities which are a fact of life in these times.

My own hybridised identity is part of the complexity of the study I explore in this book. When I began the project, I had taught French, German, English, and English as a Second Language in Australian high schools for 15 years, and English as a Foreign Language in France and Canada for three years. For several years I had lectured in second language acquisition and pedagogy. I therefore came to the job of university researcher with certain predispositions about how languages are learned and taught, and about proficiency, communicative competence and the 'good language learner'. The methodological challenge for me was to retain a space for empirical questions about language acquisition, while opening up newer, more theoretical concerns of language use, identity and representation. In my case, balancing academic concerns and rigour with the eye, ear and voice of a teacher who has spent most of her working life in school classrooms was inevitably part of the research and writing process. I claim no privileged perspective, but write as a practitioner informed with theory and research rather than as an academic who has spent time in schools. At times the position feels precarious, and I welcome the reader to add his/her own interpretive language to the multi- voiced and interdisciplinary exploration of this volume.

Jenny Miller

Acknowledgements

During the research and writing of this book, numerous people provided me with a sense of community and support. Throughout the study presented here, I was wonderfully supported by Carolyn Baker and Allan Luke. Carolyn was unfailingly generous with her time, and I benefited greatly from her astute analytical mind, her love of data, her practical orientation, and her meticulous reading. Allan pointed me towards literature and theory which enriched both my thinking and the writing process. I thank colleagues and friends in the School of Education at Queensland University for their suggestions, their collegiality, their humour, and their belief, and also Bonny Norton, Aneta Pavlenko and Tara Goldstein for their encouragement.

I am indebted also to the original reviewers for Multilingual Matters, but particularly to my editor Mike Byram, whose prompt, painstaking and constructive feedback on the manuscript helped bring this book to fruition. His suggestions were invaluable.

Like all academic authors, I also owe an immense debt to the many researchers and writers whose work I have read, and drawn upon, work which threw light on the data of the study and focused my own reflection. A special thanks to my family and friends, whose love and support provided both encouragement and much-needed diversion.

Finally I wish to thank the students and teachers who welcomed me into their classrooms, and the young immigrant students who agreed to participate in the study, and to speak with me. This is the story of their voices.

Permissions

The author and publishers would like to thank the following for permission to reproduce copyright material: *Issues in Applied Linguistics* for the diagram by Celce-Murcia, M., Dörnyei, Z. and Thurrell, S. in their article, Communicative Competence: A Pedagogically Motivated Model with Content Specifications, 1995; and Queensland University Press for the poem extract by komninos in his self- titled volume, *komninos*, 1991.

Chapter 1

Speaking and Identity

Hank:	*So, are ya Chinese or Japanese?*
Kan:	*I live in California last twenty year but, ah, first come from Laos.*
Hank:	*Huh?*
Kan:	*Laos. We're Laotian.*
Hank:	*The ocean? What ocean?*
Kan:	*We are Laotian, from Laos stupid. It's a landlocked country in southeast Asia, between Vietnam and Thailand, OK? Population 4.7 million.*
	[pause]
Hank:	*So, are ya Chinese or Japanese?*

(*King of the Hill*, Twentieth Century Fox, 1997)

Introduction

In the scene depicted above in the animated TV series *King of the Hill*, the role of Hank should be read with a thick southern US drawl. Kan, speaking with a light Cambodian accent, is incomprehensible to Hank, who in the context of the episode represents the dominant discourse. Hank has two categories for Asians – Chinese and Japanese – and is unable to hear anything different. Kan is Laotian, and is neither understood nor *heard*. Part of the humour in the scene is that Hank's southern American accent renders his English almost incomprehensible to many English-speaking viewers. The scene, which throws into relief the problem of speaking and identity, derives its humour from a situation familiar to many linguistic minority speakers, a situation which is often not funny at all.

This book is about the relationship between speaking English as a second language and the representation of identity. It is based on an empirical study of the acquisition and use of spoken English by immigrant students in Australian high schools, along with the ways in which these students represented their social identities. The book seeks to draw together understandings from the fields of second language acquisition, sociocultural and discourse theory and insights from studies of identity.

The approach taken is interdisciplinary, but the underlying theoretical position of the volume is that identities are discursively constructed and embedded within social practices and broader ideological frameworks. While second language acquisition remains a central issue, it will be tied to identity representation, discourse and discursive resources, power, difference and discrimination.

Recent literature has shown that identity is fluid, contextually realised and constantly shifting (Hall, 1996; McRobbie, 1996; Pavlenko & Blackledge, in press). What is more, the strong ties between identity and language use are well established in linguistic research (see Cummins, 1995; Gee, 1996; Hymes, 1996; Le Page & Tabouret-Keller, 1985; Norton, 2000). When students and their families arrive in Australia with little or no knowledge of English, identity seems tightly bound to the first language. It is as if the students' identity is 'in Bosnian', 'in Samoan', 'in Mandarin' or 'in Spanish'. Even when the move to Australia was one of choice, rather than the result of violence or war, the rupture with all known social networks and settings may be definitive. Some may find a strong first language community, where Taiwanese, Somali, Bosnian or Vietnamese languages and cultures remain the primary resources for daily life. However, for most high school students from non-English speaking backgrounds (NESB), establishing new networks and finding a place and a voice in new settings is part of the linguistic and therefore social identity work which must be done, and learning and speaking English is a vital part of this process.

Schools are sites where ethnicity, culture, language use and the representation of identity are played out. For immigrant students, this necessitates a renegotiation of social identity within multilingual contexts. It will be seen that this renegotiation is not conducted on a level playing field, but is tied to ideological, pedagogical and social practices which implicate power. Giroux (1992: 203) states that schools have silenced 'the voices of subordinate groups whose primary language is not English and whose cultural capital is either marginalized or denigrated by the dominant culture of schooling'. It is hoped that the research presented in this book will go part of the way in explaining how this happens.

There were four main reasons for undertaking this study. First, few studies have integrated the study of second language acquisition (SLA) in school contexts and social identity. Second, while there is a great deal of research relating to second language acquisition phenomena and outcomes, much of it has been based on testing and experimental settings (see Ellis, 1994). In his study of cross-cultural interaction between youths from south Asia and the Caribbean in London, Rampton (1995) stresses that with few exceptions, SLA research has focused on the acquisition of linguistic structures rather than on issues of social language use. This study is based on the students' spoken discourse, but does not attempt to measure their spoken proficiency as such. It therefore provides understandings about linguistic minority students of a different kind than that derived from ESL testing or proficiency ratings. Rampton (1995: 323) warns that in much educational research and debate, students figure 'as objects of concern rather than as potential partners in dialogue'. He adds that the sociolinguistic insights of minority pupils themselves are often underestimated or missing. In the case studies presented here, the students' own insights into their language learning and language use provide the core data.

Third, with the emergence of globalisation and multicultural, multilingual nation states, and rapidly changing demographic profiles in schools, there is a recognised need for studies that provide insight into the ways in which linguistic and cultural minority students negotiate and represent identity, and are themselves constructed through discourse (Luke, 1998). Such insights have the potential to inform pedagogy, curriculum and educational administration, and have implications for our understandings of educational processes, practices and outcomes. While the context of the research presented here is Australian, it has implications for other modern nation states where there are large numbers of immigrants and refugees. It has also been argued that all educators need to address the question of 'how the world is experienced, mediated, and produced by students' (McLaren, 1994: 224). And there is an increasing recognition of the need for a pedagogy which takes account of the student's expertise and identities (Cummins, 2000; Leung et al., 1997; Pennycook, 2001). An emphasis on social practices may also allow educators to interrogate their own roles and activities in shaping the social world shared with their students (Rampton, 1995).

The fourth rationale stems from my own background in ESL teaching, and my desire to understand more about how immigrant students shape and are shaped by their language use and experiences at school. I knew that some students seem to breeze through, learning English, finding friends and acquiring mainstream discourses, culture and social membership in a matter of months, while others struggle for years, remaining outside the primary discourses and mainstream membership. I wanted to understand more about how this occurred.

Language and Self-representation

Within the fields of sociolinguistics, discourse analysis, ethnography of communication and pragmatics, there is an increasing awareness that language use is a form of self-representation, which implicates social identities, the values which attach to particular written and spoken texts, and therefore the links between discourse and power in any social context. Linguistic minority students must achieve self-representation in the dominant discourses of the mainstream language if they are to participate in mainstream social and academic contexts, renegotiate their identities in new places, and accrue the necessary symbolic capital to successfully integrate into school and the wider society.

For linguistic minority students entering sites in a dominant culture, proficiency in the dominant language is therefore essential, as it is the primary resource for sense-making, and for being seen and heard to make sense (Trueba, 1989). This 'being seen and heard' is done within specific social contexts or sites, which may allow, or constrain the way students make sense of and with language, and of social situations, themselves and others. Social interactions and contexts are therefore critical to the work of language acquisition and to identity representation. Recent research suggests some students have insufficient access to such interaction, and thus opportunities to practise and learn (Norton & Toohey, 2001; Sharkey & Layzer, 2000). The more isolated the student is from the dominant language group, the more difficult this work must be. Those in schools with large numbers of students from Chinese-speaking backgrounds for example, may speak Mandarin or Cantonese almost exclusively. Functioning within a tight network of first (non-dominant) language speakers has real consequences for many of these students, whose identity work using English may be further complicated, delayed, or not even a priority (see Goldstein, 1997).

The consideration of social contexts, language use and identity representation is made more complex by two different, but related factors. To use an Australian example, it has been argued by sociologists that multiculturalism has moved Australia beyond the assimilationist model, and towards acceptance, even celebration, of ethnic diversity (Bottomly, 1997; Castles *et al.*, 1992). Yet Australian schooling is not only primarily assimilationist in its influence on ethnic minorities, but systematically disregards the cultures of minority groups (Wyn & White, 1997). The second point relates quite directly to language use. Where the first language of the student goes unrecognised, untapped and undeveloped, and where proficiency in English is or remains very limited, identity work in the public arena may be seriously affected. Working from the bilingual French/English context in Canada, Cummins and Swain (1986: 101) make this point clearly in the following terms, 'To be told, whether directly or indirectly, explicitly or implicitly, that your language and the language of your parents, of your home and of your friends is non-functional in school is to negate your sense of self'. Although a strong version of this particular argument, Cummins and Swain make a good case not just for maintaining the home language, but for continuing education in the first language, as important for cognitive and identity work. However, whether this is realistic in schools where up to 50 ethnic minority groups use 30 different languages, remains open to question. This is the case in many metropolitan Australian schools.

In regard to literate practice, Baker and Luke (1991: 261) claim that 'to not have acquired the look of a reader is a liability'. The 'look' is one way the student represents the identity of 'reader'. I will argue in this volume, that for language minority students, not to have acquired the sound of a speaker of English is equally a liability. This sound entails not just phonological skills and accent, but the use of the many discursive features that underlie any socially contextualised communicative interaction. The title of the book itself suggests that difference can be audible, rather than, or as well as visible. Control over the use of the English language opens up, but does not guarantee, the possibilities of self-representation, social interaction, academic success and aspects of the dominant culture, such as education and training, work, friends, and leisure pursuits. For high school students, in addition to using English in functional and social situations, acquiring the discourses of academic or school English is a matter of priority for the integration process and for success in the mainstream. It has been noted that immigrant students often gain 'peer appropriate grammatical skills, at least in the oral modality', provided there has been frequent and appropriate interaction in the second language (Cummins & Swain, 1986: 211). This proviso, it will be argued, is far from being a given in some schools. This study focuses on the complex practical activity of speaking, since this relates so directly to issues of self-representation, social interaction, and identity, as well as providing the primary means for adapting to a new social and cultural setting. The development of written English, though present in the study, is not a primary focus.

It seems likely that linguistic and sociocultural learnings occur in tandem, and are mutually facilitating, as meanings and understandings are learned and shared, and identities are represented and negotiated. The process involves the ability to represent one's identity in the new language, to be heard, understood and legitimated as a speaker and a social member. The burden of learning English, of communication, of adjustment to new circumstances, and of negotiation tends to be assigned fully to the linguistic minority student, particularly in mainstream schools. As Freeman (1995) explains in her study of the Oyster Bilingual School in Washington, DC, many reception and transitional programmes 'implicitly equate equal educational opportunity with English language proficiency. The student's native language is thus viewed as a problem to be overcome' (p. 44). This locates the problem and the solution firmly with the student. Freeman stresses that it is the minority student who must change, by acquiring

English, 'so that the school can treat all students equally according to language majority norms' (p. 46). In this way the responsibility of the programmes and practices to cater for diversity is deflected onto the minority students themselves. There is an alternative position, namely that those who are on the hearing side of the talk are part of the process of representation, and thus share the responsibility for the development of proficiency in English and the academic success of minority students. I will theorise and develop this line of reasoning more fully in Chapter 2. For now, it should be noted that language acquisition and use are critical parts of self-representation, but they are contingent on social practices and ideological positions. Luke *et al.* (1990: 30) remind us that language education in general is like an exclusive club, in which 'to become a member, one has to qualify, but the only way to obtain the necessary qualifications is through membership of the club'. To capture some of the complexity of the conditions and practices at work in this paradox, it is important to understand that language use involves sets of discursive practices which position speakers and hearers in particular ways. Such positioning is part of the politics of speaking (see Miller, in press). As an example, here is a piece by a Greek Australian performance poet, which provides some insight into the role and the importance of audibility, and the huge challenge it can represent for language minority speakers.

nobody calls me a wog, anymore

> nobody calls me a wog, anymore
> i'm respected as an Australian
> an australian writer
> a poet
> but
> it didn't just happen
> i had to assert myself
> as an Australian
> as an artist
> stand up and scream it
> point the finger accusingly
> thump my fist demandingly
> assert my identity
> say, 'hey!'
> 'aus tra li a!'
> 'look at me!'
> 'whether you like it or not
> i am one of you.'   komninos (1991)

The identity assigned to komninos was 'wog' – with its connotations of outsider, foreigner, immigrant. To obtain recognition as a person, the writer had to 'stand up and scream it', shout his claim to an identity. At the end of the poem, komninos wrote 'look at me'. But his poem is about speaking and what it takes to be heard. It could just as easily have ended with a plea to be 'listened to', rather than seen.

Discourse as a marker of inclusion, exclusion and difference

The problem of identity continually surfaces in any attempt to explore the relationship between speakers and discursive practices. Although we live in multilingual, culturally diverse, hybridised societies, in everyday life it is still common to experience dissonant perceptions about the way a person looks (visible difference) and the way a person sounds (audible difference). A Korean American visitor to Australia recently commented, 'Wow! I still can't believe it when Asian people speak with broad Australian accents.' She had lived with a similar phenomenon all her life, but just not thought about it. So when people open their mouths, listeners sometimes do a double-take. At school, a student may look Chinese, but speak broad Australian English; another may look like an Anglo-Australian, but be Croatian and speak no English at all. In multiethnic and multilingual classrooms, this is frequently a source of false assumptions, misunderstandings and embarrassment. Once someone speaks, the discourse marks the person as an insider or outsider. On hearing, hearers often have to rapidly and radically revise their perception based on what was initially seen. It is also worth noting that difference may also be negatively or positively valued within any social field. Accent is an obvious example here, but difference might also include other pragmatic, sociolinguistic and discourse features.

It is now widely accepted that identity is discursively constructed, that is, through speaking and hearing practices (Hymes, 1996; Pavlenko & Blackledge, in press; Ting-Toomey, 1999). The ramifications of this are widely represented in the literature. Discourse as a marker of inclusion, exclusion and difference finds perhaps its clearest expression in the current vast literature on critical discourse analysis (Caldas-Coulthard & Coulthard, 1996; Fairclough, 1989; van Dijk, 1997a) and critical applied linguistics (Pennycook, 2001). Applied critical discourse analysis shows how texts contribute to the marginalisation of minority groups (see for example, Riggins, 1997). A central focus of this body of work is that discourse, identity and social power are integrally related, and that marginalised groups, who are in many cases easily identifiable through visible difference, are most likely to be disempowered by dominant discourses. Difference, Giroux (1990) suggests, is constructed through practices that label, legitimate, marginalise or exclude the cultural capital and voices of subordinate groups in society. The exclusion of certain voices may have serious repercussions for the speakers, and their identities. Lippi-Green (1997: 17) writes, 'the evaluation of language effectiveness – while sometimes quite relevant – is often a covert way of judging not the delivery of the message, but the social identity of the messenger'.

Judgements about identity and discourse may also intersect with issues of race, class, gender and socioeconomic status. There are, quite clearly, different kinds of capital. But for many immigrants and refugees, visible and linguistic differences constitute grounds for discrimination. Highlighting the importance of visible difference, Luke and Luke (1998: 732), in their study of interracial families, argue for a reinstatement of race as an analytic category, as a 'core and defining cultural category that structures and shapes everyday motivations and common sense, social practices and perceptions'. May (2001) also suggests that ethnicity is more than a social construct, especially where ethnic categories are imposed by others. However, I want to argue that spoken discourse further shapes the lived experiences of minority students in schools, and provides the basis for another layer of discriminatory practices. Clearly there is much empirical research which documents discrimination based on visible difference. In Australia following the 11 September 2001 terrorist attacks in the United States, and in the subsequent controversy over Afghani and Iraqi asylum seekers arriving in Australia via Indonesia, Islamic citizens in traditional dress or of middle-Eastern appearance were the targets of racist attacks, both in society at large and occasionally in schools. This was all about how you look, and not about how you sound. My point is that in general, these were random acts of racism, attacks committed in the absence of meaningful interaction, and mostly against 'strangers'. In multilingual school contexts, the representation and negotiation of identity is far more complex. Before looking more closely at the school context and the study itself, I shall provide a brief contextual background.

The Australian Context

Linguistic minorities who have come to Australia as immigrants or refugees face massive dislocation and change, including great physical distance from the home country, linguistic change, often reduced social status, disruption in social and family ties, cultural upheaval, and the renegotiation of identity, along with new educational, political and social systems (Partington & McCudden, 1992). For adults and older children the acquisition and use of English often poses major difficulties, and a serious barrier to social integration. Schools are increasingly sites of convergence for a diversity of ethnic groups and cultures, for the everyday use of many languages, for the acquisition of English as an additional language and for the renegotiation and transformation of identity. Up to 80% of students in some school districts are from non-English speaking backgrounds, while in other areas there are almost no students from other language backgrounds. McNamara (1997: 561) suggests that the immigrant student's experience constitutes 'a complex renegotiation of their social identity in the new society, a process that has profound implications for their attitudes to their own language and the learning of the majority group's language'. Given the increased globalisation and mass movements of people, both free and forced, around the world, it is hardly surprising that there is so much interest in the notions of identity and the political and social dimensions of language use. Clearly we can no longer ignore social and ideological concerns when looking at language acquisition and use.

Migration

It has been argued that in countries such as Canada, the United States and Australia, for everyone except the indigenous populations, 'the common condition is being, at one's near or far origins, from somewhere else' (Hughes, 1997). In one interview, Hall (1996) stressed, 'Since migration has turned out to be *the* world-historical event of late modernity, the classic postmodern experience turns out to be the diasporic experience' (in Morley & Chen, 1996, 490). Although Australia has seen successive waves of migration since colonisation in 1788 (itself the first modern migratory wave), large-scale immigration in the post-war period has changed the face of the country dramatically. This has resulted in what Lo Bianco (1997: 109) describes as a 'demographic pluralism, which is in birthplace and linguistic origin terms the second highest in the world after Israel's'. The arrival of five and a half million people in Australia since 1945 means that from a current population of 19 million, almost one in four people was born overseas, and one in 20 was born in Asia. By the early 1970s, this mass movement of people gave rise to the policy of multiculturalism, now under threat in a changing political and economic climate. In what follows, I outline briefly some of the contemporary developments in immigration and comment on the implications of these developments for schools.

The White Australia Policy, begun in 1901 and labelled 'the public face of racism' by Welch (1996), ended officially in the mid-1970s. However, until recently the overwhelming majority of immigrants and refugees coming to Australia were white. In recent years there have been increasingly diverse immigration patterns, including large numbers of people from Asian, southeast Asian, African and Middle-Eastern countries. By 1995–6, the numbers of people from China equalled those from the UK, both supplying just over 11% of the net intake of 99,139. The most recent Census (1996) indicated high levels of linguistic diversity in Australia, as shown by the following: in 81.2% of Australian homes only English is spoken; almost 25% of the population are from non-English speaking backgrounds; and 14.6% do not use English in the home, the most widely used languages being Italian, Greek, Cantonese and Mandarin. From the mid–1990s there has also been a dramatic increase in the community use of Asian languages (Clyne, 2003). Immigrants and refugees who come to Australia are not evenly distributed around the country, but concentrated in the major cities, where they also tend to settle in particular areas or suburbs. For example, in one school district used in this study, 54% of the population were born overseas, and 40% speak a Chinese language at home (ABS, 1996).

In the mid-1990s, there was an increasingly popular perception, fuelled by the media and encouraged by some right-wing federal politicians, that Australia was being 'Asianised'. Migration became an increasingly politicised issue, associated in the media with high levels of unemployment and more 'scientific' propositions about limiting Australia's population growth. The Australian federal government acted in 1997 to reduce by 8% the future numbers of immigrants, reduced from 99,139 people in 1996 to 80,000 in 1997. In the wake of the 11 September 2001 terrorist attacks in the United States, during the Australian federal election in November 2001, refugees and asylum seekers became the most heated electoral issue, with Prime Minister John Howard campaigning with the slogan, 'We will decide who comes to Australia, and under what circumstances'. He retained government on the strength of it. The fear had shifted from Asian immigrants to Afghani and Iraqi refugees, but the phenomenon was not new.

Kalantzis (1997) claims Australians have been sold the pernicious myth that immigration boosts unemployment, along with other racialising myths that immigrants live in ghettoes, soak up welfare and boost crime rates. All of this has a political purpose, as exemplified in the 2001 election. International media articles reported the increasing incidence of racial intolerance and racialising practices in Australia, while the United Nations urged the government to implement a more humane policy towards asylum seekers. Although writing in the British context, Rampton (1995) ascribes racialising practices to essentialising culturalist definitions of ethnic groups. He claims that these 'are experienced as a set of disabling racist images, which continually threaten to insert themselves into the interpersonal relations of everyday life' (p. 11). In the wake of 11 September 2001, such images constitute a danger for people of Middle-Eastern appearance around the world, and for refugees and asylum seekers in particular.

Such disabling images lie in sharp contrast to the discourse of multiculturalism, formulated in the 1970s as a response to the diversity of Australia's post-war population, and to counter earlier assimilationist policies and practices. While Bottomly (1997) suggests that a broad section of the Australian population value ethnic diversity, and that it can even be advantageous 'to identify with migrantness' (p. 44), the status of multiculturalism as a concept is increasingly contested. In the current discourse on multiculturalism, there is a recent conceptual shift towards traditional Australian qualities, values and ideals, and away from a valuing of diversity (Lo Bianco, 1998a). Political developments in 2001–2 in relation to immigration and asylum seekers kept in remote and fortified detention centres reflect disturbing and divisive evidence of this shift. It is a shift towards the idealisation of traditional Australian qualities and virtues, and away from a valuing of diversity.

The role of schools in maintaining dominant discourses

Educational systems and schools may celebrate or devalue particular sociocultural and linguistic forms and practices, which often mean that students from linguistic and ethnic minorities are disadvantaged, and that a 'dominant culture' is maintained. Welch (1996) suggests that this keeps alive a legacy of prejudice and exclusion. Such exclusionary mechanisms also inhibit the participation and the outcomes of many students. I would also argue that these practices further perpetuate a negative reading of multiculturalism. Given the shift evident in public perceptions of immigrants and multiculturalism, we can only assume that such prejudicial views are also represented in schools. Media reports of racially motivated attacks in schools are evidence of this phenomenon. There is other more subtle evidence of the devaluing of minority students in schools. It derives from social and educational policy, and the Australian example is part of a much wider trend.

Instigated in the 1970s, and at the height of the multiculturalism policy, the provision of specialist English as a Second Language education for linguistic minority students was a genuine attempt to counter the disadvantage suffered by NESB students in schools (Lo Bianco, 1998b). As the language of Australia's primary social institutions and of power, English was advocated as the gateway to success within these institutions, and to social mobility generally. The funding of ESL programmes was aligned with a move towards social justice for immigrant and refugee students, with an integrated multicultural policy, and with a National Languages Policy (Lo Bianco, 1987) that stressed multilingualism. Lo Bianco (1998b) argues that Australia led the world in ESL provision in the 1970s. He describes the embedding of ESL within what he calls 'the five fingers of multiculturalism', namely ESL, multicultural education, first language maintenance, anti-racism, and parent participation. The contextual embedding of ESL within a range of wider social policy moves meant that ESL became a real educational priority.

By the 1980s, along with successive cuts to ESL programme funding, a discourse of 'mainstreaming' emerged in federal policy documents. Ostensibly the argument for mainstreaming ESL students was to limit their marginalisation, but the net effect was to leave many without the language support they needed (Ozolins, 1993). This was a cost-cutting exercise under the guise of equity. Cuts have continued and by 2001, with the exception of funding for newly arrived students, money formerly allocated to ESL became part of generalised literacy funding. The contextual embedding of ESL within policies of cultural diversity and minority rights was lost, and the uncoupling of ESL education from broader sociocultural contexts and from a comprehensive policy on multiculturalism set the conditions for its possible demise (Lo Bianco, 1998). Current trends constitute the biggest crisis for linguistic minority students in 30 years, a crisis that is already full-blown in the United States (Cummins, 1996; Wong Fillmore, 1998). The conflation of ESL and literacy is part of this problem.

ESL, literacy and mainstreaming

With the diversion of ESL funds to literacy and the 'literacy strategy,' Lo Bianco (2002) argues the intent of ESL has been lost, mainstreaming ESL students prematurely where they must conform to a set of standards designed for other learners. In the mainstream, the benchmarks and standards used to measure language performance derive from mother-tongue norms, and, Lo Bianco argues, mandate and presume normalcy and normal pathways, where difference is seen as a problem. A growing body of research has shown that such mother-tongue pathways may not be appropriate for ESL learners, and indeed set up the conditions for the denigration of their academic achievements (Cummins, 2000; Freeman, 1995; McKay, 1999; Shaw Findlay, 1995). The inappropriate use of literacy benchmarks for ESL students tends to identify them as failures, while deflecting attention from their need for specialist teaching and programmes (McKay, 1999).

Recently, 'mainstreaming' has been a consistent feature of federal and state policy statements, that in practice has meant that hard-pressed teaching staff have had to do more with less (Welch, 1996). The term at its worst, suggest Kalantzis *et al.* (1990: 25), has been

> no more than a euphemism for cutting 'ethnic specific' services in the hope that mainstream institutions will assume a multicultural stance following the requirements of official policy and exercising a consider-

able degree of gracious goodwill – but without the funding to support concrete initiatives.

This trend has continued for a decade, to the point where in the current bureaucratic structure in Queensland education, ESL is not even mentioned. The consequence is that where any ESL provision remains, the number of students needing specialist ESL support far exceeds those actually receiving help.

In addition to inadequate provision of ESL, the background cultures and languages of minority students are not sufficiently valued by schools (Welch, 1996). According to Welch, a 'mainstream' culture tends to prevail, even when there are large numbers of minority students and a school multicultural policy. He writes,

> The way in which a school is organised is the projection of an entire culture. While paying lip service to the equal validity of all cultures, and respect for diverse lifestyles, many schools still reflect the dominant Anglo-Australian culture. (Welch, 1996: 116)

By 'dominant Anglo-Australian culture', Welch means a white middle-class culture represented as dominant by the institutional practices of the school. The school organisation, he argues, is represented in a number of ways, for example the language of noticeboards and letters home, textbooks, evaluation and accreditation, and the language and style of parent–teacher interviews and meetings. In addition, school culture is reflected in teaching materials, texts, assessment strategies, teaching discourses, home–school liaison, the curriculum, community participation, and many other things. This may seem rather obvious, but the fact that these texts are realised through the medium of English is important. At the same time, the lack of official recognition of other languages within schools adds to the problem. We know that immigrant speakers of languages other than English bring a vast range of linguistic and other skills to the country, yet these skills may be seen as utterly irrelevant to learning in schools. Lo Bianco (1997: 118) points out, 'Children and adults who learn English as a second language do not have a mental _tabula rasa_ on which English is inscribed'. Yet this is precisely how many minority speakers are constructed in school contexts.

Representational systems may position ethnic families who do not speak English as 'other', excluding them not by design, but by default. The issues of immigration and multiculturalism have generated tensions within the Australian community, and inevitably within schools. In addition to being cut off from everything familiar, acquiring a new language and negotiating new identities, many immigrant students must also deal with the manifestations of these tensions.

Nora, one of the Chinese participants in this study, recounted an incident in which a mainstream teacher said loudly in class to her Chinese friend Alicia, 'You don't listen to what I say. You don't even understand English'. Nora tried to remember the word some of the Australian students used during lunch to describe the incident. She said what sounded like 'raisin', and then 'You know, like Pauline Hanson'. The name of Queensland's most notorious right-wing, anti-immigration, anti-Asian politician of the time was an active part of Nora's vocabulary, even if the word 'racism' was not. The incident raised a number of questions relevant to the central concerns of this volume. Here was a public, 'authorised' and totally misleading representation of Alicia, a Chinese student, as someone who didn't listen and didn't understand English. It was clear that evidence of the current debates within the wider community were alive in this school, but the incident also revealed the importance of English in representation for linguistic minority students, and the power attached to English.

The Study

The broad aim of this study is to understand the early linguistic and social adjustment of ESL students to high school, through examining their spoken discourse in a variety of contexts. My primary focus is on the development of spoken discourse in English, as speaking is of immediate and direct relevance to intercultural communication, the possibilities of social interaction and the framing and representation of social identity. The study tracked 10 students from various language and ethnic backgrounds for 18 months, from their arrival programme in an intensive English language centre, to a bridging programme in high school ESL units, and then to integration in their chosen mainstream high schools. All schools were in a large metropolitan city in Queensland.

This is a qualitative study which looks at the role of language in self-representation for students who are beginning to learn English. This involves not just the speaker and ways of speaking, but the hearer and ways of hearing. I will argue that how students are heard by English speakers is just as important as how they speak English (see also Miller, 1999, 2000). Representation is, *inter alia*, representation of social identity, a display of self in social interaction, discursively and jointly constructed in the context of social memberships. Identity may be viewed as 'an account of oneself and others in a relationship of reciprocity and mutual recognition' (Létourneau, 1997: 61). For linguistic minority students, establishing such reciprocity and recognition is part of the project of representation, a project that must be undertaken intersubjectively with other speakers of English. The case studies show that for some students this is not a clear-cut choice. In school contexts where students acquire (or do not acquire) and use (or do not use) English, a number of conditions, and institutional and social practices make it more or less difficult for English to be acquired or used. This study also identifies and documents some of the conditions and practices which promote and constrain the acquisition and use of spoken English by immigrant students. In a practical sense, students' levels of proficiency in English relate to their pathways toward full integration in mainstream classes, where they are no longer supported by ESL teachers. As students negotiate these pathways, institutional decisions are made as to where and how fast they move, based on how they speak and write English.

Although a number of data sources are used, the study places the students' own accounts in central position, in order for the reader to hear the voices of those who are often 'made voiceless in particular settings by not being allowed to speak, or silence themselves out of fear or ignorance regarding the strength and possibilities that exist in multiple languages' (Giroux, 1992: 206). Giroux has also drawn attention to the need to understand what conditions make it possible or otherwise for some groups to take up particular discourses. This study will throw light on some of these conditions. The central research questions which derive from the above are:

(1) How do linguistic minority students in the early stages of language acquisition represent themselves to other students and teachers?
(2) How are they heard and represented?
(3) What conditions at school facilitate or constrain the acquisition of spoken English by recently arrived ESL students?

Methodology

In broadening the focus of language research to include an understanding of social contexts, representation, and discourse, we need a methodology that has four critical characteristics or criteria. First, it will look at language in a sociocultural matrix, which shows sensitivity not just to proficiency in a second language, but to the social and cultural salience of language use. A socioculturally framed view of discourse means that we look not just at what is said, but how and why it is said that way, along with what is not said, what is heard, and what the consequences of speaking and hearing might be. Second, it must reveal contextual features in local settings, as the contexts of discourse provide insights into the ways in which speakers are positioned through language use. The local context helps us understand particular social conditions which make communication possible (or otherwise). Exploring the contextual layers is also important in any qualitative case study, where messy disparate influences, rather than neat, unified wholes are a fact of life. Third, the methodology must incorporate an *emic* perspective, the voice and subjectivities of both participant and researcher present in the writing. Finally, an interpretive study must allow for ongoing flexibility in the data collection and analysis, drawing on whatever fields prove productive for the project (Nelson *et al.*, 1992). Case study and ethnographic approaches have the potential to satisfy all four criteria above, but can also accommodate a focus on issues of language, representation and social membership. While generalisability is not an imperative in studies of this type, the need for credibility and plausibility remain. The key question of *what* is generalisable in any study may lead us to consider that the analytic themes (and not the specifics) may speak to a broad range of contexts and participants.

Note on practitioner researchers and reflexivity

Although the students' voices drive the narrative of this study, my own reflexivity, background, knowledge and decisions are also in evidence. In his ethnographic work on language classrooms, van Lier draws attention to what he calls the *base line*, common ground between the researcher and field, which underlies both description and interpretation. He writes,

> Behind the data set, however small, the researcher brings to the task whatever insights and experience may have accumulated over the years, and this is of crucial importance. This knowledge constitutes the base line, a sense of common ground between observer and setting, which underlies efficient description and analytic work. (Van Lier, 1998: 5)

For me, there was a strong and unavoidable sense of 'common ground' – I had worked at the intensive reception centre for ESL students, and felt at home in ESL staff rooms and classrooms, and in the corridors and playgrounds of most of the schools I visited. The problem was to work out how my own presence and activities impacted on the research process itself (Glesne & Peshkin, 1992). Although it can sometimes be harder to discern significant patterns in the familiar than in what is less well known, practical insider knowledge is useful in many areas of the research process. Practitioner researchers, Hammersley (1992: 128) suggests, benefit from experience 'based on a synthesis of information and judgement from diverse situations that is sedimented over time in the form of skills, habits and knowledge-at-hand'. Qualitative methods connote not just techniques and procedures, but also a manner of viewing and talking about what is perceived (Gubrium and Holstein, 1997). This should not mean that the researcher indulges in self-absorbed hyper-reflexivity, outpourings of autobiographical revelation, and continual hedging about the contingency of all research – a trend that has recently been widely criticised in the literature (Gubrium & Holstein, 1997; McLeod & Yates, 1997; Silverman, 1997). However, for me there remains a fundamental place in the qualitative research process for researcher reflexivity as a productive part of research procedure.

Data and analysis

Data used in this volume are selected from a three-year study of high school aged immigrant students who had only been in Australia from two to 10 months when data collection began, so that the study represents the very early phases of their arrival and integration into Australian schools. Data sources in this study included the following:

- semi-structured interviews in both English and the L1 for some students;
- student diaries;
- focus groups;
- classroom observation in ESL and mainstream contexts;
- observation of playgrounds and other microcontexts of the school;
- attendance at key school events and ceremonies (multicultural concert, student symposium on multiculturalism, Anzac day);
- talks with mainstream and ESL teachers;
- talks with school administrators;
- the collection of work samples and school documents;
- phone conversations with students;
- attendance at ESL staff meetings and morning teas;
- the collection of media articles on ethnic minorities, migration and multiculturalism;
- informal encounters with the students and their teachers.

Each data set corresponded to a different site of representation. All interviews, the videotaped focus groups, talks with administrators, one staff meeting and some phone conversations were recorded and transcribed. Detailed field notes were made during and immediately after observations, participation in school events, and informal talks with staff and students. The primary or core data sets included audiotaped interviews, student diaries, and observation in a range of contexts within the schools.

The interviews in English were viewed in part as instances of contextualised communicative competence in spoken English, but also as accounts of the students' positionings and insights into the social order of the school. As a former colleague in the intensive reception centre, I felt a strong degree of familiarity and identification with the students and staff. I was able to generate lots of data with the two Bosnian students, who spoke English quite fluently, in spite of having arrived only weeks before I met them. The Chinese speaking students, who spoke Mandarin, Cantonese or both, had far more limited English, and so interviews in their languages were conducted by native speaking research assistants, who then also translated the transcripts. These translations were cross-checked by other Chinese native speakers.

Diaries provided another set of core data from some of the participants. They were not a substitute for talk, but opened up the possibility for students to write about speaking and identity. Diaries constitute a form of communication which takes the heat off the speaker. There is no wait time for responses, no awkward long pauses, no pressure to respond, no agonising search for an unknown or forgotten word. Students can formulate in their own time what they want to say, and the discourse is not overtly shaped by the researcher. As the researcher and as a former ESL teacher, I had observed how students may be made voiceless. I was also aware that some students have a greater facility in writing than in speaking English, partly due to the nature of their prior language learning. The use of diaries also opened the way for students to use narrative accounts, a form that while not particularly valued as a school genre, allows the student creative freedom in the discourse. As Drake and Ryan (1994: 49) point out, 'A narrative format allows students to present views of the world that are not necessarily filtered through a perspective that assumes uniformity of experience'. I was also interested in the ability of narrative, in which experience and responses are constructed and located in text, to provide a resource for the display of identity (see Schiffrin, 1996). Several students from China and Taiwan wrote prolifically in their student diaries, which contained reflections on their learning and social experiences. These were written in English with myself as the intended reader. One student, Nora, wrote 8000 words in two months. By contrast the Bosnian students told me quite eloquently and emphatically that they would not be writing any diary – Milena because she already wrote a diary in Danish to maintain her Danish and contact with former friends in Denmark, and Alex because he had never written in a diary and was not about to begin one. These were clear representations in themselves.

Hornberger (1995) has outlined the importance of linguistically informed approaches, particularly discourse analysis, to ethnographic research. She writes, 'notions of situated discourse and multiple and alternative social roles and identities . . . are fundamental to all of the sociolinguistically informed approaches to ethnography' (p. 244). However studies concerned with social identities have often been resistant to incorporating methods such as discourse analysis, and reluctant to theorise how social members position themselves and are positioned by discourse (Antaki, 1996). The analysis used here sought to find ways to understand each case in its specificity and complexity. A range of discourse analytic methods was used in the analysis. Luke (1998: 55) stresses that interdisciplinary techniques of analysis may involve 'a series of text analyses that use different analytic tools, but which are nested within an overall set of social theoretic frameworks and sociological questions'. The tools I selected included, but were not limited to, the five interrelated systems of discourse outlined by Gee (1996), namely prosody, cohesion, discourse organisation, contextualisation signals and thematic organisation; aspects of critical discourse analysis (Caldas-Coulthard and Coulthard, 1996; Luke, 1998); and of membership categorisation analysis (Antaki & Widdicombe, 1998; Baker, 1997).

Overview of Following Chapters

In this chapter, I have provided an orientation to the major issues and the contextual background for the case studies presented in this volume. I have suggested that spoken communication implicates both speakers and hearers in practices of representation, through which identity is both constructed and negotiated. I have also suggested that within these practices lies the possibility of discrimination based on the audible difference of the speaker. In Chapter 2 I will develop a strong theoretical framing for these claims. I will argue that traditional second language acquisition (SLA) research is inadequate to theorise links between discourse and social identity. I then use Bourdieu's sociological theory to make some of these connections, along with work from Gee (1996). I discuss the issue of acquisition versus learning and the role of speaking or *voice* in self-representation in school contexts. Chapter 3 provides a scene setting for the following data chapters, in which I introduce the students. Using transcripts from two focus groups, I also begin to explore how contextualised communicative competence in English is tied to representation and social identity.

Chapters 4, 5 and 6 comprise the main data chapters and are detailed case studies of five students – a Taiwanese girl and a boy from Hong Kong, a Bosnian girl and two mainland Chinese girls. The cases present many contrasts in terms of the students' language use, construction of identity and self-representation. In Chapter 7 I synthesise issues from the data chapters and propose a model for the move towards representation, which includes the key notion of audible difference. I argue that there is an economy of reception which radically affects the lived experiences of linguistic minority speakers, and which can only be addressed by challenging social and institutional practices which limit the representation of these students in schools.

Chapter 2

Language, Identity and Audibility: A New Theoretical Framing

Introduction

> *We came to the school and like, I didn't have, I didn't have many friends, or most of the time I just stayed up here, up in ESL, because there was no people who spoke my language then. It was only me. So all these Australian people, they are nice but like, now they really won't, you know, talk to you. Now, when I know English, I was so confident in myself and everything. I can be with anyone I want. But then when I came, like, no one really didn't care, like you just, you're just by yourself. Most of the time I spent in ESL here. It was really hard on you then.*

(Neta, a Year 11 Bosnian student)

> *If your English is as fluent as Australian students, the Australian students do not really see you that much differently. I saw them talking to those Asian students whose English is good in the same way as they would to other Australian students.*

(Helen, a Year 11 Taiwanese student)

The observations of Neta and Helen above draw our attention to the intensely social nature of language use, and issues such as the linguistic and social isolation of ESL students, the consequences of speaking in a way that is recognised by speakers of the dominant language, perceived fluency, access to native speakers and the problem of being seen and heard as different. But there are gaps and silences in these brief excerpts. Neta segues effortlessly to 'now when I know English'. How did this happen (since the nice Australian people didn't talk to her)? Who gets to be someone 'whose English is good'? Although socio-linguists have stressed the relevance of language to social life, there is limited research that combines linguistic insights with sociological perspectives, particularly in school contexts. Hymes (1996: 88) states that there is a need within academic institutions for what he terms 'the peculiar combination of social theory, ethnographic perspectives, and linguistic skills'. The case studies in this volume are an attempt to represent this 'peculiar combination'. This chapter moves across a number of related theoretical fields and considerations, including a brief overview of insights from second language acquisition (SLA) theory, current critiques of SLA research based on broader social models from discourse-related work, and understandings from Bourdieu's social theory. In this way it sets out the groundwork for theorising links between language, identity and audibility.

Notes from SLA Theory

Although it will be seen that within agency there are different kinds of capital which students can draw on, the interrelationship between a student's acquisition of English, and experiences within and beyond school often define the landscape of academic success and opportunity which lies ahead for the student. Second language issues and theory are therefore of considerable significance in this study. To ignore or to downgrade them is to imply that dedicated ESL teachers, using practices based on SLA theory and perspectives, do not make a difference. Clearly this is not the case. SLA theory has developed from the study of the learning of foreign languages in schools and the learning of second languages (particularly English, or ESL) by immigrants (Ellis, 1994). It is this second branch of SLA research which is of primary interest here, particularly as it applies to the acquisition of spoken English (the dominant language) by immigrant students in Australia. The SLA field has provided practitioners with a number of critical understandings for their work. These include understandings of the contrasts between first and second acquisition; interlanguage; macroskills, grammar; SLA pedagogy; the influence of age on arrival and length of residence; the importance of prior learning; communicative competence; and the types of language competence valued by schools, particularly in relation to context-embeddedness and cognitive demand (Cummins & Swain, 1986; Ellis, 1994; Lightbown & Spada, 1999).

For almost two decades, SLA research has sought to come to terms with various forms of communicative competence, from the language needed to communicate effectively and interactively in a range of social contexts, to the language needed to perform cognitive and academic tasks in classroom contexts (Cummins, 1984). Recent insights into language competence make it clear that learning a second language is far more than replacing one symbolic system with another, and increasingly there has been an awareness of social language use in specific contexts, which goes well beyond acquiring a set of linguistic patterns. In a meticulous elaboration of Canale's (1983) model of communicative competence, Celce-Murcia *et al.*

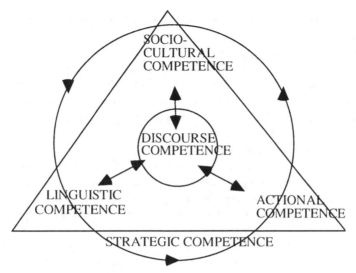

Figure 2.1 Model of communicative competence (Celce-Murcia *et al.*, 1995: 10)

(1995) presented the schematic representation of communicative competence shown in Figure 2.1.

Note that in this model, Celce-Murcia *et al.* choose the term 'linguistic' rather than 'grammatical' competence, to stress the inclusion of lexis and phonology in this category. They also include sociocultural rather than sociolinguistic competence, in order to suggest that a knowledge of linguistic resources is notionally distinct from knowledge of sociocultural rules and an understanding of contexts. This is a refinement of the interrelationship of sociocultural and linguistic patterns of use. Here is a brief summary of the categories included in Figure 2.1.

(1) **Discourse competence**
    Cohesion, deixis (personal pronouns, spatial, temporal and sequential references), coherence (interrelationship of utterances within the text), generic structure, conversational structure.
(2) **Linguistic competence**
    Sentence patterns, morphology, lexis, phonology, orthographic systems, systematic aspects of formulaic utterances.
(3) **Actional competence**
    Matching communicative intention with linguistic form, especially in spoken discourse (rhetorical competence in written forms), repertoires of flexible and conventionalised language functions such as greeting, giving

information, expressing feelings, desires and opinions, solving problems, and persuading.

(4) **Sociocultural competence**
A knowledge of factors relating to social contexts (participant and situational variables), stylistic appropriateness, cultural factors (sociocultural backgrounds, dialect differences, cross-cultural awareness) and non-verbal communication (body language, use of space, non-vocal noises, silence, touching).

(5) **Strategic competence**
Competence in avoidance and reduction strategies, compensatory or repair strategies, time-gaining strategies, self-monitoring and interactional strategies (appeals for help, meaning negotiation, responses, comprehension checks, e.g. whether the interlocutor can hear you).

Celce-Murcia *et al.* stress that their model is a 'pedagogically motivated construct', with clear application to language acquisition, to teaching and learning. These categories eliminate the notion of language acquisition as the learning of overt linguistic forms, focusing instead, in Fine's (1988: 12) terms, on 'the acquisition of the relation between social uses of language and the discourse patterns that result from those uses in the specific language context'. Celce-Murcia *et al.* remind us that in terms of knowledge, these may be separate. This model highlights how complex, socially and culturally situated and contextualised the mastery of another language actually is. Speakers can get the grammar right but the discourse wrong through a sociocultural misunderstanding, as in the case of a Korean student who greeted me with 'Have a nice day', unaware that this is normally said on leaving, rather than on meeting someone. Clearly it is also possible to get the discourse right, but with limited linguistic competence, in conventional terms. Linguistic competence, however, is highly prized by schools, particularly in written assignments. The notion of competence also raises the question of who is considered competent in a language. Is the goal to sound like a native speaker? Are native speakers all competent? Although currently contested (Leung *et al.*, 1997; Lippi-Green, 1997), native speaker competence has often been assumed within the field of applied linguistics, and SLA in particular. For example, scales measuring second language proficiency frequently reserve the highest levels for those who are near-native or native-like in their production and understanding of the language.

The integrated nature of language competences outlined above, and the likelihood that school draws on and values very specific aspects of language competence, make it clear that for linguistic minority students, the acquisition of English is a multi-layered process of great complexity.

The extent to which language competences are learned in classrooms and / or acquired through sociocultural interaction is a matter of ongoing research (see also Lantolf, 2000). At school, students must master specific areas of spoken and written language to function socially and to succeed academically, things such as the grammar, phonology, communicative strategies and an understanding of academic and other sociocultural norms. But even where a student has substantial aptitude for language learning, as exemplified in the literature on good language learners (Cook, 1991), these areas require a great deal of work.

SLA research provides valuable concepts which help us to think about what it means to learn another language, or to become bilingual. However, the theoretical positions associated with SLA research have increasingly been subject to a critique which implies casting the theoretical net somewhat wider, in order to capture more of the context and complexity of language acquisition and use.

SLA Reconsidered

Ongoing critique of the assumptions and methodology used in second language research has suggested an overuse of research instruments such as surveys, which do not show language acquisition as a process (Williams, 1992), inadequate attention to sociocultural and psychological factors, which may be as or more significant to acquisition than linguistic factors (Firth & Wagner, 1997), an overreliance on theory developed from the mea-suring of differential performances in a testing context (Edelsky, 1991), and conceptual inflexibility which admits 'no room for the view that a person's linguistic identity might be socially defined and interactionally negotiated' (Rampton, 1995, 323). Although Canale's (1983) model of communicative competence included sociolinguistic and discourse factors, these have not featured in much SLA research, which has continued to seek out models of teaching and learning that stress the role and responsibility of the individual learner. As Nunan, (1995: 155) puts it, 'In the final analysis . . . it is the learner who must remain at the centre of the process, for no matter how much energy and effort we expend, it is the learner who has to do the learn-ing'. However commonsensical the appeal of such a statement is, it accords insufficient weight to social and contextual factors, expresses a skewed per-spective on language learning and use, and does not incorporate an understanding of how discourses work, or how language is related to issues of social representation, power and identity. Norton Peirce (1995: 12) writes,

> Theories of the good language learner have been developed on the premise that language learners can choose under what conditions they

will interact with members of the target language community and that the learner's access to the target language community is a function of the learner's motivation.

Norton Peirce's view here is in direct contrast to that of Nunan, for whom the burden of learning resides with the learner, irrespective of conditions which may obtain. The community may or may not open up possibilities for learners to practise and to participate in social events (Norton & Toohey, 2001). Finally, Rampton (1987: 49) suggests that SLA research 'runs the risk of remaining restrictively preoccupied with the space between the speaker and his [*sic*] grammar, rather than with the relationship between speakers and the world around them'. This relationship is to do with discourses (languages in use), rather than language or second language *per se*.

From language to discourse

Two key elements in the theories of language as discourse have had a major impact on language research. First, the view of language practice as socially constituted embodies the assumptions that discourse cannot be viewed in isolation from its cultural and social context, and that we are positioned by and through our language use. Second, since linguistic relations are social relations, they are also power relations, and the power of language to legitimate and maintain ideologies is a recurring theme in the literature. We speak often of learning a language, as if there were only one, or one with finite content. In fact, learning a language entails mastering many languages, or sets of discursive practices. The complex and dynamic processes involving language, membership, culture and identity are central to the position advocated by Gee, who places discourses at the heart of the matter. He defines Discourses, with the characteristic capital D, in the following way,

> Discourses are ways of being in the world, or forms of life which integrate words, acts, values, beliefs, attitudes, and social identities, as well as gestures, glances, body positions, and clothes. A Discourse is a kind of identity kit which comes complete with the appropriate costume and instructions on how to act, talk, and often write, so as to take on a particular social role that others will recognize. (Gee, 1996: 127)

This definition loads the term 'discourse' to groaning capacity, yet as I mentally apply it to the contexts of family, colleagues and friends, the inherent value of Gee's definition seems to strike home. We all have our identity kits, our linguistic repertoires and routines designed to make us recognisable to others. Using myself as an example, on any one day I may move through the discourses of, for example, censorious parent, ESL teacher, sympathetic colleague, university lecturer, dissatisfied shopper, intimate friend, emailing lobbyist, and so on. Through these discourses I construct and negotiate a range of identities to serve specific purposes, memberships and contexts. Such identity kits, linguistic repertoires and routines are designed to make us recognisable to others, and effective agents through our communicative practices. Our knowledge of language is therefore far more than a knowledge of words and how to combine them to form grammatical sentences. This is in contrast to the language learner in much of SLA theory, who has been constructed as a kind of ahistorical stick figure, appearing without a past, existing outside of any social context (McKay & Wong, 1996). The learner's relation to the social order *outside* the classroom seldom enters into the picture (see also Auerbach, 1995; Pennycook, 2001). Gee's definition of Discourses implies viewing the linguistic minority student not as a learner of any particular language, but as someone who needs to acquire a range of discursive practices in addition to those already possessed.

A number of researchers have suggested reconceptualising aspects of second language research to incorporate discourse and sociocultural perspectives (Firth & Wagner, 1997; Miller, 1997). Table 2.1 opposes fundamental concepts inherent in SLA with concepts underlying discourse approaches. Although the oppositions are more complex than a simple binary suggests (they are not either/or propositions), they illustrate the incorporation into language research of insights from other disciplines, and open up the possibility of new questions for the field.

In Table 2.1 it can be seen from these 'oppositions,' which are actually dimensions or continua, that the conceptual shift from language to discourse suggests a more complex orientation to language use and to research. This involves moving away from the decontextualised figure of the learner (implied by the left side of the table) towards a conceptualisation in which all speakers and hearers are implicated.

Native speakers of standard languages

The shift implied by the table necessitates questioning the traditional native speaker/non-native speaker binary, and the assumptions within notions such as 'standard English'. Teachers are often complicit in promoting a standard language ideology which rejects or marginalises certain varieties of English. Lippi-Green (1997) reminds us that standard language and non-accent are abstractions, idealisations which do not really exist, and argues that the opposite of standard appears to be non-standard or substandard. She suggests that 'these terms automatically bring with them a uni-directionality and subordination which is counterproductive to a dis-

Table 2.1 Contrasting orientations in SLA and discourse studies

SLA	*Language as discourse*
'decodable' meanings	situated, contextualised, and negotiated meanings
cognitivist and mentalist orientations	social and contextual orientation
focus on individual competence	focus on competence realised socially through interaction
native speaker as an idealised source of perfectly realised competence	competence realised by all speakers to varying degrees in a range of social contexts
native/non-native binary	collaboration of all speakers in discourse
standardised language as the goal	standardised language as a myth
neutral communicative contexts	ideologically laden contexts with real consequences for participants
focus on formal learning environments	focus on discourse in a range of settings or social fields
learner as 'subject'	speaker as a social identity, enacted in particular social situations
search for generalisable rules and methods	understanding of the contingency of local contexts
lack of an emic perspective	centrality of participant perspectives
focus on development of communicative competence	focus on contextual and interactional dimensions of discourse
good language learners can learn	social hierarchies and structures impinge on learning
difficulties predominate in studies	consideration of communicative successes and agency; problems viewed as contingent social phenomena

cussion of language variation in linguistic terms' (p. 60). The attribute of 'native speaker' may be conferred as much by symbols and attitude as by language ability and knowledge (Davies, 1991). Lippi-Green also draws attention to the ideological aspects of standard language, 'a bias toward an abstracted, idealized, homogenous spoken language which is imposed by dominant bloc institutions and which names as its model the written language of the upper middle class' (p. 64). The deconstruction of conventional notions of native speaker competence is also stressed by Rampton (1995) and Leung *et al.* (1997), who emphasise that majority language speakers are also done a disservice by the assumption that they speak, and are affiliated to, an undifferentiated standard English. They propose replacing the blunt notion of native speaker competence with three concepts which refine the notion of what it is to know and use a language. These are the concepts of language expertise, language affiliation and language inheritance. Language expertise refers to what you know about language(s), including linguistic and cultural knowledge; language affiliation refers to an attachment, allegiance and identification with the language, and therefore focuses on connections between people or groups; language inheritance constitutes one's language background, and is to do with continuity between groups. For many speakers, there may be limited allegiance to the language inheritance, and a blurring of and within the conventional categories of native and non-native. This work is particularly relevant to the language competence of immigrant students, whose language expertise, affiliation and inheritance in the first language is likely to be disrupted on acquiring discourses in their second or third language.

The categories of native and non-native are clearly problematic, yet Kaspar (1997: 309) has pointed out that such terminology has a role to play in the context of second language research. She writes,

> The constructs 'nonnative speaker' and 'learner' focus upon the aspect that is *common* to the studied agents, and relevant in the global research context (or discourse universe) of L2 study generally and L2 acquisition (SLA) specifically.

Kaspar's concern is that in SLA, the 'A' stands for acquisition, and that this must remain the primary focus within the field. While it is important to challenge tired, misleading or decontextualised assumptions about the nature of language, I agree with Kaspar that the pragmatic dictates of research involving second language may make the use of terms such as 'native speaker' both appropriate and inevitable.

Having said this, a broader perspective of language as discourse moves us beyond the notion of a speaker as deficient, to an appreciation that all language use varies and is contingent on social contexts, in which power is implicated. Further, the concept of native and non-native do not explain the enormous variation that occurs on the level of language practice and use. While not contesting the significance of individual differences in language acquisition and use, the individual-in-a-social-context becomes a worthier object of study. In addition to measuring the immigrant or Aboriginal child's communicative competence in English on scales, or calibrating their proficiency in literacy and oracy, researchers need to allow for the contingent, social and contextual features of language in the right-hand side of Table 2.1. In this way, some of the weight of communicative competence can be redistributed from the shoulders of the language minority students to other participants in communication. In addition, connecting patterns of their everyday lived experiences with larger configurations of discourse and power and identity, and refocusing on their real-life contexts is needed to get a fuller picture.

In the case of minority groups, issues of language and power are also linked to processes of inclusion and exclusion. Seeking to understand these processes in institutional contexts has been a priority on the agendas of many educational researchers in recent times. Giroux (1990: 43) argues that,

> ... it is important that educators possess a theoretical grasp of the ways in which difference is constructed through various representations and practices that name, legitimate, marginalise and exclude the cultural capital and voices of subordinate groups in society.

Aspects of Bourdieu's theory provide one way to grasp the construction of difference in discourse and social practices. He explains the relationships between language use, sociocultural contexts and power through the concept of cultural or symbolic capital. However before turning to Bourdieu, I wish to focus briefly on institutional practices which affect linguistic minority students in schools.

School and the ESL Student

Part of the institutional role of any school is to integrate and sort persons and groups. Gee (1996: 143) describes schools as 'public spheres of secondary Discourse, involving interactions with people well beyond the initial social group or local community'. Partly because of this, schools may also be sites where individuals experience the clash of conflicting discourses from home, class, gender, youth culture and academic work, discourses which meet and often fail to mesh. Participation in these discourses forms part of the daily project of negotiating social identity, a key phenomenon of school life. The problem for students, who must negotiate and somehow accommodate this range of discourses, is even more acute for those students whose first language is not that of the dominant majority in the school. Some learn to sidestep the secondary discourses, continuing to function in their first language. To what degree are they then involved in 'public spheres of secondary Discourse'? In addition, minority students face multiple memberships, experiencing mainstream discourses and cultures through the school and peer group, but also often continuing to operate as members of their ethnic and language groups.

Within this context, there are two issues to consider. First, it has been suggested that certain aspects of discourse are acquired rather than overtly learned, and that they stem from interaction and participation in social, communicative contexts. This is a given in the literature on discourse, but runs counter to aspects of SLA theory, which is based on the premise that languages can be taught and learned formally in classrooms. Second, there is the issue of the specific type of English that is valued on the linguistic market of school, and by implication, the subordination of forms of English and other languages which do not conform to this value or standard.

Acquisition versus learning

To what extent are second languages learned? To what extent are they acquired? Answering such questions entails serious dilemmas for both teachers and students. Gee (1996) makes an explicit comparison between the concepts of first and second language on the one hand, and primary and secondary Discourse on the other. Primary Discourse, acquired in informal settings through face-to-face interaction, is the basis of one's first social identity. Secondary Discourses are developed in a more conscious way through apprenticeship to institutions and other groups. The acquisition / learning distinction is pivotal and Gee draws a convincing analogy between Discourse acquisition and learning on the one hand, and first and second language acquisition and learning on the other. The dilemma that Gee (1996: 144) presents is that discourses are acquired via enculturation 'in natural, meaningful, and functional settings', rather than learned through overt teaching. Acquisition in this sense requires the complicity of people who have already mastered the Discourse. Knowing 'about' the language is therefore not knowing how to 'do' the language. In Gee's terms, knowing 'about' the language is what can be taught and learned, as opposed to acquired. He argues that good teaching should lead to metaknowledge about the interrelationships of the primary and secondary Discourses to each other, to the self and to society. That is, good teaching facilitates learning. What is not elaborated by Gee is that good classrooms can also be 'natural, meaningful and functional settings', where teachers create the conditions for acquisition, via apprenticeship, as well as assist students to gain the metaknowledge necessary to process the second language and relate it to their first. This is not to underestimate the difficulty of such a task for both teacher and learner. As Gee (1996: 146) writes, 'Non-mainstream students and teachers are in a bind. One is not in a Discourse unless one has mastered it and mastery comes about through acquisition not learning'.

Spolsky's (1989) notion of natural acquisition contexts for language learning parallels Gee's concept of acquisition. Natural acquisition contexts, according to Spolsky, include learning for communication, unmodified language input, and being surrounded by native speakers. Such contexts provide a real-world social context for learning, along with a primary focus on meaning. ESL students, who are learning English in an English-speaking country are in a natural acquisition context, as opposed to a formal learning situation, where students are instructed in a foreign language. These students supposedly travel on buses and trains, go shopping, see movies, talk to other students, field phone calls and emails – all in the second language. There is, one would suppose, ample opportunity for multiple interactions and practice, which Spolsky stresses are essential for natural acquisition. This supposition will be raised again later in the data chapters of this volume. However, it is worth pointing out that in the initial phases of their schooling, Queensland ESL students may be in an intensive formal language learning programme, where different conditions obtain. Initially, the teacher is the only one in the classroom fluent in English; there is limited access to native speakers; the language input is highly modified; and there is much controlled practice of forms. Although these students are also using transport, shopping and talking to friends, their classroom experiences may more resemble those of a foreign language classroom than a natural acquisition context.

Here is the dilemma for teachers and non-mainstream learners. If Discourses are acquired rather than learned, what and how are teachers to teach? For example, a focus on form is part of contemporary language learning programmes. Yet SLA literature acknowledges that an overt focus on rules is only helpful for some aspects of language learning (see Doughty & Williams, 1998). Persistent error correction, for example, has little impact on the learner's internalisation of structures (Lightbown & Spada, 1999). Although students may not learn much from the corrections on their work, the sad fact is that for many students, those red marks locate exactly where their writing will be found wanting, by the teacher and others. Within a frame of literacy that is socially constructed and institutionally located (Freebody & Luke, 1990; Gee, 1996), a level of grammatical accuracy is essential. Gee problematises this situation in the following terms.

> These non-mainstream students often fail to fully master school-based dominant Discourses, especially the 'superficialities of form and correctness' that serve as such good gates given their imperviousness to late acquisition in classrooms without community support. (Gee, 1996: 146)

The 'superficialities of form and correctness' are critical to the kinds of English most valued in schools.

For linguistic minority students, there is some tension in the arguments about acquisition and learning. It is likely that the problem is not as simple as the summary: languages are learned, while Discourses are acquired; but this may be a useful platform to work from. I have also suggested that school requires specific forms of discourse which potentially disadvantage minority students. Literacy, claims Gee (1996), has historically played the dual roles of both liberator and weapon. The metaphor might presumably be extended to Discourses. The acquisition and use of English is essential for students wishing to participate in social and institutional practices, and in the wider society. However, the notion of a standard English discourse, or school English, may be used as a weapon against those from language minorities (and others), who are outsiders to the Discourse(s). It seems clear that we cannot view the competence of the speaker in isolation from social practices, speaking in isolation from hearing, discourse in isolation from relationships of power. These are all interrelated in systems of communication.

Insights from Bourdieu

The theoretical work of Bourdieu provides a scaffold which strengthens our understanding of language practice and its relationship to the material social conditions surrounding this practice, while foreshadowing the consequences of particular forms of language use. For Bourdieu, linguistic relations are also relations of symbolic power. Above I suggested that a move to discourse perspectives, as opposed to traditional SLA perspectives, opens up new questions about language use and language learning. In his *Outline of a Theory of Practice*, Bourdieu (1977a) provides a powerful warrant for this move, based on what he sees as the limitations of structuralist linguistics to theorise how language works in the context of the social conditions of language production. In the following section, I revisit these limitations briefly, and then focus more directly on Bourdieu's concepts of *linguistic habitus, linguistic capital* and *linguistic market*.

The charm of a game devoid of consequences

Bourdieu's (1991) primary objection to traditional structural linguistics is that it focuses on the internal construction of text, while ignoring the sociohistorical conditions and practical character of text. He is therefore opposed to the presuppositions of Saussurian and Chomskyan linguistics, which treat language as an autonomous and homogeneous object, drawing parallels between Saussure's *langue/parole* and Chomsky's competence/performance definitions. For Bourdieu, there are two major problems with these approaches. First, such binary analyses assume language production which is more idealised than real, and the binaries themselves do not do explanatory justice to the complex practical activity of speaking. The essence of communication often lies not *in* the communication itself, but in the social conditions which make the communication possible (or impossible?). For example, the conditions in classrooms shape communication in particular ways, including the way meanings are expressed and heard. The relationships in classrooms and schools are also part of the communication. Second, the idealisation of linguistic practices does not take into account the strategies speakers use to adjust to relations of power within any interaction, or indeed the fact that linguistic exchanges *are* 'relations of symbolic power in which the power relations between speakers or their respective groups are actualised' (Bourdieu, 1991: 37). Bourdieu's objection to traditional linguistics, then, is that it is intellectualist in orientation, treating language as an object to contemplate, rather than an instrument of agency and power.

Central to Bourdieu's conception of linguistic practice is the notion that it must be analysed and understood within its cultural context, taking into account the social conditions of its production and reception. In simple terms, Bourdieu argues that linguistic relations = social relations = power relations, and they occur within particular contexts or social fields. Symmetries and asymmetries of status and symbolic capital are inherent in every social interaction. Bourdieu makes this connection repeatedly in *Language and Symbolic Power* (1991: 34). He writes,

> ... bracketing out the social, which allows language or any other symbolic object to be treated like an end in itself, contributed considerably to the success of structuralist linguistics, for it endowed the 'pure' exercises that characterise a purely internal and formal analysis with the charm of a game devoid of consequences.

Work by Fairclough (1989), Gee (1996) and Lippi-Green (1997) highlights the fact that there are serious consequences for language users not operating within dominant discourses. These consequences can be explained by Bourdieu's concepts of habitus, linguistic capital, and linguistic market, in which all linguistic products are not equally valued. Bourdieu (1991) suggests that authority and power derive from the linguistic habitus and its different values in different sites of exchange.

In his introduction to *Language and Symbolic Power*, Thompson (1991: 18) reminds us that in Bourdieu's terms,

> ... differences in terms of accent, grammar and vocabulary – the very differences overlooked by formal linguistics – are indices of the social positions of speakers and reflections of the quantities of linguistic capital (and other capital) which they possess.

Such differences are therefore indices to the listener about the speaker. Lippi-Green (1997: 73) observes that accent, for example, often functions as 'the last back door to discrimination'. Accent is of course part of the linguistic habitus.

He says it so well it must be true

The linguistic habitus has been defined as a 'subset of dispositions acquired in the course of learning to speak in particular contexts' (Thompson, 1991: 17). These dispositions determine the linguistic practices of a speaker, along with the value that linguistic products receive within social fields or 'markets', such as schools, workplaces, or sporting clubs. Furthermore, these durable transposable dispositions are inscribed in the body, visible and observable to all. Thus age, race, gender, sexuality and class are embodied dispositions which have real consequences for the uptake of the linguistic products of speakers. Part of the symbolic capital of any individual, the linguistic habitus, is one element of embodied cultural capital. Included in the linguistic habitus are phonological, morphological, syntactic and semantic representations. The habitus enables spoken interpersonal interactions, along with participation in culturally valued literate practices, and is also necessary to maintain normalised relationships with others. The linguistic habitus is interrelated with other local fields of discourse and practice, and also with other forms of cultural, economic and social capital.

It is also important to realise that the linguistic habitus is realised through a process of legitimisation, entailing a set of social relations or an institution, and the joint participation of speaker and listener. The right to speak and the power to impose reception is intrinsic to this. In Bourdieu's (1993) terms, this participation is between the authorised speaker and the believing listener. That is, a speaker must possess the authority to speak, part of which is derived from the listener. In the context of schools for example, Bourdieu (1993: 65) argues the following:

> In order for the teacher's ordinary discourse, uttered and received as self-evident, to function, there has to be a relationship of authority and belief, a relation between an authorized emitter and a receiver ready to receive, and it is not the pedagogic situation that produces this.

Bourdieu stresses that an institution, action or usage is dominant when it is tacitly rather than overtly recognised as such. The hearer may therefore tacitly accept or deny the authority of the speaker to speak, and if symbolic capital is not recognised as such, it is not capital.

An irony of the legitimisation process, however, lies in the fact that such tacit recognition amounts to what Thompson (1991) insists is the active complicity of dominated individuals in their own subjection. In his words, 'symbolic power requires, as a condition of its success, that those subjected to it believe in the legitimacy of power and the legitimacy of those who wield it' (p. 23). In the dominant discourse, the manner of speaking is integral to the legitimising process, as shown by Bourdieu's (1993: 66) statement, 'One of the political effects of the dominant language is this: 'He says it so well it must be true''. The implication is that the reverse may also be applied to those subjected to the dominant discourse. That is, if you have the 'wrong accent', non-standard pronunciation or faulty syntax, in Bourdieu's terms, you may also lack credibility, and the affirmatory role of the believing listener. Such aspects of the discourse will be negotiated on the linguistic market.

The linguistic market and language values

The French title of *Language and Symbolic Power* is *Ce que parler veut dire: l'économie des échanges linguistiques*, which places language use firmly in the domain of linguistic exchange in the economic sense. In other words, one's language practices are a product of the interplay between the linguistic habitus and the properties of the market itself. Bourdieu (1993: 62) writes, 'the language used in a particular situation depends not only, as internal linguistics supposes, on the speaker's competence in the Chomskyan sense, but also on what I call the linguistic market'. He stresses further that language is used with a view to its acceptability, or its value, on a specific market.

Clearly, learning the 'acceptability' of a specific instance of language use entails more than mastering a genre or discourse. It also implies an analysis of how a particular practice is situated in a particular social field. Part of this analysis is knowing the market. In the educational field, an official bureaucratised institutional field, there are concrete values assigned to such knowledge and the acceptable use of language, in the form of grades awarded. It has been argued, for example, that senior school external exams reward cultural competence that is acquired outside of the class-room (Freebody, 1990). The market therefore has the power to reward language which is approved, received, or legitimated, and to sanction and censor that which is not. However, Bourdieu makes it clear that acceptability is not simply grammaticality. Values assigned to the social conditions of language production mean that, as Bourdieu (1991: 38) writes, 'Grammar defines meaning only very partially: it is in relation to a market that the complete determination of the signification of discourse occurs'. Recall here Canale's (1983) notion that grammatical competence is only one aspect of overall communicative competence. However, Canale's model places discourse, strategic and sociolinguistic competence firmly within the domain of the individual speaker. In SLA theory there is often reference to social fields, but there is little sustained analysis of fields of power, identity and value. By contrast, Bourdieu's concept of *market* brings into relief the importance of how our competence is valued by others.

Linguistic products are not equally valued, and they may be differently valued in different markets. In simple terms, speakers are heard quite differently by interlocutors in different fields. One of the practical competences of a speaker is, as Thompson (1991) suggests, to know how to produce expressions which are highly valued on the market, that is, to be able to manipulate the discourse to work in one's own interest. Clearly not all speakers have access to this kind of competence, especially across classes, or across languages. A speaker's competence which is highly valued in some fields may therefore be almost worthless in other fields. Inevitably, discrepancies arise between what Thompson (1991: 21) calls,

> linguistic markets and the forms of censorship associated with them, on the one hand, and the capacities of individuals from differing social backgrounds to produce linguistic expressions appropriate to those markets, on the other.

Lippi-Green (1997) builds a powerful case that in the educational field, the odds are stacked against those who do not produce or demonstrate 'appropriate' use of the dominant discourse. The vast majority of students she is referring to are from socially and linguistically diverse backgrounds, and she shows that their linguistic varieties are not valued by educational authorities, bureaucracies, teachers or employers, that is, those authorised to control the linguistic market. To understand this phenomenon more fully, it is pertinent to look at what Bourdieu says about schools as institutions.

Uneven playing fields

It has been seen that the value of utterances is a product of the relationship of the linguistic habitus and a particular linguistic market. All utterances, according to Bourdieu, are inseparable from the institutional context or field where they occur, an institution being 'any durable set of social relations which *endows* individuals with power, status and resources of various kinds' (in Thompson, 1991: 8). Utterances are therefore 'underwritten' by the social relations inherent in the institution, relations which authorise members in various ways. Thompson (1991: 8–9 continues,

> The efficacy of performative utterances presupposes a set of social relations, an institution, by virtue of which a particular individual, who is *authorised* to speak and *recognised* as such by others, is able to speak in a way that others will regard as acceptable in the circumstances.

Once again, we have here the notion of the authorised speaker, recognised through 'acceptable' language use as legitimate by others. Administrations and teachers are obvious examples of recognised authorities within schools. In their formal capacities, it is they who confer and oversee the values of the market, and who award the grades. Bourdieu (1991: 45) argues that teachers are responsible for inculcating mastery of the 'official' language, and are 'empowered *universally* to subject the linguistic performance of speaking subjects to examination and to legal sanction of academic qualification'. In this way, schools set the values of different linguistic products, at least for purposes of assessment and credentialling. These values authorise particular students in turn, while disempowering and disadvantaging others. Within the field or market place of school, the conditions of reception are already skewed against those who have not acquired the 'basic, deeply interiorised master patterns' of the dominant discourse (Bourdieu, 1991: 192). The use of these master patterns raises a question as to whether teachers can actually do anything to change the life chances of individual students. Bourdieu (1993: 67) suggests, for example, that it is the teacher's moral duty to correct a student's grammar, since failure to do so disadvantages the student in other fields and markets. He writes,

> A teacher who refuses to correct his pupil's speech is perfectly entitled to do so, but in doing so he may compromise his pupil's chances on the matrimonial market or the economic market, where the laws of the dominant linguistic market still prevail.

The implication here is that teachers *can* change mental and bodily structures which Bourdieu has already defined as social structures. But how are teachers to alter deeply interiorised patterns, inculcated since birth? If grammar only partially determines meaning (Bourdieu, 1991), how effective is correcting a pupil's utterance, and what is its purpose? We could also ask what else is occurring along with the correction of the student's language. Luke (1992) suggests that certain language practices inscribed at the site of the school are actually inscriptions of the authority and power relations within the institution itself, onto the student. Although Bourdieu suggests that a teacher's intervention could help change patterns which might affect a student's life chances, his primary argument is that schools serve primarily those who are ready in advance to learn what school has to offer, while disadvantaging those who are unprepared, excluding them by neglect. This view explains in part the apparent ease of success of some students, and the struggle of others.

Lessons from Bourdieu

There are several lessons that can be drawn from the above. First, it has been seen that Bourdieu provides cogent reasons for rejecting structuralist linguistics and depoliticised sociolinguistics alike as means for understanding critical aspects of language. The social and cultural contexts of language production and reception are part of the text, help frame the text, and ultimately render 'value' in the form of symbolic capital to a text, whether spoken or written. This is the critical theoretical notion that is largely missing from SLA theory (Norton, 2000; Norton Peirce, 1995; Pennycook, 2001). Second, within this framing, certain forms are privileged or authorised over others, with part of this authority emanating from the listener. Recognition from the field is crucial to the symbolic power of the speaker. Authority is also derived from the linguistic habitus, engaged in a particular linguistic market and a particular field. Saying something well, and therefore appearing to speak 'true', highlights that one's manner of speaking, quite apart from substantive content, is part of the legitimating process. How one is *heard* is therefore immensely important. And for Bourdieu (1977a), this relates not just to what the speaker sounds like, but also to the embodied dispositions of the linguistic habitus. Finally, it has been shown that these principles operate within schools as institutions, where practices and values are not a product of learned rules, but of cultural, economic and social capital gleaned elsewhere.

Bourdieu, described by Jenkins (1992: 176) as 'good to think with', offers a direction for understanding social practices, including linguistic practices, as situated encounters framed within institutions, such as schools. This direction is summarised by Thompson (1991: 31) in the introduction to *Language and Symbolic Power*.

> The first step in creating new social relations, alternative ways of organising social and political life, is to understand the socially instituted limits of the ways of speaking, thinking and acting which are characteristic of our societies today.

In this book I propose to take this kind of first step, and to begin to deconstruct the 'socially instituted' ways of hearing second language speakers.

. . . and beyond

Bourdieu's (1991) concept of habitus is defined as a set of dispositions with four characteristics. They are structured (by the social conditions in which they were acquired), durable (ingrained in the body), generative (of a practical sense of how to act and speak), and transposable (to other fields). While it has been argued that Bourdieu's notions of habitus, capital and field enable us to think critically about social language use, some take exception to the determinist stance affiliated with the notion of habitus

(Jenkins, 1992; Nash, 1990). Thompson (1991) suggests an overreliance on determinist class structures within the work of Bourdieu, classes which are more theoretical constructs than actual social groups. This approach, he warns, tends to 'misconstrue a whole series of questions concerning the ways in which agents mobilize themselves through representation' (p. 29). Nash (1990: 446) similarly finds that the idea of habitus contains insufficient recognition of agency, of the power of self to make choices, and is ultimately an 'inherently ambiguous and overloaded concept'. It presupposes stable people in a stable world, a virtually unthinkable and unworkable notion in contemporary times.

One way through this problem resides in using Bourdieu to think against Bourdieu, a theoretical pathway well established by the theorist himself (Jenkins, 1992). Returning to the nature of the set of dispositions which comprise the habitus, we see possibilities for a more dynamic interpretation. That is, if dispositions constituted by particular social conditions are generative and transposable to other fields, these other fields may provide new sets of social conditions, and therefore generate new dispositions. As people move across boundaries, geographic, ideological, social, cultural and linguistic, they may acquire new ways of speaking and acting, new ways of being. Bourdieu also provides us with an understanding that linguistic practices cannot sensibly be studied in isolation from power relations and capital relations in social fields. But to see how language use is linked in everyday contexts to issues of social identity, we need to turn to recent conceptualisations of identity and the role of discourse, and speaking, within these.

Theorising Links Between Discourse and Identity

> The reflexive project of the self, which consists in the sustaining of coherent, yet continually revised, biographical narratives, takes place in the context of multiple choice as filtered through abstract systems. (Giddens, 1991: 5)

The substantial body of recent writing and research concerned with the notion of identity encompasses a dazzling diversity of terminology, including social identity, ethnic identity, cultural identity, linguistic identity, sociocultural identity, subjectivity, the self, and voice. Hall (1996: 2) has described identity as a key concept, 'an idea which cannot be thought in the old way, but without which certain key questions cannot be thought at all'. Some of these questions are closely related to discourse, and the understanding that we are shaped by and through our use of language (Le Page & Tabouret-Keller, 1985; Tabouret-Keller, 1997; Weedon, 1987). Giddens' (1991: 3) view that the self is reflexively made 'amid a puzzling diversity of options and possibilities' (p. 3), reminds us that all experience is mediated through social practices, language use and our own reflexive responses. Many recent critical works have stressed the constitutive link between discourse and social identity (Gee, 1996; Hall, 1996; Heller, 1994; van Dijk, 1997b). Two premises which such works share are the notions of shifting multiple identities and the discursive construction of identity, which incorporates the key notion of representation.

Towards a notion of shifting multiple identities

Although the concept of identity has been a preoccupation of many theorists and writers in recent times, there has been a fundamental shift away from unified, originary, essentialist notions of identity (Hall & du Gay, 1996), towards identity conceptualised as a process of continual emerging and becoming. Tied to this is what Hall (1996: 1) has described as an 'anti-essentialist critique of ethnic, racial and national conceptions of cultural identity'. Unitary labels and hard binary oppositions are rejected in favour of the conception of multiple identities, 'points of temporary attachment' (p. 6), which are fluid, dynamic, contradictory, shifting, contingent and processual. Hall stresses that identities are not unified but increasingly fragmented, not singular but 'multiply constructed across different, often intersecting and antagonistic discourses, practices and positions' (p. 4). Nor are identities given through race, gender, community membership, kinship and so on. This is not unlike Giddens' (1991: 14) idea that identity 'forms a *trajectory* across the different institutional settings of modernity'. The word 'trajectory' evokes concepts of movement, evolutionary development, and change – all of which are coherent with contemporary conceptualisations of identity.

Although the contemporary conceptualisation of identity is that it is always in process, and never complete, Giddens reminds us that we need not think of ourselves as fragmented, forced by diversity into some kind of mass schizophrenia. He writes,

> It would not be correct to see contextual diversity as simply and inevitably promoting the fragmentation of the self, let alone its disintegration into multiple 'selves'. It can just as well, at least in many circumstances, promote an integration of self . . . A person may make use of diversity in order to create a distinctive self-identity which positively incorporates elements from different settings into an integrated narrative. (Giddens, 1991: 190)

The concept of 'making use of diversity' is an important one, and presupposes a certain level of linguistic and symbolic capital. That is, using diversity in this way implies the notion of agency, in which one draws on a range of language and other resources. Building 'the integrated narrative' therefore is not a given, but an ongoing project involving the acquisition of the discourses of the narrative.

The discursive construction of identity

In her powerful book on the ideological ties between language use and subordination in the US, Lippi-Green (1997: 5) describes language as 'the most salient way we have of establishing and advertising our social identities'. In her analysis of the attempt to destroy the identities of the indigenous tribes of North America, she describes how the focus of the attack became the languages of the tribes. This marked the astute realisation that without their languages, the tribes would lose the strongest unifying feature of their tribal identities. A similar claim could be made against the authorities which removed indigenous children from their families in Australia in the first half of the twentieth century. Forbidding these children to use their native languages was an attempt to destroy their primary sense of identity, which was embedded in their indigenous cultures. Similar motives lay behind the prohibition of Catalan in Franco's post-war regime in Spain. Anyone who doubts the powerful connection between identity and language need look no further than the nationalist movement in Quebec, for which the French language has and continues to be a cornerstone. That is, Quebeckers represent themselves as a distinct society and culture on the basis of their historical experiences as francophones (Heller, 1994). It is worth noting however that Le Page & Tabouret-Keller (1985) caution against any easy equivalence between language and ethnic identity or national consciousness, demonstrating the linguistic and ethnic diversity and complexity within any purported group.

In a review of recent conceptualisations of identity, Hall (1996: 4) emphasises that it is discursively constructed. He writes, 'Precisely because identities are constructed within, not outside, discourse, we need to understand them as produced in specific historical and institutional sites within specific discursive formations and practices, by specific enunciative strategies'. Rampton (1995) makes a similar point, stressing the importance of the specificity of local sites, and arguing that studies of identity must attend to local and autobiographical histories, along with representational resources and contexts. According to Hall, the notion that identity is discursively constructed has several implications. First, identity must be seen as processual and never completed. Second, identity takes place within and not outside of representation. That is, identity both produces and is produced through discourse practices, which may be paradoxical and imbued with aspects of race, class, status and gender. An example of the tie between identity and representation is offered by van Dijk *et al.* (1997: 145). They point out that 'the ways members of one ethnic group speak among each other are of course related to their position in society, and how they are spoken to and about by dominant group members'. Third, identity and representation involve a two-way process or articulation between the subject and the discursive practice, and between speaker and hearer. Evidence of this is the way we adjust our speech according to whom we are with, how we view those people, and how we are viewed.

In the field of second language research, the discursive construction of identity has been stressed by Miller (1999, 2000), Norton, (1997, 2000); Norton Peirce (1995); Pavlenko and Blackledge (in press); Rampton (1995) and others. Norton Peirce (1995: 13) writes,

> It is through language that a person negotiates a sense of self within and across different sites at different points in time, and it is through language that a person gains access to – or is denied access to – powerful social networks that give learners the opportunities to speak. (1995, p. 13)

The process of acquiring new linguistic, social and cultural practices has been described by Pavlenko and Lantolf (2000) as a 'self-translation,' a transformation of self through discourse necessary for discursive assimilation, in which one is heard and read by others. Rampton's concepts of language expertise, affiliation and inheritance are all related to identity. Affiliation in particular connotes active use of and identification with a particular language or dialect. The language we are affiliated to reflects how we wish to speak, but also how we are positioned to speak and how we are heard. Norton Peirce also proposes the related idea of *investment* in language learning and use. She claims that investment signals better than motivation the socially and historically constructed relationship between language learner and target language, as well as ambivalent attitudes towards practising and using the language. The link between discourse and identity is undisputed by these and many other writers, but there is a need to look more closely at the relationship between language, identity and social membership, particularly when a second language is being acquired and used.

Enacting identity

In *Social Linguistics and Literacies* (1996), Gee builds a powerful case that discourse patterns are among the strongest expressions of social identity. He shows how we shift our identity positions and discourses to express solidarity with particular groups, using language variation to manifest membership and to demarcate particular social identities. Gee outlines a theory which integrates the notions of language, identity and membership in a simple yet elegant way.

To grasp what is entailed in the process of enacting identity, it is worth recalling Gee's definition of Discourses, as 'ways of being in the world, or forms of life . . . a kind of identity kit' (p. 127), the point of the process being that we assume social roles that others will recognise. Being recognised by other members signals that we are insiders to that group. Gee points out that an 'insider' of any group or discourse must get things 'right' – say the right thing, while being the right who, doing the right what. He states simply, 'It's not just what you say or even how you say it, it's who you are and what you are doing while you say it' (p. viii). Gee describes the key notion of the 'insider', the person functioning within the Discourse, and acting as gatekeeper to those who would enter. A direct implication is that there are also 'outsiders', those who get it wrong.

Identity, the 'who we are and what we are doing', Gee (1996: 69) argues, is enacted through a three-way simultaneous interaction between (a) our social or cultural group memberships, (b) a particular social language or mixture of them, and (c) a particular context. It is useful to envisage Gee's notion as a simple integrated diagram, as shown in Figure 2.2.

We could also hypothesise that any change to one aspect of the diagram will flow on to other aspects. That is, each new context has consequences in terms of social practices, memberships and language use. This graphic representation of Gee's idea allows us to extrapolate to situations and interactions from everyday experience. For example, as I move from my son's soccer match, to a university lecture, to a family dinner, to a store where I'm trying to change an unwanted gift, my social memberships

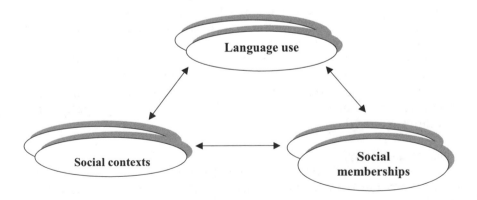

Figure 2.2 Enacting identity

move from footy parent, to academic staff member, to family member, to ingratiating but hopeful customer. The language used in each of these contexts changes significantly to reflect these contexts and social memberships.

It should be added that it is not enough to be seen and heard in language interactions. Gee takes his cue from Bourdieu, namely that the speaker must also be authorised, recognised and accepted as a group member, having 'word-deed-value combinations' acknowledged as legitimate by others (p. 127). In this way one is apprenticed to the Discourses and social practices of the group. For this to happen, the speaker must be heard as a user of the group's language, understood and acknowledged as a legitimate speaker of that language. We could say that for the purposes of integration of immigrant students into the mainstream, being visibly different is sometimes less important than being audibly similar. For example, the huge contrast between the linguistic and social practices of Australian born Chinese students (known as ABCs) and adolescent Chinese or Taiwanese immigrants is evidenced on a daily basis by teachers and other students in many schools, as will be seen in later chapters of this book. Where the speakers are excluded from native speaker groups, some isolation from the mainstream culture is likely (see Miller, 1999, 2000). Through talk, the speaker flags his/her identity, and demonstrates that he/she is a candidate for group membership. This two-way process, whereby what we do and say engages directly with how others hear us and what they do back, is intrinsic to the process of enacting identity, and critical for conceptualising the social and linguistic adjustment of linguistic minority students.

The model of Gee's theory above represents aspects of identity discussed so far. It accounts for ways identities shift across a range of contexts, and for the pivotal role of language use, or discourse, in identity construction. By implication, it also involves the potential for inclusion within or exclusion from particular social groups, and in particular contexts.

Sites of identity representation

The notion of sites of representation is a useful one which throws into relief the textualised and contextualised nature of the discourses of identity. As we move from one site to another, encountering different partners in interaction, we invoke different representations of our identities, and draw on different linguistic resources. Within school there are, for example, many sites one could observe – visualise the ESL classroom, the mainstream English classroom, the school assembly, the handball court, the tuckshop queue, a corridor, the administration lobby, the manual arts centre, the music block, the place under B block where the in-crowd sits, the home economics staffroom, the bus stop outside the school. As the eye roams like some wild hand-held camera, we hear the different discourses, and take note of their resonances. Each of these sites affords linguistic minority students different opportunities, constraints and conditions to speak, and to represent themselves through language use. Beyond the school, other sites present other possibilities, constraints and conditions.

In regard to such sites of representation for minority students, it is impossible to avoid the question of which particular language is in use. There are presumably sites of first language use, sites of second and third language use, and sites where these overlap and intersect. How we speak and are heard within sites seems critical to social identity work. Furthermore, the sites are themselves value-laden, as are the discourses within them. Sites of representation can therefore be compared to Bourdieu's *fields*, social spaces where discourse and social activity take place. These sites are places in which identity is enacted, where social interactions, cultures, languages and identities are made manifest, where the 'insidering' and 'outsidering' is done, where spoken discourse is heard or not heard, is validated or remains unacknowledged, where membership is made available or denied. Identity is thus accomplished through social activity and practices, spoken and written texts, and particular sites of activity and representation. This is compatible with Gee's conceptualisation of enacting identity through social memberships, a particular social language or mixture of languages, and contexts. However the idea of representation is critical. It is the focus of the concluding section of this chapter, where I return to language use, and specifically to speaking as a means of self-representation.

Speaking and Self-representation

Voice and representation

For many theorists, particularly those working within the field of cultural studies, the notion of representation is often tied to a metaphorical use of the term *voice*. Giroux's (1992) concern is with the politics of voice and difference, that is, the wider issues of how students function as agents, and how they are rendered voiceless in certain contexts, or silence themselves as a result of intimidation, real or perceived. Giroux signals that racialising practices in schools often involve the silencing of the voices of linguistic minority students, whose cultural capital is not valued by dominant school cultures. This is a slant on racism qualitatively different from that manifested by overt violence, or racial slurs. There is no direct attack implied here – just a denial of the right to speak and be heard, and the non-hearing of first languages other than English. At this point, the term *voice* undergoes a qualitative shift, from its metaphorical sense of an authorised claim, to a more literal yet highly symbolic sense – spoken voices. Students from subordinate groups are silenced because they are unable to represent themselves through their first languages at school. And they are heard as different.

Speaking is therefore a critical tool of representation, a way of representing the self and others. It is the means through which identity is negotiated, and agency or self-advocacy is made manifest, via a process of legitimisation, whereby speakers are authorised to represent themselves. Speakers may also be marked as belonging to specific groupings by their use of spoken language, which may provide for hearers an index to class, gender, age, ethnicity, social status, education and countries of origin. In English-speaking countries, the dominant group speaks the dominant variety of English, the so-called unmarked or unaccented form (Lippi-Green, 1997). Children who lose their native accents are thus judged to have no accent. And there are social, personal and academic rewards for those who sound the same as the dominant majority. Linguistic skills in English are therefore symbolic resources not equally available to all persons, and are heavily endowed with social currencies. To explore this further, we need to look more closely at the physical representation of voice, the practical activity of speaking.

Speaking and audibility

Speaking, and what Bourdieu (1977b: 648) calls 'the power to impose reception', cannot sensibly be divorced from listening, or the conditions of reception. Bourdieu (1993) stresses that in any communicative interaction, there has to be a legitimate emitter, a legitimate receiver, a legitimate situation and a legitimate language. Legitimacy derives from the cultural or symbolic capital of the speaker and listener. Capital must thus be recognised and acknowledged as such to function as capital. The notions of legitimacy and authority are also found in Gee's (1996) conception of Discourses, in which the word-deed-value combinations must be recognised and acknowledged as 'right' by the interlocutor. The importance of this for ESL students in schools cannot be stressed enough.

To be authorised and recognised as a legitimate user of English by others, you must first be heard by other legitimate users of English. If you speak another language, or English with an accent, or in other ways that are heard as non-standard, there are often consequences for the speaker. Normally in spoken interactions, the responsibility for keeping the communication alive is shared. In cases where the speaker is not fluent in English or has an accent, speakers and listeners have to work hard sometimes to 'foster mutual intelligibility', which requires both an effort of will and a degree of social acceptance (Lippi-Green, 1997: 70). However, the dominant speaker may refuse to carry any responsibility for the communicative act. What Lippi-Green calls 'language ideology filters' come into play whenever an accent or a hesitant 'non-standard' voice is heard, causing the listener to reject what she calls 'the communicative burden'. Implied in the process is a negative evaluation not just of the accent and other non-standard features, but of the social identity of the speaker. What the listener brings to the message, and his or her willingness to listen may powerfully impact on the effectiveness of the communication. Lippi-Green cites one study in which students who saw that a lecturer was Asian were actually incapable of *hearing* objectively, showing that racial and ethnic cues may be more critical than accentedness. In this instance, the visible cues were overriding what was actually heard. It is significant that this was not a close social interaction, but a mass lecture situation. The example does show the complex interplay between visual and aural cues, but what if the students were to communicate with the lecturer on an individual basis when they needed help? Would a better hearing be granted? The interaction may be reminiscent of the scene between Kan and Hank at the start of Chapter 1, or the student may share some of the responsibility in the communication, in listening to and understanding the lecturer. It would be in their interests to do so. Others might reject the idea of even approaching the lecturer based on what they had 'heard' so far. This is a complex problem, and will remain a focus throughout this volume.

The theoretical framing I have undertaken in this chapter opens up traditional SLA concerns such as communicative competence to include broader sociocultural contexts, discourses, linguistic and cultural capital, audibility and the representation of identity. This is the background against which we need to look at the huge challenges facing students whose first language is not English. Developing proficiency in the language involves communicative competence, but also the acquisition of social and academic discourses and linguistic, social and cultural capital. Further, to be accepted as a legitimate member and participant at school, one first needs to be audible to mainstream groups. In the first instance, this means speaking loudly and clearly enough, and in a variety of the discourse that can be readily understood and acknowledged by other speakers. Communicative competence has a role to play here. However, audibility is more than this. Being audible to others, and being heard and acknowledged as a speaker of English, may determine the extent to which a student can participate in social interactions and practices within the educational mainstream. Being audible also provides the means of self-representation, as well as the essential underlying condition for the ongoing acquisition of English through practice, and continuing identity work.

This is where the school context becomes so important. Conditions at school, including social and institutional practices, may or may not provide an environment which favours the development of second language competence in a range of discourses. Here then are the issues to be explored in the three main data chapters of this book, which present five students' stories. To set the scene for the detailed case studies, the following chapter provides a snapshot of the students just before they left the intensive language centre, which I have called Newnham High School (pseudonym). It is time to enter into the detail of the students' lives, to hear them speak, and to think about the issues above in the 'light' of their voices.

Chapter 3

On Leaving Newnham: The End of Arrival

Introduction

In the previous chapter I suggested that while contextualised communicative competence cannot be ignored in any understanding of language acquisition by linguistic minority students, it is important to take an integrated perspective which includes social contexts, memberships and interactions, that is, the ways in which identities are represented through language use. Such a perspective also throws light on how speakers position themselves, and are positioned through discourses and social practices (Norton, 2000; Norton & Toohey, 2001; Pavlenko & Blackledge (in press); Rampton, 1995). In this chapter I introduce the cohort of students from which the case study participants were selected. Using data from two videotaped focus groups, I want to explore and to problematise the notion of contextualised communicative competence and to look further at the links between speaking and social interaction. The focus groups were held at Newnham High School (pseudonym), an intensive ESL reception centre, at the end of the on-arrival programme for these students. It was important to talk with them before they left Newnham, as this was the end of the first phase of their learning English in Australia, the end of arrival. This was also the last opportunity to see the students all together. After the summer holidays they would be in five different schools. Their recent visits to their new schools was one of the subjects discussed in the focus group. Because Newnham High is an unusual school, it is useful to understand some of its features, before moving to the focus group data.

Newnham State High School

Newnham High School is a federally funded intensive English reception centre for high school age migrants and refugees. I had worked at this school intermittently for over a decade, and always found it the least stressful and most rewarding school teaching I have experienced. Com-

50

prising approximately 160 students aged 12 to 19 years from 20 to 30 nationalities, it offers an intensive ESL programme to students for six months on average prior to their move to high school ESL Support Units and then to mainstream integration. The Newnham school population varies a great deal over time, depending on patterns of migration and humanitarian programmes responding to various international crises. There is a diversity of ages, ethnic backgrounds, languages, cultures, socioeconomic status and circumstances of migration within the Newnham population. The one common factor is that students arrive at the school with little or no English. Newnham does not fit easily therefore into the definition of a speech community developed by Gumperz and Hymes (1986: 54), that is, a community sharing rules for the conduct and interpretation of speech, and rules for the interpretation of at least one linguistic variety (p. 54). The only linguistic variety in common for these students is English, which they are acquiring. English functions therefore as a lingua franca, and there are naturally vast differences among the students in terms of levels of proficiency. Some need just a few weeks at the school to 'acclimatise', while others who have had almost no schooling in their country of origin, interrupted schooling, or learning disabilities, tend to stay a year or more.

Newnham is like a collection of imported speech communities in one site, as well as being an integrating community in which nascent English skills are practised and developed, while twenty or so other languages continue to be spoken. Sometimes students speak their first language intentionally to other students who don't understand. In this case, the first language is used to exclude (or include other members who may be nearby), and may function as a source of humour or even of abuse. I have on occasion witnessed a torrent of derision in a language unknown by the interlocutor, resulting in a sense of powerlessness that is almost tangible. Even when the L1 is used with a humorous motive, the effect is discomforting. However, the overwhelming impression of the interactions amongst Newnham students is one of intercultural and multilingual harmony and acceptance. Walking around the school at lunch time one notes that the majority are in their first language groups, but others are engaged in interethnic cross-cultural interactions in English – on the basketball courts and soccer fields, in the library, on the computers, or just sitting in groups around the grounds.

Many features of Newnham are expressly designed to smooth the way for students to feel they belong to the school community. The school provides a strong positive model of interculturalism and anti-racism; the guidance officer speaks Mandarin and Cantonese; all teachers are qualified ESL specialists and many speak another language; there is a strong emphasis on pastoral care and providing access to community and government services for students and their families; there are low teacher–pupil ratios and there is also the pervasive and much-valued presence of numerous bilingual teacher aides, including speakers of Spanish, Serbo-Croatian, Vietnamese, Cantonese, Mandarin, Arabic, German and French. Students enrol at the school year-round, and within days of arriving in the country. There is a brief assessment of their spoken and written English, and they are placed in one of twelve classes, depending on their English language proficiency. The beginner classes are therefore multi-age, with students aged between 12 and 19. Every five weeks a class exits to one of seven high school ESL units, where intensive ESL support continues prior to mainstreaming. There are frequent staff meetings to determine if any students should be moved to a more or less demanding level, or need extra support. There is therefore a constant spiralling towards exit and adjustment to the students' needs and rate of progress. After the beginner level, students are placed whenever possible in age-appropriate groups.

Newnham also plays a significant role in providing images of 'Australian' cultural identity and social practices to students. There are excursions and outings, sports and swimming carnivals, three-day camps in the bush, visits from students from other schools and members of the community. The students receive intensive language-focused tuition in English, Mathematics, Science, and Physical Education, but there is no formal summative assessment in any subject, although ESL bandscales (McKay, 1995) are used to assign levels to the macro-skills of listening, speaking, reading and writing for each student. The emphasis is on learning the discourses of the subjects as intensively as possible, but in a non-competitive and very supportive climate. In addition, many practices of regular high schools are modelled, such as daily classroom administrative routines, the afternoon of sport or electives, visits from performing artists, the tuckshop, and the access to sports fields at lunch time. I once noted the sports field looked just like the mainstream version. There were 32 boys playing basketball, 16 boys playing soccer, and not a single girl playing either. Like any school, Newnham is a complex mixture of social identities and heirarchies enacted within a range of micro-environments. I do not want to represent the school as an idealised site, devoid of contradictions, conflicts and the occasional fisticuffs. However, students often write and say that they love this school, which made their language and settlement needs priorities, and many return to visit whenever possible. Compared with regular high schools, Newnham is intimate, supportive and nurturing, and students often experience the move to high school, which several former students had told me was 'real school', as quite traumatic (Miller, 1999).

The Videotaped Focus Groups

The purpose of these groups, as explained to the students, was to talk about the ways they had learned English in their own countries (where relevant) and at Newnham, and to discuss their experiences at Newnham and their knowledge and expectations of high school. The group context was to facilitate their interactions with each other as well as with me. As I felt students might be inhibited in a group of 10, I formed two focus groups, largely on the basis of age, ending up with an older group (15–16 years) and a younger group (13–14 years). The groups were videotaped, and the tapes were then fully transcribed. Students marked with an asterisk are those featured in the main case studies. Names used are pseudonyms.

Group 1 participants

Name	Age	Country of origin	DOA	LOR
Tina (F)*	15	Taiwan	10.7.96	5 months
Milena (F)*	16	Bosnia	21.9.96	2.5 months
Alex (M)	15	Bosnia	5.8.96	4 months
Sinitia (M)	14	Rumania	16.8.96	5.5 months
John (M)*	16	Hong Kong	29.9.96	2.5 months

Group 2 participants

Name	Age	Country of origin	DOA	LOR
Nora*	14	China	5.5.96	7 months
Alicia*	13	China	5.12.94	2 years
Carlos	14	El Salvador	15.1.96	11 months
Silina	13	Samoa	29.5.96	8.5 months
Bun Tan	14	Cambodia	28.9.95	1 year 2.5 months

* Included in the main case studies
DOA = date of arrival; LOR = length of residence;

The students had been in Australia for between two and a half months and two years. By chance, most of the younger group had arrived much earlier, and spent longer in the intensive programme. Alicia had spent a year in Queensland primary school before being referred to Newnham.

Four students in the groups were noticeably more proficient speakers in English than the others. These were Milena, Alex and Sinitia in the older group and Carlos in the younger group. After watching and listening to the videotapes, my interest was initially drawn to these differences in communicative performance and to consider their implications for self-representation in a group situation. What did certain students do that made me hear them as competent speakers? How did this relate to other conditions in their acquisition and use of English? As the study progressed, I gained increasing insight into the contextual and sociocultural features which impacted on the everyday experiences of these students. However, I began by looking with a language teacher's eye and ear at their spoken English, hence the initial focus here on the traditional SLA concept of communicative competence.

Prior to the videotaped focus group sessions, each group spent one 'warm-up' session with me, in which we played language games, and students became more familiar with each other, as they had come from different classes. Even within this 45 minute period, the communication games provided some sense of group cohesion, and a level of confidence in speaking in front of the others. It was also important to create a climate of acceptance and of valuing what was said, while keeping proceedings light-hearted. This was to minimise the anxiety many learners feel in relation to their oral skills (Norton, 2000; Tsui, 1996).

The relaxed atmosphere of the warm-up sessions was counteracted to an extent by the surface formality of the videotaping conditions. The taping was done in an office of the administration block, an official room not normally used by students, and we sat in a U shape around a table. Although the cameraman was a teacher aide well known to the students and to me, the videotaping of students was relatively unusual in the school at this time. During the focus groups, I had a folder on the desk in front of me and a set of questions or prompts, which also perhaps reinforced the formality of my role as teacher/group coordinator. However, it should be added that I was known in this role by the students, having taught most of them on occasion in my relief teacher work. The situation was not designed to provide spontaneous talk (which is technologically much harder to capture and record), but resembled more a semi-structured interview, or class discussion. It is worth noting that this context, and my known teacher role, account for certain asymmetries in the talk, and rendered 'normal' such things as the allocation of roles, the use of preplanned questions, the 'directing' of the talk, a level of formality appropriate to student–teacher relations (from students and researcher), and the use of prompts and scaffolding. In these terms, the focus group data is certainly talk, but a different register of talk from spontaneous naturally occurring conversation or individual interviews. The participants may also have felt positioned as 'ESL students in a study'.

Of interest in the transcripts from these two videotaped groups are the responses given by students to specific questions and issues, but even more significantly, the patterns of talk and levels of interaction which emerged in spite of the formalised context and allocation of roles. Finally it should be added that a focus group of five (plus researcher) provided the possibility for the more proficient speakers to take the floor, but a real challenge for those used to avoiding speaking in English for a number of reasons. In a group of five, it is less easy to hide, and obvious to an observer when one member is silent. In the individual interviews, I had focused on personal issues and autobiographical details, trying to build up a profile of the individual student and his/her background. This was familiar material for the students, who had frequently drawn on their biographies in the Newnham curriculum. For the videotaped groups, the focus shifted to the study of English, ways to learn a language, the students' use of their first language and of English, and also their expectations of high school.

Note on transcription symbols

The following conventions, based on Psathas (1995) were used in the transcripts.

(.)	untimed micro-interval
(2.0)	2 second pause
<u>good</u>	underlining indicates emphasis
(( ))	transcriber's description
[	overlapping talk

The Problem of Communicative Competence

What struck me from the first in analysing the video data, was that although the students were all exiting what may be described as a full immersion ESL programme, where they had access to some first language (L1) support, their levels of fluency and confidence in spoken English were very diverse. Many factors may of course account for this, but it seemed likely that there was a dynamic relationship between their levels of spoken English and their interactions in a range of contexts within and beyond school. By this I mean that opportunities to use English with English speakers scaffolded their developing confidence, and their progress in the language (see also Norton, 2000). Length of residence did not seem to correlate with communicative performance. The most fluent speaker of English, Milena, had been in Australia just over two months, whereas Alicia (from China) had been here almost two years, first in primary school then at Newnham. Their case studies are presented in Chapters 5 and 6.

Before dealing more closely with the relationship between speaking English and social interaction, I wish to address the notion of communicative competence. In Chapter 2, I developed an argument for a very contextualised view of language acquisition and use. Recent interest in social and discursive approaches to the concepts of knowledge and competence aim to restore some of the sociocultural complexities and unique contextual circumstances to our understandings of second language use. However, I would also argue that communicative competence, as outlined by Celce-Murcia *et al.* (1995) encompasses many of these understandings. That is, the development of linguistic, strategic, discourse, sociocultural and actional competences are critical for language learners. I would also argue that Cummins' (2000) framework for academic language learning cannot take place in the absence of communicative competence. The notion of contextualised communicative performance perhaps engages more of the current thinking about the politics of language use, but it should be acknowledged that for learners and teachers the development of 'communicative competence' is fundamental to what they are doing everyday in classrooms. It underpins their curriculum, their tasks and activities, and all assessment procedures. As a teacher and a researcher, I feel the tension around the terminology, and I cannot resolve it other than to say communicative competence is essential to a contextualised communicative performance. While I understand that the focus groups were an unfamiliar context for the students in this study, clearly some students were able to communicate more effectively in this context than others. That is, their levels of spoken English impacted on their level of participation in the focus groups, and indeed on my role as interlocutor and focus group facilitator. What did the students who seemed so competent in their use of English actually do? How was this competence constituted? We know that oral language discourse consists of a number of competences, or discourse proficiencies, including cohesion, comprehensibility, effective use of prosody, elaboration, complexity, grammaticality, a sensitivity to sociocultural context and conversational control. However, I started not with a predetermined checklist, but with the videotapes and transcripts. From the data, I identified seven aspects of language use which I perceived as related to these students' contextualised communicative performance in the focus groups. These are briefly outlined below.

Some elements of contextualised communicative competence

A.   *The use of extended or elaborated discourse*
     When asked about learning English in their own country, Carlos said,

> When I was in school ... we have only every day, have English. But you have to buy a book, but in the book is write all () it's English, nothing Spanish, a̲l̲l̲. You have to write and you have to make some passages ...

The teacher say to speak English, she say to open the book, to read, to do things.

In the focus group interview, Carlos regularly explained things in response to questions, giving examples, generalising, and elaborating ideas. Contrast this with Nora's answer in relation to learning English in China.

(**R** = researcher)

Nora:	We, every day we had one lesson for English. Nearly three years *((Nora speaks very softly, almost inaudibly))*
R:	For three years. And what sort of work did you do in English? (2.0) What sort of lessons? (3.0) Did you read, did you write?
Nora:	Yeah
R:	Did you have to speak at all?
Nora:	No
R:	You didn't have conversations
Nora:	No

A feature of the talk here is the predominant question/answer format. Nora in fact only spoke when nominated by me to answer questions, and several long pauses show that she was having trouble either understanding or responding. Her last three turns are minimal, although she seemed to understand the questions. Several students answered similarly in single words or short phrases.

B. The use of generalisations in English
Certain speakers in the group regularly picked up a point which had been raised, and encapsulated it in a generalised statement. For example, when asked about the new high schools they had just visited, the following interaction occurred.

Milena:	It's nice. You're not supposed to do many things, you know you can't do what you want. I mean, it's just an Australian school, you know. And I have heard that Markwell High is a better school than others. And I talked to one guy from Sandford (High), and he said that Sandford is better than [Markwell
Sinitia:	[Everyone says that the school you go to is the best.

Milena: Just, if you wanna learn, then every school is good for you, you know?

Milena begins by indicating the restrictions she'd heard about at high school. After fleeing Bosnia, she had lived for three years in Denmark, attending schools in Copenhagen. I heard her comment that 'it's just an Australian school', accompanied by a raised eyebrow, as a slight put-down of Australian schools. She then turns to comparative views of two neighbouring high schools. Sinitia intervenes here, shown by the overlap, with the summarising generalisation, 'Everyone says that the school you go to is the best.' Milena's last turn then generalises the relationship between motivation and school quality or reputation. She is also concerned with the acceptability of her statement, shown by the tag, 'you know.' This is, in Gee's (1996) terms, a contextualisation signal, showing both Milena's position and her assumptions as to the positions of others. Sinitia and Milena often constructed the talk between them, taking complementary conversational roles, listening, responding to, building on or contradicting what the other had said. They seemed to have similar levels of proficiency in English and were able to pick up on an idea, develop it, and generalise from it.

C. Point making, using examples

In the last excerpt, Milena made a point about 'just an Australian school', which was not lost on me. I heard her point as 'Typical Australian school – what could you expect?' There were numerous examples of such point making, or expression of a point of view in the focus group data. During talk about TV viewing habits, several students named programmes they liked. Carlos then made a different point about TV.

Nora: Hercules
R: Sorry?
Nora: Hercules
R: That's very simple English in Hercules. ((*All laugh, Carlos the loudest*))
Alicia: Simpsons, Sale of the Century, The Price is Right
Carlos: I don't like to watch too much TV, because you don't have time to do your homework. You have to, to make yourself, to have time to listen to the radio, to watch TV, make another things, you have to make your time, everything, because if you don't make nothing, you always watching TV, you don't have a job, you have nothing.

Nora and Alicia in this excerpt named TV programmes, whereas Carlos was making a point about other activities taking precedence over watching

TV. He uses repetition and paraphrase to construct a moral position about television viewing. Milena and Sinitia also used examples to make a point about how English is learned at Newnham.

R:	What do you do in classes that helps you a lot?
Sinitia:	We talk a lot
Milena:	and teachers explain things
Sinitia:	Even in my country, when we had English lessons, we would ask the teacher in our own language, what that word means (.) but here you ask in English, and you get the answer in English.

Milena also provided a cohesive link, the coordinating conjunction 'and', between Sinitia's first turn and her own, an aspect of conversational competence. Expressing a point of view and providing examples or contexts to support it reflects communicative competence, including linguistic, discourse and sociocultural elements, which allows the student to participate more fully in spoken interaction.

D. Use of markers of casual discourse, including the adolescent 'like'

The more competent speakers used colloquial expressions and aspects of prosody often used by native speakers. These included 'wanna', 'gonna', 'or something', 'you know', 'you know what I mean,' 'kids', 'guys' and the ubiquitous 'like', which marks the speech patterns of so many anglophone adolescents, as shown in the following examples.

Sinitia:	when I write a letter to my country, my language starts to be, like, weird.
and	
Alex:	when is the next time, we're gonna, like, talk?

As I listened to these students, I increasingly understood 'competent' as having had lots of exposure to English, and the chance to talk to people in English. That is, access to conversations in communities, as stressed by Norton and Toohey (2001), seemed an increasingly important criterion for the development of the language features outlined here.

E. Reflection on metalinguistic issues and language learning processes

In considering how Newnham had helped him learn English, Carlos said,

Carlos:	Because when you speak English, it's different when you write, because if you speak English, sometimes the words the same. But when you write, different. You know what I mean?

The grammar is not 'standard', but the point is clearly made about the lack of correspondence between the phonology of English and some written forms. We talked about homophones, and about the dreaded 'ough' in English. Carlos was able to express this significant metalingusitic awareness. Similarly, Milena had clear views on ways to learn a language, as shown in the following interchange.

R:	What are some good ways to learn a language?
Alex:	Read books.
Sinitia:	Speak with Australian friends.
Milena:	That's how I learned Danish, so I'm using that way to learn English . . . I speak a lot in English,'n just read something and translate, take a book and a dictionary.

At the age of 11, Milena moved from Bosnia to Denmark, and she learned Danish in the three years her family spent there. She picks up Sinitia's idea of speaking to Australian friends, using the referential 'that's how'. She then claims to be applying this method, along with others which had worked for her when she learned Danish. Her translation work, for example, was quite independent of school, done in her own time.

Several students rejected my suggestion that students could use English amongst themselves as a strategy for language practice, if they shared a common language.

Milena:	It's weird if I speak English with Alex.
Alex:	It's stupid.
Milena:	Here it's just so weird you know to speak other languages with your family,
Sinitia:	Sometimes when you speak with somebody else from your own language, from your country in English, you get embarrassed or something, maybe you use the wrong word, and you start to laugh.
Milena:	It's weird.
Sinitia:	You don't have to stay and think what word you use.

The claim here, perhaps hardly surprising, was that within one's own language group, there is a strong affective and practical motivation to use the first language. This is partly because language is so closely bound to identity, although Sinitia also draws attention to the time needed to retrieve words in English and the humour when a wrong one is used. Using or practising English in such contexts seemed inauthentic to these students, and was rejected in terms of being 'stupid', 'weird' and 'embarrassing'. So much for the time-worn urgings of ESL teachers (including myself) to 'use English amongst yourselves.'

F. *The use of expressions 'found' in the talk of others*

Although there was clear evidence in the videotapes of students listening to and responding to each other, on several occasions students picked up on a word used in the talk by someone else, and then used it themselves. Sinitia reused Milena's term 'weird', while Carlos understood and later used one of my formulations. After he had summarised the need to 'make your time' instead of watching TV, the following exchange occurred.

R:	So you have to be organised.
C:	Yeah, organised.

He recognised this word, and repeating it made it easier to retrieve next time, which he did a few minutes later.

R:	You know in high school you'll have a lot more homework. What do you think about that?
Nora:	It's too hard [smiles broadly]
Carlos:	You have to organise.

Tuning in, identifying and recycling words and expressions seemed an important part of the work language learners need to do in conversation.

G. *Use of humour*

Humour is generally considered to be strongly defined by particular sociocultural contexts, as well as related to ethnicity and language. My own experiences as a student in France showed that understanding and using humour in a second language often entails quite advanced levels of language proficiency. While all students appeared reasonably relaxed and happy as the videotaping proceeded, some showed a propensity for using and understanding humour. While the context, the 'moment', and non-verbal characteristics are often important in humour, some examples are given below. They were small moments, but (some) students found them funny, as I did.

R:	Has Newnham helped you learn English?
All:	Yes, yeah.
Carlos:	Too much
R:	Too much? ((*All laugh*))

R:	Are there things you still need to improve? ((*I meant in English*))
C:	My behaviour

R:	How do the teachers learn more about you?
Alex:	Next day they knew everything.

It is perhaps contentious to draw conclusions about humour and language competence. However, there were occasions when only the more 'competent' speakers laughed. And ESL teachers know that their jokes have more chance of being understood as the class progresses. There was evidence that the students who laughed also watched programmes on TV such as 'Full Frontal', which consists of comic sketches, satire and parody. Although the humour is often physical, strong listening comprehension skills are needed to understand the gags.

All of the above features provided evidence of the competence which underlies contextualised communicative performance. The use of elaborated patterns, generalisations, examples to illustrate a point, colloquial expressions, comments on language learning itself, and expressions discovered in the process of talking with others were evidenced by those students who felt comfortable speaking English. These features marked the differences, in linguistic terms, between these speakers and their more tentative and silent peers. It is perhaps worth noting that for ESL learners in this beginning context, communicative competence is not the same as grammatical accuracy, as many of Carlos' utterances attested. His errors seldom impeded comprehensibility. Communicative competence is also more than being able to say a lot. The Samoan student Silina had what appeared on the surface to be considerable oral fluency, and she liked to take the floor. However, analysis of the talk often showed a lack of cohesion and relevance, and a failure to make a connection with her listeners. The following interaction relating to the work load at high school is an example.

R:	You know in high school you'll have a lot more homework. What do you think about that?
Nora:	It's too hard *((smiles broadly))*
Carlos:	You have to organise
Nora:	Because in China, in high school too much homework.
R:	Too much? *((Nora nods))* So what do you do?
Nora:	Always do homework *((writing gesture))*
Silina:	*((a long talk here, but meaning and relevance not clear. Includes the following))* My country, when you finish all things, we talk about when you go to high school, we have camera like this one, and I was going to high school, but my sister she's work . . .

Although Silina said a lot, her voice was often soft, and the words unclear. As a listener, it seemed to me that the links to other speakers and an orientation to the topic were often missing. Prior to the focus groups, Silina's teacher had emphasised that she loved to hold the floor, but that this frequently annoyed other students, perhaps because they found the discourse difficult to follow. The teacher also commented that Silina seemed to say everything that came into her head. In the teacher's words, 'She doesn't have a thought that she doesn't express'. Making choices about what is said, how and how much, in fact comprises an essential part of effective communication.

Students who displayed aspects of communicative competence as described above, such as Alex, Milena, Carlos and Sinitia, were able to interact more in the conversation, taking longer and more frequent turns and responding to others. Those with less facility at this point offered minimal responses to questions, and only when nominated, needed more prompting and scaffolding, and tended to use stiff formulaic utterances, with little or no elaboration. A lot of smiling was used, by me and the students, to defuse tension and to communicate acceptance, lack of comprehension and other things. The amount of data from these focus groups was limited to two 50-minute sessions, but provided insights that oral competence is a set of continua, an ongoing and developmental process for these students. The point however is that the more you talk, the more you *can* talk. This seemed to me to be the critical link between speaking and interaction in social contexts. It was also true for Eva, the adult learner in Norton (2000) and the child Julie in Toohey (2000). Their success in language use was in part due to their access to peers, to talk and to social interactions. As Norton (in Norton & Toohey, 2001: 315) writes of Eva,

> whereas some workplace practices constrained here access to and participation in speaking English, others permitted her access: in time, space was made for her to participate more actively in the social and verbal activities of her community.

Norton and Toohey (2001) also suggest that the agency of the learner is also important for taking opportunities to participate as they arose. Milena had an openness to new experiences and new friends which had scaffolded her development of competence in Danish and in English. For other students, entering new social networks is more intimidating and problematic.

The Language of Lunchtime

On the basis of the features of communicative performance described above, I identified four of the 10 students who appeared to be confident and 'competent' users of spoken English. These were Milena, Sinitia, Carlos, and Alex. In addition, Silina also seemed a competent speaker on familiar topics. The other students, for whom speaking still posed many problems, were Tammy, John, Nora, Alicia and Bun Tan. Although no conclusions were drawn at this time, it seems impossible not to mention that in broad terms, these two categories contained five speakers of non-Asian languages and five speakers of Asian languages respectively. That is, the speakers of Mandarin, Cantonese and Cambodian were all hesitant speakers of English. Even though a cohort of 10 is small, this seemed improbable. What else came into play for the Asian students?

The opportunity to use English beyond the ESL classroom has a strong bearing on competence in speaking. Such interactions provide intensive speaking practice, opportunities for listening, negotiation and output. From my knowledge of Newnham, the individual interviews with the students, and the focus group data, there were three main possibilities outside of the classroom where informal social interaction occurs. These were the school morning tea and lunch breaks; other sites in everyday life outside of school; and weekends or holidays. Experiences of using English in these three situations varied greatly.

Lunchtime at Newnham finds the students speaking 20 to 30 different languages, with English being the lingua franca for those who choose or are obliged to mix outside of their language groups. Sinitia spoke English all day at school, largely because there were no other Rumanians for most of his stay at Newnham. He was also aware of ways to mix and find new friends, saying, 'If you find friends the same age, like, even you do things like they like doing, you play basketball or something'. After school, he also regularly swam in a friend's pool, where only English was spoken. Carlos spoke both English and Spanish at lunchtimes during soccer matches, depending on whether he was talking to the Bosnian or El Salvadorean players. Bun Tan claimed to use English only 'in lessons', as did Tina, Nora and Alicia. Tina added, 'I eat lunch with my friends so I speak Mandarin'. Nora's hope for her new high school was that she would meet more English-speaking friends.

'Outside school' contexts mentioned by students included shopping (Tina); buying railway tickets (Carlos); and church and home (Silena). Carlos spoke English regularly with his Australian neighbour, Sinitia with Australian friends and Bun Tan with his Australian-born cousins, of whom, he said with some disdain, 'They can't speak own language', by which he meant Cambodian. Although Bun Tan was not yet a fluent speaker in the ways described above, his talk was often very resourceful.

R: What's your new school like Bun Tan?
Bun Tan: Not bad Miss.
R: Yeah. What's not bad?
Bun Tan: I don't know.

R:	What about the uniform?
Bun Tan:	It's not good like ah, at Waverly High School it's very nice than Sandford.
R:	What does Sandford uniform look like?
Bun Tan:	Like a leaf, you know?
R:	Green
Bun Tan:	Yeah, green and white. And the pants is grey, short pants.

Hearing that his uniform was 'like a leaf' as the colour green is an index of one of the ways ESL teachers hear NESB students. Bun Tan had forgotten the word 'green', but confirmed my inference in his last turn. Another example occurred as he compared Newnham and his new high school.

R:	Is the high school different from Newnham, Bun Tan?
Bun Tan:	Yeah, because the high school have bigger than Newnham. Like experiment, have many. Newnham have, it's not many.
R:	Not many what?
Bun Tan:	Experiments
R:	Experiments. You mean for science?
Bun Tan:	Yeah.

Bun Tan mentions science to illustrate how the high school was bigger than Newnham. At high school they did more experiments, presumably in laboratories. Bun Tan substitutes the verb 'to have' for the verb 'to be' three times, but is still able to convey his meaning, and provide the key word in answer to my question 'Not many what?' The flow of talk with Bun Tan was very asymmetrical and may simply have reflected the power differential encoded in a conversation between a teacher and a student. But my intuition was that he was still really struggling with English. How many listeners would be prepared to do this listening work, to decode, draw inferences, generate the questions and so on?

Holidays also provide potential for learners to speak English. Students were about to have a six-week break from school, and I wondered how they would spend this time, and what part English would play in their language use over this period. The answers were quite revealing, and consistent with what has been suggested above. Tina was going back to Taiwan for two weeks, and apart from a weekly lesson with an Australian tutor on her return, said she would not speak any English. Nora would go to the council library. Alicia had no plans, but said she might accompany Nora to the library. Both Nora and Alicia said they would not really have a chance to speak English over the six weeks. Both Carlos and John said they were going to sleep, but their statements contrasted in length and complexity of turn, as follows.

Carlos: Sleeping, because when it's hot you don't have nothing to do.
R: You could go swimming.
Carlos: Yeah, but you have to pay.
R: What are you going to do, John?
John: Sleep.

Alex said he was going to do 'Everything I can, I don't know, I go to friends, I go to Gold Coast, everywhere.' Sinitia was off to Sydney to visit friends for Christmas. There was a clear sense in this part of the talk that those who 'went out', or travelled away from home (not including to Taiwan), would be in situations where they might interact in contexts where they would need to use English. For those who remained at home, or in the council library (a symbolic place of silence), there would be minimal interaction involving speaking in English.

As this phase of the study did not really include much classroom observation, it is unclear how much English was spoken by these students in classrooms at Newnham. My own observation over many years was that it was possible for some students to say next to nothing in class, communicative pedagogy notwithstanding. What did seem clear from the videotaped focus groups was that opportunities to use English beyond the classroom had a critical impact on the speaking resources of these students. Nora, Alicia, Tina and John did not speak English at school during lunch, spoke only Mandarin/Cantonese at home and over the summer holiday, and had little contact with English speakers generally. Milena, Alex, Sinitia, Carlos (and Silina and Bun Tan to some extent) were actively bilingual within and outside of school, and during the six week holiday would 'go out,' see people, and use English. It is worth adding that for many boys at Newnham, sport provided an arena for bilingualism, and multilingual swearing. Both Bun Tan and Sinitia spoke of playing basketball, while Alex and Carlos mentioned soccer. Although the girls could have joined in, it was not a practice for girls at Newnham to play sport at lunchtime, and they remained within their language groups.

'Nobody can hear Anything'

Newnham students travel considerable distances to get to the school, and virtually all come by train, as there is a station close by. During the focus group, I suggested this was perhaps an avenue for using English. Carlos responded as follows,

> With friends, when you want to make (.) a new friend, when you want to buy a ticket, because if you say in your language, nobody can hear anything, because they just say 'What? What?'

In an important sense, to speak a language other than English in most Australian social contexts, is to be inaudible. We go 'What? What?', neither understanding, nor 'hearing'. This is just one reason why mastering the dominant language is so essential for these students. Early attempts can be fraught with anxiety, especially in a public context. Carlos said that he could not be heard or understood in Spanish. It was my feeling that several of these students could also not be heard using their current levels of English. Too few speakers of English would be willing to take on the communicative burden of listening required to decipher the meanings.

Was there a threshold to reach, before one could be heard and understood? Both Tina and John, who are the focus of the next chapter, found it immensely difficult to be understood in English. Tina commented in an interview in Mandarin, 'sometimes when I said something, they did not understand, so I don't want to speak'. This brief statement implicates the identity, agency and legitimacy of the speaker, the power of the hearer, and the process of 'othering,' issues to be taken up more fully in the following data chapters. With all students except Milena, Carlos, Alex and Sinitia, understanding the gist and flow of their discourse in English still required an ESL teacher's ear, an ear that decoded 'like a leaf' instantaneously as green, and 'experiments' as science. Whereas most people are unwilling to take the time and effort required to listen to what one of my Samoan students whimsically called 'fresh English', teachers become attuned to the phonology and idiosyncrasies of various accents, to grammatical anomalies, to deducing meaning from context. With the three Chinese girls, Tina, Alicia, and Nora, the softest and most hesitant speakers in this group of students, I was often simply unable to hear much of what they said in English. Metaphorically inaudible when they used Chinese outside the home or school, and literally inaudible when they spoke English, I felt that the path toward representation within the mainstream school and culture would not be an easy one for them. The public at large does not have 'an ESL teacher's ear', and many people are simply not prepared to do the intense listening work required to understand varieties of English which are heard as nonstandard (Lippi-Green, 1997).

Conclusion

The central topic of these videotaped group talks was the learning of English. The students' responses and accounts showed that although they were all about to exit Newnham and enter high schools, they were at very different points in their levels of spoken English. The seven aspects of communicative competence outlined in the first section seemed to characterise the more fluent use of English which some students displayed. These aspects were part of their communicative performance in the context of the focus group. Furthermore, it was evident that those who were more advanced had, or had sought, opportunities to use English beyond the classroom. Such interactions, at school, at home and on holidays, provided important social and cultural information, as well as vital linguistic exchanges, and the chance to practise listening, speaking and 'being heard'. For students who remain isolated from such interactions, it seems likely that the acquisition of English, and social integration may be much slower.

Leaving Newnham constitutes for these recently arrived ESL students what may be seen as the close of the first phase of their linguistic, social and cultural integration in Australia, the end of arrival. After the summer break, these students would enter the second phase in regular high schools, a new context for their language learning, and many other learnings. Although most students enjoy the Newnham programme, they were looking forward to the challenges of high school, and new chances to learn, and to meet Australian students. In the following data chapters on five of the students, I explore some of the issues above, along with the key research questions raised in the first chapter.

(1) How do linguistic minority students in the early stages of language acquisition represent themselves to other students and teachers?
(2) How are they heard and represented?
(3) What conditions at school facilitate or constrain the acquisition of spoken English by recently arrived ESL students?

I would like to conclude here with an excerpt of a misunderstanding which occurred in the focus group as Nora and I spoke of her new high school. It shows her hopefulness, but also the challenge of the path which lay ahead. I had asked why she was looking forward to high school.

Nora:	It's great. Because I had more than friends. (*(I don't understand, but go for one interpretation. It is the wrong one.)*)
R:	You've got more friends there. Do they speak Chinese?
Nora:	No.
R:	What language do they speak?
Nora:	English
R:	People you know? These are friends you know already?
Nora:	Ready?
R:	(*(realising we're on different tracks, and that I would have to own up to not following)*)
	No, sorry, I didn't understand what you said.
	(*(Nora now makes a repair. She makes her statement louder, slower and clearer)*)

Nora: If I go to high school, I can more than friends.
((The light dawns. I now recognize Nora's generalisation of 'more than' for 'more'. A function of the overzealous teaching of the comparative?))

R: More friends. You can meet new people.
((Nora nods, relieved.))

Nora and her friend Alicia are the subjects of Chapter 6. In the next chapter I focus on Tina and John, whose silences and seeming resistance to speaking English both fascinated and at times exasperated me.

Chapter 4

Tina and John: The Self as Different

'Why are you trying to get data from kids who can't talk to you?' This question from an academic colleague brought laughs but no answer. My central themes were clear enough, namely the contexts and memberships of social language use, audibility, contextualised communicative competence, agency, identity and difference. I wanted to explore these themes by looking more closely at two students who did not present as 'the good language learner', who had difficulty participating in the focus groups, who spoke quietly and hesitantly, and had not ventured far from their first language groups at Newnham. I wanted to understand their moves towards self-representation in English in their new schools. What opportunities would they have for speaking English there? How would they be heard and inducted into the mainstream discourses of the school by teachers and others? Their stories have some elements in common, although it will be shown there are also significant areas of contrast. Tina was a 15-year-old Taiwanese girl, and John, a 16-year-old boy from Hong Kong. They arrived in Australia within two months of each other. They both attended the Newnham intensive on-arrival programme, and exited at the end of 1996 to enter ESL units at two different high schools. Their family circumstances were similar, as were some of their experiences at high school. In the first half of this chapter I look at Tina, and then at John in the second half.

My colleague's question had implications for both methodology and content. It firmed my resolve to conduct first language interviews with students who found it difficult to communicate with me in English, and much of the data used here comes from interviews conducted by postgraduate research assistants in Mandarin and Cantonese. These interviews themselves raised certain methodological and linguistic concerns, which are worthy of comment.

First Language Interviews

After meeting with the Mandarin- and Cantonese-speaking research assistants to clarify the purpose of the interviews, discuss the students and the context of the research, I provided them with a schedule of questions and some simple strategies for qualitative interviewing (see Seidman 1991). They first transcribed the interviews, then translated them into English. For all transcripts, I relistened to the original Chinese tapes with the research assistants, while following the English transcript as best I could, and asking questions as we went along. In these sessions, we clarified some parts of the interview, added in pauses, laughter, and other comments. Later I had the translations checked by other bilingual speakers. After this process, I felt confident that the students had been ably represented by the research assistants and the transcripts.

In the English transcripts of the interviews, the written English of the two postgraduate student interviewers was very proficient, but not grammatically 'standard'. Here are two simple examples:

Example 1. (D = the interviewer; J = the student)

D: Do you intend to stay here for a long time or root in Australia?
J: But we will go back to Hong Kong.
D: That means after you have got the citizenship.
J: Yes.
D: You will sure go back to Hong Kong, won't you?
J: Sure. My mother does not know English, how can she communicates with other in Australia.

Example 2. (F = the interviewer; N = the student)

F: You haven't been to other schools?
N: No.
F: So you straightly came here after you arrived?

This presented me with the dilemma of whether to 'standardise' the text or leave it. In most cases I left it, unless the meaning was unclear. In those instances, I clarified the meaning with the interviewer. I was less concerned with 'correcting the grammar' of my colleagues than with including their voices in the text. They of course were interviewing in their L1, and I do not read their translations as defective, but as the meaningful, real world language use often produced by non-native speakers (Firth, 1996).

Tina

Tina, aged 15, arrived in Australia from Taiwan on 7 July 1996. She came with her mother and 16-year-old brother, her father remaining in Taiwan to work. She and her brother were immediately enrolled in the Newnham intensive reception programme, where they remained until December. Although they had learned English at school in Taiwan for three years, their spoken English was minimal. The family lived in a high rise unit in an exclusive suburb near a university. On weekends, Tina regularly visited Chinatown in the city, or travelled 20 kilometres across town to another suburb, renowned for its strong Chinese community, its Chinese businesses, shops, restaurants, karaoke clubs, and cinemas. When asked why the family had chosen to live so far from the Chinese community, Tina said that her mother thought there were too many Taiwanese in that area, and that it was 'crowded'. A Taiwanese acquaintance later informed me that some absentee Taiwanese businessmen choose to locate their families away from 'unwanted influences' such as 'a range of Taiwanese people, in particular other men, from all walks of life'. In the family apartment, Tina's family was isolated from friends or other speakers of Chinese, hence her weekend outings to more familiar territory. Tina remained at Newnham for 20 weeks, and then after a family holiday in Taiwan, she started at Taylor High's ESL unit in January at the start of the school year, along with Nora and Alicia (see Chapter 6). Approximately 30% of Taylor High's 800 students were from non-English speaking backgrounds, including large numbers of students from Vietnam (11%) and Taiwan (12.4%). Tina joined this group, where her sense of being Taiwanese, her language use and her experiences in classrooms drew her towards a representation of herself as 'different'.

'No Matter Where I Go Still Taiwanese'

In the course of the Mandarin interview (M.Int), Tina stressed her strong identification with Taiwan, its lifestyle, her friends there, and Taiwanese friends here. She said she felt Taiwanese. When asked to say more about this feeling, she said,

> Because everyone around me is still Taiwanese, no matter where I go, still Taiwanese. What I feel here is the same as what I feel in Taiwan.   (M. Int. p. 5)

There are two ways to read this, namely that wherever she goes, she still feels Taiwanese in her head, or alternatively wherever she goes, people around her are Taiwanese. Both readings are supported by the text and the context of its occurrence in the interview. This sense of both being and being surrounded by 'still Taiwanese' seemed in part a powerful mental and social construct, a way of thinking and acting. It is also in part an identification with particular people and spaces both at school and across other sites. Let us look at some of these in more detail.

The sense of being Taiwanese

In a banal but important way, our names reflect who we are, how we know ourselves, and how we are known. The name Tina was chosen by one of Tina's English teachers in Taiwan, because it sounded a bit like her Chinese name. Like many students from China, Hong Kong and Taiwan, Tina used an English name at school in Australia. In my view, this is in part a concession to the incompetence of English speakers in understanding and saying 'non-English' names, and in part a conscious decision to do with integration into and acceptance by the English-speaking community. At school, there is often confusion about Chinese given names and family names, so an English given name simplifies things. Tina was asked about her name in the Chinese interview.

F:	What do your parents call you at home?
T:	My name.
F:	Which name?
T:	The Chinese name.
F:	How about the English name?
T:	No.
F:	Who would call you your English name? Is it at school?
T:	Some of them call me Tina, some would still call me my Chinese name. They would call me my Chinese name. (M. Int. p. 1)

It is perhaps a small point that Tina first equates 'my name' with her Chinese name. She goes on to agree that she has two names ('my name' and 'my English name'), saying that both names were used at school. She then self-corrects this, implying that at school she was known by her Chinese name. 'They' in the last sentence of Tina's last turn were her Chinese-speaking friends. It seemed mainly her teachers (and I) used her English name.

I first spoke to Tina at the end of her 20 weeks in Newnham, just prior to the school holidays in which she was returning to Taiwan. She said she missed her Taiwanese friends, her school and her teachers. In Taiwan she had played basketball, but commented that 'here no girls play, only boy'. On many occasions during Newnham lunch hours, I had observed that the boys colonised the basketball courts, outnumbering the girls by about 20 to one. Tina had also left her piano in Taiwan, and so was unable to play music in her new home. She missed the crowds of Taipei and the shops open late every day of the week. Her new city seemed quiet and boring by comparison. She had lost a neighbourhood of friends, now finding herself in a forbidding landscape of silent empty streets and luxury high-rise apartments where she knew no one. Her new-found school friends were also from Taiwan, but lived far away. Together they bridged the gap between themselves and those they had left behind, through talk in Taiwanese and outings to 'Taiwanese' places. When asked what she and her friends talked about, she said:

T: What we talk about? What, what, we always, (2.0) gossip
          about someone. No, we often talk about the things happening
          in Taiwan, the big events happening in Taiwan, we write, the
          friends in Taiwan write to us and tell us about them. So, we
          often talk about this.
F: Do you often write to your friends and classmates in Taiwan?
T: Yeah.   (M. Int. p. 6)

Such talk was an evocation of life in Taiwan, but also evidence of the girls' solidarity and identification with Taiwanese events, people and language.

My strong intuition was that Taiwan's 'big events' were a greater focus
of attention for these students than any events in Australia. Giddens (1991)
reminds us that in new personal and social domains, processes of
reappropriation and empowerment gradually take place, but these are
frequently accompanied by a sense of expropriation and loss. The appro-
priation of English discourses was occurring, but slowly for these students.
Tina and her friends were reappropriating aspects of their Taiwanese identities and memberships in the new social environment, through the
medium of their first language. They were contesting the sense of loss of
their home country on a daily basis, as they represented themselves as Taiwanese, both within the context of school and on weekend outings.

Social language at school: 'My friends are all from the same place'

When Tina returned from her holidays in Taiwan, she was placed in the
ESL unit at Taylor High School, along with Nora and Alicia, but she was also
integrated into Year 9 mainstream Mathematics and Geography. Early in the
school year, she had stressed that she hadn't made any new friends at Taylor
High, saying 'all my friends, they come from Newnham so, I knew them
already'. At the time of the Mandarin interview, Tina had been at Taylor
High for six months. The following brief interchange is from this interview.

F: If a new student came, say from Taiwan, and she wanted to
          know something about Taylor High, what do you think you
          would tell her?
T: Lots of Taiwanese are here, so don't worry.   (M. Int. p. 3)

This response offered some insight into Tina's own coping mechanism (in
both social and linguistic terms) in the high school. Other Taiwanese students
provided for Tina the haven of her first language, and strong links to Taiwan.
As a Mandarin speaker, her group of friends also included students from
mainland China. Her answer 'Lots of Taiwanese here, so don't worry', also
provides a clue to her position on language use at the school. Just after she

started at Taylor High, she had told me that she didn't need to speak English at school. Several months later, the Mandarin interviewer prompted the following exchange.

F: You once said to Ms Miller that at Taylor High you didn't need to speak English. What is it like now?

T: The same.

F: Why?

T: Because (2.0) the friends of mine speak the same language, the same, they are all from the same place, all come from Taiwan, China or Hong Kong. So it is not necessary to use English.   (M. Int. p. 2)

By Tina's own account, these students were clearly *not* from the same place – but for Tina, speaking the 'same language' made it seem so. The same place was 'the land of Chinese speakers.' Most of the students from Hong Kong spoke Cantonese; however, some of them were bilingual, and so were able to speak to the students from Taiwan and China in Mandarin. This set apart these students as having a particular membership, that of Mandarin and Cantonese speakers, who stayed visible as a strongly cohesive group within the school, often within mainstream classes, but particularly at morning tea and lunch times.

I suggested to Tina early in the year that it was very noticeable that at lunch time the Chinese-speaking students all sat together, to which she commented, 'All Taiwanese, or Vietnamese, or some overseas students are under C Block. And other blocks are Australian.' The Chinese and Vietnamese students, both boys and girls, sat on the ground in small friendship groups, under the length of the building. Was there a kind of lunch-time segregation at Taylor High based on language or racial lines – Asian language speakers under C Block and English speakers under other blocks? In fact, it was more complicated than this. As Tina mentioned, some of the groups were Vietnamese, and I observed there was also a physical separation of the Chinese and Vietnamese areas under C Block, with the Vietnamese groups clustered more to one end. Furthermore, Mandarin and Cantonese are not mutually intelligible, so the monolingual Cantonese-speaking students tended to be together. Some European ESL students also congregated under C Block. This location was therefore held by students affiliated to a range of languages, who belonged in general to the category 'ESL students'. It should be added that the students under C Block were overwhelmingly of Asian origin, and so their visible ethnic difference was possibly also a factor in the apparent segregation of students at Taylor High. Tina had noted that the other blocks in the school belonged to the category 'Australians', by which it will be seen she meant white Anglo-Australians.

I observed similar lunch-time seating arrangements at John's school (see later in this chapter). In both cases, the students congregated under the building which contained the ESL classrooms, their first point of contact and primary site of affiliation with the school. Such arrangements tend to be self-perpetuating, as new students arriving in the school join what is a pre-existing and highly visible group. In doing so, they position themselves, and are positioned by other students and staff, as ethnically and linguistically 'other'. Tina emphasised that even students who had been in Australia for four or five years, and spoke 'good English', remained in the Chinese speaking groups at lunch. I had in fact heard broad Australian English from some students in some groups, and surmised that for these students, being under C Block was a matter of personal choice. I asked Tina directly on one occasion why she thought the Taiwanese students liked to stay together, to which she replied, 'I stay with them because language is not pretty good and I can't talk to Australian very much, so I stay with them'. For Tina, who lacked confidence in using English, staying in the Chinese-speaking groups was in part a matter of pragmatic necessity. The language field where she had both a command of the language and knowledge of its patterns of use was Chinese (see Hymes, 1996), and she was not yet able to move freely across language fields.

For her first six months at Taylor, Tina remained primarily in the ESL class, apart from Year 9 mainstream Maths and Geography. In the ESL classroom, over half the class spoke Mandarin or Cantonese. In the classes I observed Tina rarely used English in this context, except to answer a question from the teacher. Her experience of using English in the mainstream context is taken up later when I discuss her academic work. Overall, the school context for Tina was entirely compatible with her notion that everywhere she went was Taiwanese, although there were 800 students in the school, close to 90% of whom were not Taiwanese. Her sense that all her friends spoke the same language and came from the same place was a generalisation. Yet it highlighted the degree of Chinese language affiliation felt and enacted daily by these students, as well as the powerful links between language, social affiliation and representation (Rampton, 1995). School was one site where Tina and others were able to 'enact identity in Taiwanese', as part of a Chinese speech community. Hymes (1996: 32) suggests that the boundary and internal organisation of a speech community is not 'a question solely of degree of interaction among persons . . . but a question equally of attributed and achieved membership, of identity and identification' (p. 32). As a social member, Tina represented herself as Taiwanese at Taylor High School, thereby deriving her social identity from group membership and a process of social categorisation and differentiation (Tajfel, 1981). By the same token, these students were attributed a Chinese identity by other students, in a way that further limited their interactions. Tina's limited access to conversations and interaction in English was not helped by her home or out of school environments. This tended to reinforce her sense of identity as Taiwanese.

Tina out of school

So far in this chapter, I have framed Tina's sense of identity in terms of her sense of being Taiwanese, mixing with Taiwanese friends, and moving in a Taiwanese world. For her, wherever she went, places and people were 'still Taiwanese'. At school, as we have seen, this did not entail moving very far. For six months, most of her lessons were in the ESL unit in C Block. Eight of the 14 students in this class spoke Mandarin. She had only to descend the stairs each morning tea and lunch time to remain in a Taiwanese world. On weekends she regularly visited a Chinese community 20 kilometres from her home.

Early in the year when I asked her about her long trips to the Chinese suburb, she said,

T: Uh (2.0) my friend says uh, you know there are many Chinese
            food and very delicious so I go to try.
R: Is it true?
T: Yup   (Int. 28.2.97)

I felt sure that the object of these long outings was not just food, but a range of social and language practices which supported her Taiwanese sense of belonging. Several months later in the Mandarin interview, the topic cropped up again.

F: Do you go out with your classmates or friends after school?
T: Rarely in weekdays, but <u>at weekend,</u> I would. *((Tina used the*
            English term 'weekend' here, i.e. code-mixing))
F: Where do you normally go?
T: Ehh, most often, go to city, then Sandford (suburb pseudonym)
F: Why Sandford?
T: Because there is Karaoke over there, and then more Orientals,
            more friends.
F: So, your friends live in Sandford?
T: Not all of them, but some live there.   (M. Int. p. 4)

In the time elapsing between the two statements, she has altered her simple and functional motivation of having great Chinese food to a more explicitly social interest in doing things there with Taiwanese friends. My mental image of Tina singing her lungs out in a Chinese Karaoke club jarred seriously with the reserved, reticent and minimally responsive (in English) student I had come to know, a girl who was quiet almost to the point of inaudibility. Did she lead a double life? Did she really sing out loud on the weekend in public venues?

When at home in the apartment with her mother and brother, Tina was immersed in her first language. Mandarin was spoken at all times, and her family had no Australian friends. Tina said they had 'foreign friends', from China and Taiwan. The family's only Australian acquaintance was a private tutor Tina's mother had hired for one hour per week to help with the children's English. Tina also mentioned that she had never heard her brother, who attended the same high school, speak any English. Nor, of course, had he heard her using English. In one interview, Tina said she had stopped watching TV in English, a medium often advocated by ESL teachers for language learning. When asked why this was, she explained that they now had a video player, and hired four or five videos a week in Chinatown, either in Mandarin or with Chinese subtitles. This meant that apart from some mealtimes, when the TV was occasionally on, Tina was effectively cut off from this influential source of English, as well as the social and cultural knowledge it provides, particularly for youth cultures. Television programmes provide a major topic of conversation in schools, as the most casual eavesdropper could attest. It also struck me as somehow sad that the only person who ever spoke to Tina in English outside of school was paid to do so, namely the tutor.

In addition to the family practices and routines mentioned above, the family returned to Taiwan regularly for holidays. She told me before leaving that there would be no chance to speak English for these weeks. She was very happy to be going back. In June of the following year, her mother returned to Taiwan, leaving the two children for three weeks. During this time, Tina was at school for one week, but for the two vacation weeks, she mostly stayed at home in the apartment. In the September holidays, she also remained at home. At the start of these holidays, she wrote about her feelings in her diary. This was one I had given her, and she was writing in English for me as the intended reader, but also I think for herself. All diary entries are reproduced as they were written, with no correction.

> *Ya! The holiday is beginning from today. I love holidays! Don't need to do any homework. Don't need to get up at 7.30 a.m. . . . . However, most of my friends went back to Taiwan. No-one could go shopping with me. I may stay at home the whole holiday!*
> *I am so lonely!*   (Diary: 20.9.97)

Her next entry was eight days later. She wrote,

> *I can't endure anymore. This holiday is too boring. Until now, I just went out one time – went to the library and return two books.*
>
> *The weather begins hotter: my heart falls deeper. I start to hate holidays. But I still don't want to go to school! I want to . . . want to . . . go back TAIWAN.*   (D: 28.9.97)

Tina's one outing had been to a place of silence, the library. Her repetition of 'want to' and choice of upper case for 'Taiwan' reveal her strong feelings at this time. She was relieved to get back to school after these holidays, noting in her diary that at least there she would have 'someone to talk to.' I noted also the marked difference between her written skills and oral skills in English. This was expected, for reasons outlined at the end of Chapter 1.

At the end of the 1997 school year, she returned once again with her mother to Taiwan. When she came back after one month, she joined Nora, Alicia and me on an outing to a shopping centre, to look around and have lunch. We met at my home, and when she arrived, she barely greeted me, and then chatted in Mandarin to the others. I was aware that she had not spoken in English for several weeks. We shared our holiday experiences, Alicia recounting her holiday trip to Hong Kong and China and showing dozens of photos. I asked what Tina had done in Taiwan. 'Eating, sleeping and shopping', came the reply. I joked that she could have done that here, but it fell rather flat. However, bit by bit (and the going was extremely tough, a veritable 'blood-out-of-a-stone' effort so familiar to teachers at times), she revealed the story of her 17-year-old brother, who had remained in the apartment by himself for the month. When she said her brother had stayed here, I asked if he could cook. No, was the reply. I then asked what he had done about food. Tina said, 'Nothing'. It emerged that he had eaten very little, not gone shopping for food, and had lost a lot of weight. I asked why he didn't order pizza. She said he did not know how to do this, on the phone, or in person, and claimed she had never heard him do anything like this using English. In one month, he did not go anywhere, or do anything, except play on the Internet. My ears pricked up – surely he had to use English for this. No, again. He had a Chinese computer and keyboard and was chatting with others in Taiwan. I felt uncomfortable prying any further. Tina did not volunteer any of this, but gave short answers to my questions. I was frankly amazed as I imagined her brother, starving in his luxury high rise apartment, in an affluent suburb, because he did not feel able to communicate a pizza order in English. Tina also mentioned that although he knew how to get a bus into the city, he did not know how to go to the local shopping centre using public transport. For the entire month of December 1997, he remained a hungry prisoner in their apartment.

I tell this story, not because Tina was the same as her brother, but because it helps build a picture of her home environment, and the deep isolation of her family, surrounded yet seemingly untouched by the majority language and social practices associated with it. And I was confounded by the story, and the conditions which could explain how someone is unable to order a pizza after living in a country for a year and a half. To explore this further, it is necessary to focus now on the issue of language use, and specifically of speaking English.

Choosing not to Speak English

Moving from one country and culture to another poses many challenges to one's sense of identity and identification (Lantolf, 2000; Trueba, 1989), in which the primary mode of self-representation, speaking, must undergo complete transformation. Pavlenko and Blackledge (2000) propose the idea of self-translation in the new country. Guiora *et al.* (1972: 112) suggest that of all language skills, speaking is psychologically the most demanding, necessitating fundamental changes to 'one of the basic modes of identification by the self and others, the way we sound'. The theory of ethnolinguistic identity (Giles & Johnson, 1981; Heller, 1987, 1988) also provides insight into language as a salient marker of social identity and membership. According to this theory, language signals membership of particular ethnic groups, where backgrounds, behaviours, lifestyles and values are shared. Members may compare their social group to out-groups, emphasising in various ways their positive distinctness as a group. Culture shock may also be part of the social distance which some immigrant and refugee students establish between themselves and other groups (see Brown, 1987). I have already described the groups under C Block at Taylor High, who spoke their first and sometimes second languages rather than English. For these students, 'the way we sound' was Chinese or Vietnamese. Tina acknowledged that her Maths and Geography lessons in the mainstream provided virtually her only opportunity to talk in English to 'Australian' students. There are two aspects to consider in regard to Tina's use of English. The first concerns the perspective I obtained in talking to her over a period of 15 months, in terms of her developing communicative competence in English. The second relates more to her accounts of speaking English, and what this meant to her.

I begin with an extract from an interview with Tina a month after she had started at Taylor High's ESL unit. Previously, she had completed 20 weeks at Newnham. This group interview also included Nora (N) and Alicia (A).

R: and is it all in that building (.) all in ESL rooms or do you go to other classes. Tina?
                (4.0)

A:	Same class
T:	no () Year 9 (*inaudible*) (*mastree?*)
R:	Bit louder?
T:	Yeah?
R:	Yeah. Speak louder
	(2.0)
R:	Cos I
	((*Tina giggles, looks exasperated*))
T:	Say (.) Year 9 students will go to (mastree) in mathematics
R:	to which one and maths?
T:	Sorry?
R:	Year 9 will go to:
T:	(manstree) (2.0) uh high school
N:	mainstream
R:	Mainstream (1.0) high school (.) OK (1.0) Year 9 go to mainstream maths. Are you in Year 9?
T:	Yes (Int. 28.2.97)

This excerpt contains elements which were in fact patterns in Tina's spoken English. First of all, I call on her by name. Only once in this interview, which runs to nine pages, did she ever speak without being called on. Second, her first turn is inaudible, and I ask her to speak more loudly. Her question 'Yeah?' reveals her virtual disbelief that more volume was needed, followed by her exasperated expression on realising that she still needed to speak more loudly. Third, she uses a word I can't understand, the word 'mastree' or 'manstree'. She uses it three times finally paraphrasing it with 'high school,' but still I don't get it. Nora then enters the talk, pronouncing the word clearly in her last turn – 'mainstream'. In my relief at finally understanding the word, and simultaneously making sense of Tina's paraphrase of high school, I use a series of four affirmations of the connection made: 'Mainstream, high school, OK, Year 9 go to mainstream maths'. For me, it was almost a celebratory moment. However, Tina revealed later that such episodes helped account for why she avoided speaking English.

The following is an excerpt from her interview in Mandarin, four months after the talk above. The Chinese interviewer (F) refers at the start to the mainstream Maths and Geography classes which Tina attended.

F:	Do you have any difficulties in the class?
T:	No.
F:	Why?
T:	Because I can understand all of what they say, just I do not like to speak.

F: You don't like to speak. Is that because you don't want to talk,
            or you have difficulty in speaking?
T: Both. Because sometimes when I said something, they did not
            understand, so I don't want to speak.
F: You feel that they don't understand?
T: Sometimes, perhaps because of my accent, different accent, so
            sometimes they don't understand. Then I don't want to speak
            any more.   (M. Int. p. 2)

Having observed Tina in the geography class, and seen her work, I was aware
that she followed the lessons, and I was aware of her silence. The silence, as she
indicated, was caused by the frustration of knowing that while she understood, she could not make herself understood. Her use of the pronoun '*they*'
groups the Australian students, those whom she could understand but
who did not understand her, in one oppositional category. It was not the
first time she had said she did not like to speak. In the focus group at
Newnham six months before, she said of her English lessons in Taiwan,
'My teacher wants us to speak English but we don't like'. This reticence,
together with experiences where she could not make herself understood,
such as in the 'mastree' episode above, meant that over time she simply
chose not to speak English. She attributes the non-comprehension of her
interlocutors to her accent, 'different accent'. Not being understood meant
not only that she went unheard, but that she was effectively silenced.
However, her own agency in abandoning attempts to speak English must
not be discounted.

    At the same time she was aware that not speaking English meant her
proficiency in the language could remain limited, as shown below. The
translation from Mandarin is by the Chinese interviewer.

F: What do you think about your English improvement?
T: A little bit
F: A little bit? Not big?
T: No
F: Why is that?
T: Because I don't talk often
F: If there was a chance, would you be willing to talk, or not?
T: A little bit not
F: How is that? Because they are not willing to talk to you, or:
T: Yeah   ((*firmly*))   (M. Int. p. 6)

While one could argue Tina was 'fed' the last reply by the interviewer, other
data showed she felt the Australian students were indeed unwilling to speak
to her. Ironically, she had spoken more English in the intensive ESL reception

programme at Newnham, where English, however halting, was the lingua franca. Moving to high school meant she lost her non-Taiwanese NESB friends with whom she could experiment and practise in English.

T: After I came to this school, I seldom talk (1.0) speak English. Before, when in Newnham, there were some friends from, not Australian – there was a chance, sometimes to speak English, but now, here, no.

F: Is that because there are so many Taiwanese students or:

T: Yeah, and the Australian classmates won't actively talk to me, so I won't go to talk to them.   (M. Int. p. 5)

'Now, here, no' – I found the juxtaposition of these three small words quite powerful: a time, a place, a rejection. There is not a little irony in the fact that in moving to a mainstream 'Australian' context, you may lose the chance to speak English, opportunities which are available with friends who are 'not Australian'. Tina had moved into an Australian high school in which she countered the prospect of speaking English with 'now, here, no'. There is a stand-off here – she feels the Australians won't talk to her, and she won't 'go to talk to them'. As we have seen from the physical organisation of students at lunch time at Taylor High, that is, outside of the classroom, to talk to Australian students would indeed mean *going* somewhere, since none are generally available in the space taken up by the Asian students. It is a move that Tina, along with many others, was unprepared to make. At this time, in the ongoing renegotiation of their social identities, Chinese ethnolinguistic identity played a powerful role for these students. One could also argue that any renegotiation of identity was quite limited. If the negotiation of identity involves an interplay between self-representation and the positioning imposed by others (Pavlenko & Blackledge, in press), Tina and her friends both positioned themselves and were positioned by others as Chinese speakers. In terms of their social group membership, choice of language and social context, their identities as Taiwanese or Chinese students were on display for all to observe and hear (Gee, 1996).

Seems they Don't Like the 'Black Hairs'

At this point I would like to consider further Tina's view that speaking to Australians was difficult, and particularly her feeling that they wouldn't talk to *her*. Neta, a Bosnian student from an earlier study, had told me what happens when you don't speak English well.

Because if you don't, you just don't feel confident, like to talk to them, to be with them, you know you think they don't like you, or something like that.

The absence of any comprehensible interaction may lead students to assume the worst, namely, that they are not liked. Tina said that Australians were unwilling to talk to her, and in the following excerpt, she offers an account of this.

T: Seems that they don't like the 'black hairs'. Because I have a classmate from Bosnia now in my class. If we go to (a mainstream) class together, they, they know that she is not Australian, don't speak much English, but go to talk to her not me.
F: Why?
T: Don't know.
F: Where is she from?
T: Bosnia. Blondy hair.   (M. Int. p. 5)

In each case, 'they' refers to the Australian students. By 'black hairs' she was referring to Asian students. She makes the point here that the act of speaking to one student and not another in fact constitutes a racialising practice on the part of Australian students, a differentiation made on the basis of whether someone looks Anglo or Asian. I had asked where the student was from, to which she answered not just the country, Bosnia, but what was for her a critically defining physical characteristic, 'blondy hair'. She had used the expression 'black hairs' and made a similar point to me at other times. She had also conveyed this theory to Nora, who mentioned it in her diary. Nora wrote after one incident with a teacher,

> *Before Tina told me some thing about the teachers likes the foreigners. I don't believe she, now I realize that. I just don't know why the teachers always likes forniger, they always like white skin, gold hairs?*   (Nora's diary, 18.6.97)

Tina's 'visible difference' racial interpretation of who talks to whom, also extended on one occasion to what she perceived as certain discriminatory practices by teachers in regard to Asian students. She recounted the following anecdote to me during one school visit.

> On Wednesday has, ah, sports and some people think that's () it's not important and want to go home and they will just walk through the fence and go to station. If Australian walk through that, the teacher will (.) not stop them and we will walk through that and they stop us and call parents and send letter to home so our parents go mad.   (Int. 18.9.97, p. 3)

Once again, 'they' and 'them' refers to the Australian students, the second 'they' meaning the teachers. This is opposed to 'we' and 'our parents', referring to the Asian students. Curious, my teacher background got the better of me at this point and I could not help conducting a kind of cross-examination.

R: So you think they discriminate. Are you sure they just let the Australian students go?
T: Yeah we saw that. We follow them.
R: And you were all Taiwanese students.
T: All Taiwanese and Chinese.
R: What about in class? Do they differentiate between Asian students and others?
T: No.   (Int. 18.9.97, p. 3)

To me, Tina was depicting an extraordinary scenario, a gateway to escape through which only Australian students could pass, and where Asian students were arrested and reported. There was no way of knowing whether Tina's assessments were warranted, or if there were other quite reasonable explanations for the phenomena she was describing. What was indisputable was that this was how she reported these incidents, and that her categories of 'black hairs' (Asian NESB students), 'blondies' (European NESB or Australian students) and Australians (mostly Anglo mainstream students) were parts of her own sense of identity and inclusion in the first group, and exclusion from the other two groups. The pronominal 'we' and 'they' signal Tina's awareness of in-group and out-group memberships within the school. Tina was representing herself as a member of the 'black hairs', an out-group, the name itself a reference to visible physical difference. I recalled two other occasions where she had viewed her appearance in a negative light. On the first occasion I offered copies of individual photos I had taken of Tina and other students. She refused her copy out of hand, saying she looked terrible. Another time she wrote in her diary of the unwelcome prospect of having to wear glasses.

> *After school, I went to ~~the~~ a opthalmologist to check my eyes, and the results was – my eyes were inflammation so I can't wear contact lenses. It was a pretty bad news for me! I can't wear the contact lenses any more! Oh! my God!*   (Diary, 15.8.97)

It is hardly unusual for adolescents to be concerned about their appearance. Yet I wondered if Tina saw wearing glasses as a problem to be added to the distinctiveness of her being Asian, and having black hair. This is conjecture, but seems plausible in the light of her categories about visible difference.

Hall (1996: 4) stresses that identities are 'the product of the marking of difference and exclusion', a point also made in Grundy's (1994) study of Australian identities in primary school discourse. Grundy suggests that rather than taking as its point of departure the individual or unique self, the shaping of identity draws on 'the establishment and maintenance of categories of likeness and difference' (p. 21). The notion that identity derives from group membership and differentiation draws on the socio-psychological theory of Tajfel (1981), who identified four processes which link identity formation and group memberships. These are social categorisation, a developing awareness of social identity, social comparison, and the search for psychological distinctiveness. Tina represented herself as different, and the Australian students as different from her. We can infer this from a simple incident during a school excursion to a Chinese restaurant. She noted later in her diary, '*I was so surprised most of the Australian could use the chopsticks. I thought they might use the folks [forks] and spoon before.*' In this instance, she had to shift her perception of Australians as wielders of forks and spoons. The visit to the restaurant evoked a point of similarity, rather than difference.

As another layer in the identity process, we saw above that Tina attributed certain racialising practices to one category. In regard to the Australian students, she perceived that their failure to talk to her was because she was Asian, not a 'blondy hair' like her friend from Bosnia. In the case of the teachers in the sports day incident above, she believed that the 'visibly different' Asian students were the ones singled out for punishment. Luke and Luke (1998) frame such perceptions as part of the 'them and us' divide which indeed relates to what is commonly a silenced racial difference. These perceptions are also assessments derived from comparisons between in-groups and out-groups. Tina's story exemplifies the notion of identity established within and across differences, and an understanding of self in relation to other groups. Identifying herself as a 'black hair' showed her sense of identification, belonging and allegiance to the Asian students at the school, but also conveyed her exclusion from the dominant mainstream groups. She was thus an insider to the group from Taiwan, China and Hong Kong, seeing ethnic origin as of critical defining importance, but saw herself as an outsider to the Australian groups and also the European ESL group, members of whom she perceived were heard and spoken to by the Anglo Australians. Unlike her blonde Bosnian peer, she felt she had not yet been spoken to or heard as a speaker of English.

The Academic Context

It would be misleading to depict Tina as someone who simply refused to speak English, saw the world divided into 'black hairs' and their more favoured white counterparts, and whose identity was anchored inexorably to her ethnicity. We know that identity is not fixed, solid and immutable, but is constantly enacted as a web of intersecting practices in a variety of contexts. Moerman (1993: 96) refers to 'epiphanies of identity', which are 'occasioned, accomplished, transitory, and locally organised'. Tina's realisation that some Australians could eat with chopsticks in a Chinese restaurant was one of these small epiphanies. Over a period of 12 months, I observed her moving towards a more confident level of self-representation in the mainstream context at school. For six months, she remained in the ESL unit for all but two subjects. Her Taiwanese school reports showed that she had been academically quite strong in Taiwan, and found Year 9 Maths extremely easy. In Geography, I had seen her neat and well-organised notes, peppered with Chinese characters, good results on assignments and her teacher's comments of 'Clear, neat, accurate work' on one test. Tina had commented to me that there was little demand to speak during these lessons, and that most of the time was spent 'writing, taking notes'. She was good at this.

At the end of the first semester, she was fully mainstreamed into Year 9, doing the subjects Maths, English, Geography, Science, Health and Physical Education, Chinese, Home Economics and Computer Studies. Just before this happened, she wrote in her diary, '_I am a bit scare. I will go to mainstream and there are all Australians._' This of course was only partly true.

The mainstream classes at Taylor High were very ethnically diverse, with 30% of the school classified as non-English speaking background students. On at least three occasions I was embarrassed by assuming individuals were ESL students, only to find they had been in Australia for all or most of their lives. I had approached them in mainstream classes, because they looked Chinese for example, and then asked how long they had been here. I should have known better, and was in fact operating on Tina's premise of visible difference. One Filipino boy told me he had come to Australia aged two. Some students looked Chinese, but spoke broad Australian English, and sat with Anglo Australian friends. The point is worth reiterating – if you sound the same, you may not be seen as different by your peers. I had been focusing so much on Chinese speakers that in another class observation, I missed the Croatian boy who had arrived a week earlier, a Serbian girl and a light-skinned Salvadorean girl. This is all painfully obvious, but it struck home to me on these occasions that the category of visible difference was utterly useless as an index of language background, affiliation or competence, equally unhelpful as an indicator of membership or social identity, and gave no indication as to academic participation or success. Why did Tina place so much store by visible difference? The mainstream students may have been 'all Australians' but they looked like every colour under the sun. Tina's fear of mainstream integration dissipated after her first day in the mainstream classes. She wrote in her diary,

> Today is the first day at school. I was so nervous. My first lesson was computer, I have some friends there, I felt better. Then, I had Science, English, finally Maths. I have friends in all of those lessons. I think I'll be good in mainstream.   (Diary, 8.7.97)

Her last sentence here was one of the most positive things she had ever written or said. She felt positive about the mainstream context. Yet note in this brief entry two references to her friends (from the ESL unit), who in fact would provide the conditions for her ongoing use of Mandarin in class. ESL students often remain a quietly isolated group within mainstream classrooms, having little interaction with other students (Sharkey & Layzer, 2000), and few chances to practise English. A particular challenge for Tina over the next term was a number of oral presentations in class and in one class, she finally got to work with a group.

'Doing something with Australians'

In Geography, the teacher randomly selected groups of three to do research on Africa and present their findings orally. Tina wrote,

> My group decided to do the Zulus of Africa. And I am doing the 'Art' of Zulus. This is my first time doing something with Australians. I hope I could do as well as them.   (Diary, 25.8.97)

Although the Australians are still 'them', the ones she wants to do as well as, it is *her* group, and she has a specific role in it. Tina had arrived in Australia 13 months earlier, and been at Taylor High for seven months. Her account of this oral project as the first time she had done something with Australians is even more significant in this light. To her, it was worthy of noting in her diary, and it signalled a new range of practices, both socially and linguistically. Later in the diary, she writes of the project's outcome.

> Today is the due day of our geography assinment and oral. I was the second speaker of our group. I was so nervous and my voice was shaking. My group used fourteen minutes to discribed the culture of Zulus. When we finished the class, we went to ask Mr L what result did we get. It's a A-. We thought it's a pretty good result.   (Diary, 15.9.97)

In this excerpt, there is no mention of 'they' or 'them'. The cohesion of the group is expressed by the use of first person pronouns, as in the examples: 'our geography assinment', 'our group', 'my group', 'we finished', 'we went', 'we get', and 'we thought.'

Around this time she also wrote about two other orals in English.

> *Today we had a English Role Play. I was working with Sarah, a Australian girl. We are doing a girl and a boy are fight for a dog. We just prepared for ten minutes. I was so scared when I was in front of the class. We finished it about 1 minutes. and Ms Ball said I was doing very well. I was glad and I know I was doing my utmost.* (Diary, 5.9.97)

Tina again mentions the fact that her partner Sarah is Australian. But from this excerpt and the one above, we start to see Tina inscribing herself as a legitimate mainstream class member, joining her voice to those of others, focusing on the time factor, as many students tend to do, and feeling she has done her best and been acknowledged. The teacher's comment that she'd done well clearly reverberated for her in a positive way, as shown by her concluding sentence. The final excerpt below shows further evidence of these shifting representations in her school work.

> *Today we had an English Oral . . . I was working with Sarah and David. We are doing a TV interview of two girls – Lara and Pearl who just save their sister from a fire accident. I was the interviewer. Because we had three members in our group, so we need to speak for three minutes. However, we just speak for two minutes and forty-seven seconds. So we didn't got a very high mark. I got a B–.* (Diary, 18.9.97)

The obsession with time continues, fed by the set parameters of the talk, and in practice, often by an overzealous peer doing the job of timing. Although Tina implies in this excerpt that David had to play one of the girls, I noted that the activity now sounded routine; nationalities are not mentioned, and nor are the feelings of nervousness or fear.

In the excerpts above, Tina represents herself not as a 'black hair' or as different in any way from the other students. Within the mainstream context, she had begun to shift from positioning herself as an ESL student, and as different. Her end of year report contained a creditable list of results (A for Maths and Chinese; B for Geography, Science, Home Economics and Computing and C for English and Health and Phys. Ed.), and a series of computer-generated comments selected by teachers. Tina had told me rather smugly that she did nothing in Chinese but chat to her friends and still got an A. Her teacher of Chinese commented on the report that she 'could participate more in class', but was then obliged to select the rather inane computer-generated comments that Tina could understand listening passages in Chinese, had good pronunciation and knew most of the vocabulary taught. Her English teacher commented that Tina had 'difficulty with diction and pronunciation' and wrote 'with some lack of fluency'. By way of contrast, the Maths comment was that Tina 'communicates clearly in the language of mathematics'.

Ambiguity, van Maanen (1988: 127) claims, 'is an accurate characterisation of lived cultural experience'. So far, we have seen that while Tina chose to represent herself as Taiwanese through her membership of particular groups and language affiliation, on moving into full mainstream classroom integration, she encountered new social memberships and contexts which slowly began to affect her language use. Her tentative initiation into mainstream school tasks brought her a degree of recognition, and some sense of success and identification with those she had labelled the 'Australians'. At the same time, I had observed her ambivalent attitudes to speaking English and to English speakers. At the end of one year at Taylor High, six months of which had been in the mainstream, she had a better than average academic report, but in terms of her social practices and language practices outside of the classroom, she was still an outsider to the mainstream groups, remaining firmly within the Chinese-speaking community. She ended the year by once more returning to Taiwan for a holiday. I now turn to John, whose experiences and accounts offer some parallels and some contrasts with those of Tina.

John

Sixteen year old John arrived in Australia with his mother and three younger sisters in late September, 1996 under the business migration programme. His father remained in Hong Kong for business reasons, and the family settled in to the suburb of Sandford (pseudonym), one of several suburbs adjacent to each other in the metropolitan area, all of which are renowned for their large ethnic Chinese communities. John's two younger sisters went to a primary school and a preschool respectively. John told me that his neighbours were from Hong Kong, and several other friends from Taiwan and Hong Kong lived close by. Around 40% of Sandford's population speak a Chinese language at home. After only nine weeks at Newnham, John and his 13-year-old sister moved to the ESL unit of Sandford High School. Overall, 35% of Sandford High's students were born overseas. Of its 1070 students, 14% were from Asian countries, 8.5% from Europe (excluding the UK) and 1.2% were from the Middle East. There were five ESL teachers and approximately 90 students in the ESL unit. More than twice this number had been assessed as needing ESL support, but funding did not allow it.

John's family spoke Cantonese at home, and John stated in the Chinese interview, 'No one can speak English in my family except my younger sister' (the one at preschool). John also said the family had 'several cars', but emphasised that they did not go anywhere, as his mother didn't drive. Both the cars and his absent father were to play critical roles in John's experiences in Australia. When I asked if his mother was happy here, he said, 'I don't think so. She is not always happy because in here nothing with her to do.' In what follows, I begin by discussing John's use of spoken English, and then explore his language and social practices in three sites at Sandford High, namely an ESL class, a mainstream class, and the lunch time context.

Speaking English

My first talk with John was about 10 weeks after he had arrived in Australia. Two months later at his high school, we spoke again and I noted on the transcript the difficulties of these talks.

> John speaks in a very jerky staccato way, with long pauses. Because John's answers are often brief, or reflect that he didn't understand my question, I am constantly searching for something to keep the talk going, or to paraphrase the question; lots of negotiation needed. Spoke briefly to one of his teachers. John had been away for a week in the first three weeks of school (Chinese New Year?), and apart from that, the teacher said he had not said five words.   (Int. 14.2.97)

At times, we were able to keep the conversation flowing. This is an excerpt from our first talk, just before John left Newnham.

R: Tell us about why you came to Australia.
J: Because they think (1.0) we (.) we (.) come to Australia (.) we study level will be better. In Australia is easy to study in university.
R: And in Hong Kong: ((*I thought his point was about comparison*))
J: Is (.) is (.) difficult to go to university
R: Why?
J: because the university the (4.0) the (3.0) I donnow how to say the word
R: Selection? (2.0) exams?
J: No
R: What is it about?
J: It's about if the university (.) can study about 200 people in one class (.) but Hong Kong have more high school and then have more studen() (1.0) and then another (.) more another (.) can't go to university (.) they need to another   (Int. 10.12.96)

John is clearly trying to convey quite complex information here, but finding it difficult. However, he tries to use my turns to build his responses. For example, my 'Why' prompted his 'because' and my 'What is it about?' prompted his 'It's about'. I was struck by the length of his last turn. He did not recognise the word 'selection', although his own account of the difficulty of getting to university in Hong Kong basically revolves around competitive selection.

There were several instances in this talk where he simply did not understand words or questions I used, where we had real difficulty understanding each other. The following shows one of my turns, in which I asked a question, then paraphrased it four times, before John responded.

R: When you arrived here were you very surprised? (2.0) Or: surprised at anything about this city? (2.0) Or found things very different? (1.0) Your first impressions (1.0) What did you notice here when you came first?

J: Australia is very large country. If you go to buy something you need to buy a car. (3.0) It's not the same as Hong Kong.   (Int. 10.12.96)

Those first four questions, which seemed to drag interminably, drew a blank, until John finally chipped in after the fifth reformulation. There were also several examples of miscommunication in the interview, one of which now follows. I had just asked him if there were Chinese people living in his area.

J: My (inaudible) is with me to coming here
R: Sorry?
J: My (labour), my house labour, they are all come from Hong Kong.
R: You mean the workers in your house, your house labour
J: Yeah
R: What do you mean by labour?
J: They live in (.) near my house
R: And what do they do in your house? (2.0) ((*the penny drops*)) Oh your neighbours. Sorry, I heard labour, I heard wrongly.   (Int. 10.12.96)

John's mispronunciation, and my wrong assumption meant that we were on different wave lengths throughout these turns. I took responsibility for mishearing to mitigate the problem. Phonemically, he was one consonant out – neighbour and labour are close, but the semantic difference disrupted the meaning completely. Sometimes it seemed that the burden for John as speaker and the burden for me as listener were very great. The reverse was also true. The work needed on both sides, and in both directions, must be taken into account as we consider why some students eventually give up even trying to speak English, and also why many English speakers are unprepared to do such work. A second example of the intense negotiation, and further pitfalls, is taken from the first interview at Sandford High.

R: And you, how much time are you in the ESL unit, and how much time are you outside?

J: Outside is (1.0) in (.) in the formu ((sounds like 'formal')) class?

R: Yeah, in the mainstream classes

J: Uh, one day have seven period, and three (.) three period, three period in ESL, and no, sorry, three period in form(u) class and and all is in ESL classroom.

R: So, (2.0) OK, and what subjects are you doing in the mainstream?

J: Mainstream? ((*John does not seem to be familiar with this term. He uses rather 'form(u)' class*))

R: Are you doing any subjects, like, not in the ESL unit, or are you in the ESL unit all day?

J: (inaudible)

R: Sorry I misunderstood. Tell me again about your day. Are you in the ESL unit?

J: Yes

R: All day?

J: It's not all day.

R: So..

J: Uh, three period is outsi(de) ESL.

R: Which subjects?

J: Uh, woo(d) work, and (2.0) science, and maths.   (Int. 14.2.97)

In terms of talk, this is an example where my question in line 1 is answered 20 lines later, and it took 14 turns to get there. Among other things, we had to encounter and steer around words I didn't recognise ('formu') and words John didn't know ('mainstream'); negotiate inaudible responses; initiate backtracking, agree; disagree/clarify; and reformulate. We were both labouring here under what Lippi-Green (1997) calls the 'communicative burden'.

During our first talk, the topic of Newnham came up, and John made the point that with students from so many countries, he needed to use English to 'talk to another people', that this was easy to do, and that his English was getting better as a result. However, it was clear that while he talked at times to other students, his friends were from his own language group, or from Taiwan, as John spoke both Cantonese and what he termed 'Chinese' (Mandarin). These friendships within his own language group continued at Sandford High, and by May, my question as to whether he thought his

English was improving was greeted with a very emphatic 'No'. I noted in transcripts of our talks after he moved to high school, there was no turn in English as long as the one from Newnham, in which he'd explained the problem of getting into university in Hong Kong. In June, John was interviewed in Cantonese, and he expressed concern about retaining his level of English.

D: You have no confidence in keeping your level of English.
J: Not much confidence
D: In what ways do you think that you can improve your English?
J: No ways.   (C. Int. p. 6)

To see John's concern and his comment in perspective, it is important to understand the contexts in which he used and did not use English. He made this clear on several occasions, as in this excerpt from the Cantonese interview.

D: Then, is there any time that you speak English in school?
J: When I talk to teachers.
D: That means you will only speak English in the classroom and speak no English outside the classroom.
J: No, I will not.
D: Do you have any Australian or English speaking friends?
J: (pause) Greeting only. There is little communication between us.   (C. Int. p. 6)

As a brief aside here, I was struck with the strong AB pattern of the interview in Cantonese, consisting of numerous questions and brief responses from John. It sounded a little like an interrogation (and looked not unlike the pattern of our talks in English), but according to the interviewer, it was amiable enough. He commented however that John seemed quite depressed. John's claim that he only spoke English to teachers or in class was reiterated on other occasions. I wanted to observe this, and felt that interaction in English was more likely to be maximised in an ESL class than in a mainstream context, and the following description is of one of John's ESL lessons from about three months after he had started at high school. After this, I look briefly at a woodwork lesson. Both lessons provide some insight into how students position themselves, and are positioned by pedagogical practices.

An ESL Lesson: The Short Story

When asked about English classes during the Cantonese interview, John had said, 'I have no English class. There is only ESL class. ESL is my English lesson.' The interviewer, a university student from Hong Kong was unfamiliar with the term 'ESL'.

D:	What is ESL?
J:	It's just like your tutorial class in University.
D:	Tutorial.
J:	Yes. Those students who have no lesson will attend this ESL as an English class.
D:	Then, what do you do in this class?
J:	We have got some work to do. The teacher in this class speaks much slower and uses more simple English. She also assists us in completing the tasks. (C. Int. p. 4)

John seemed to represent ESL as a substitute for 'real English', but it occurred to me later that there was a chance he had no idea what ESL stood for. He invokes the ESL students as 'those students who have no lesson', that is, no mainstream lesson. In this representation, ESL is what you do when you are not doing 'real' subjects. The focus of the ESL lesson described here was a short story, chosen by the ESL teacher from a unit often done by Year 10 students in mainstream English.

There were only four boys in this ESL class, and the teacher's name was June (pseudonym). The boys were all in Year 10. John, Leo and Keith were from Hong Kong, and Ivan was from former Yugoslavia. As we walked to the library where June had booked a small withdrawal room, she explained to me that due to ESL timetabling, she saw John only twice a week, which meant he had not finished reading the short story 'Precious Pet' to be used in the lesson, whereas the other boys had completed the reading. The story was three pages long, and had a sheet of questions attached. These had been set for homework. In the library, June and the four boys sat around a very large table, while I positioned myself a table away, at the back of the small room. The seating plan was as shown below.

I noted the alignment of the Hong Kong boys together at one end of the table, and the distance they put between themselves and the teacher and Ivan. John, Keith and Leo chatted in Cantonese while I spoke briefly with

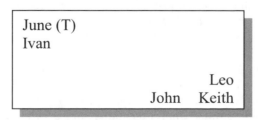

June. She then started the lesson by asking questions about the story, aiming specifically to bring John up to speed on the plot and characters of the story. John read one sentence, struggling (Keith and Leo were speaking in Cantonese again and did not appear to be listening). The teacher then explained what John had read, adding that the owner of the dog Silky was always described in the story as a 'great galumphing creature'. Noticing that Keith seemed distracted, she asked 'Is that right, Keith? The owner is always described as 'a great galumphing creature'?' Keith's answer to this was 'Yeh'.

The boys switched constantly to Cantonese, using every stumbling of another student as a window of opportunity for chat. The story was not particularly easy, but they had been reading it for several lessons, and had been set the worksheet. I was aware of how hard the teacher was working, trying to get the boys to listen to her and to each other, and to talk. June then ran through the plot, doing what seemed like 98% of the talking, actually narrating the story, with the odd oral cloze question. 'Sometimes Zondra let Silky out into the . . . ?' When she asked questions, the boys' answers were usually one-word in length. For example,

June: She hasn't got the key. What's she going to do?
Keith: Find.

John then read from the last two paragraphs of the story, which he found very heavy-going. I include an excerpt here to indicate the level of difficulty he faced.

> But Zondra, that great galumphing creature with the warm, lolly-sticky hands, cheered up considerably when on Alien Day (which celebrates the colonisation of Earth) she was given another pet – one that looked almost like Silky. Zondra wrapped her great scaly green arms around her new precious pet and vowed to be extra careful in future. This cute little human would never escape. Never.
>
> (from *Precious Pet* by Margaret Wild)

I felt the lexical density of the text was a major stumbling block for the students. Had I drawn up a list of words likely to be unfamiliar to these students, it would have included galumphing, lolly-sticky, cheered up, considerably, celebrates, colonisation, wrapped, scaly, precious, vowed and escape – that is, 11 words in 7 lines, an impossibly dense text to be read with any ease or enjoyment (Nation, 1998). June asked the meaning of the word 'alien' and insisted John look it up in his electronic dictionary. He did this, then June asked the group, 'Where could aliens come from?' – 'ET' from John; 'UFO' from Keith, but softly. Keith then took over the reading. It was slow, and unclear. He changed words and omitted final consonants. June asked him to repeat some of these. As Keith continued reading, John made a comment in Cantonese, which amused both Keith and Leo. As Ivan read, the boys talked quite volubly in Cantonese, not listening to the reader or the teacher, who continued to ask the odd question.

The boys were having a lot of trouble with this story, set in the future when the earth has been colonised by aliens, with humans made into domestic pets. While the level of the story seemed to me to be appropriate for Year 10, it was utterly beyond this group. For the teacher, there was the added complication that John had not read all the story and the others had, although this wasn't really in evidence in the boys' answers. They all seemed hesitant and unsure, and often did not understand the questions. Only Keith had a finished worksheet of answers, and tried on several occasions to give this to Leo and John to copy. June finally confiscated his sheet. In the last segment of the lesson, June asked if they'd found the ending a surprise. She repeated and paraphrased her question. After much hesitation, Leo said, 'Little'. John was given some work to do from the sheet, and told not to copy Keith's, whose sheet was now returned to him.

Even around this one table, the boys had spoken far more Cantonese than English. Ivan was quite excluded. As the boys left, I spoke briefly with June, who said that Keith had just arrived from Newnham, but perhaps had the best understanding. She described the boys as 'reluctant to talk', 'an extremely weak class', and 'unable to retain anything'. We speculated that it might be difficult for them to cope with Years 11 and 12. I reflected later on John's participation in this class. Was this an example of his speaking English 'only in class?' His attention and allegiance in this lesson had clearly been to the other two boys, one of them newly arrived, rather than to the work, the class or the teacher. The lesson allowed for answering questions in English, but the presence of Chinese speaking peers, and possibly the difficulty of the text, overrode any potential interaction. I wondered if John might speak more English in mainstream classes, if say, he were not with Chinese speaking friends. To be honest, I doubted it.

The Woodwork Lesson

John's three mainstream subjects at Sandford were Woodwork, Science and Maths. For several other lessons each day, he was in the ESL unit. After a few months, he also started mainstream Geography. Early in the year, he told me that the Maths, which he'd already done in Hong Kong, was not too difficult. However, he had not done Woodwork, and found it hard, and the Science topics were also new and difficult. There was another problem in the mainstream classes. He said, 'Science, mm, the form(u) class teacher is speak too fast. I'm difficult to understand', meaning 'I find it difficult to understand'. He reiterated this point four months later during the Cantonese interview.

D: Can you tell me more about these subjects? Are they difficult beside not understanding the English.
J: I filled nothing in the examination paper of Geography and Mathematics.
D: Can you tell me why?
J: I don't even understand the questions in the paper.
D: What about in classroom? Do you understand what the teachers teach?
J: I can't understand because they speak too fast.
D: Is language the main barrier to your learning?
J: Yes, they speak too fast. When I understand the first sentence, the second sentence is passed already. So I can't understand in the class.   (C. Int. p. 4)

There are two points to note in John's account. On the one hand, his mainstream teachers provided a critical contrast to the ESL teachers, whom he'd told us spoke 'much slower and use simple English'. Mainstream teachers spoke too fast for him to follow. On the other hand, he was unable to read and understand written text on exam papers, even in a subject he did not find difficult, such as Maths. Combined, these two problems represented formidable barriers to John's academic success in the mainstream. I also speculated that he had not been ready for the move from Newnham to high school.

What was it like to sit for months in classes, for hours each day, not understanding what was being said, what was going on, what was required to be done? At the start of the year, he had told me about another school site which was a mystery to him, where teachers spoke too fast. This was the school assembly. He had no idea what they were talking about. 'I just boring sit down', he said. This, it occurred to me, could apply to 90% of the student body during most school assemblies, but John was an outsider to the ritual, excluded not just by boredom, but by language. It seemed, as the months went by, that this did not change very much.

One mainstream lesson I observed was a Year 10 Woodwork lesson. There were 14 boys and one girl in the class. They stood around six work benches, each student working on making their own coffee table. I sat at the back of the room. There were three ESL students in the class. One, an Iraqi boy, Ranid, whom I recognised as a former Newnham student, worked alongside an Anglo Australian and an Australian-born Lebanese student. They chatted and helped each other occasionally. The other two ESL students were John, and a boy called Danny from Taiwan. John and

Danny had a work table to themselves. They worked quietly and did not communicate at all. After the lesson, I asked the teacher about John, and his participation in class. He said that both John and Danny kept to themselves, didn't integrate at all, and didn't ask questions. He added that it was very hard to talk to them, and that what they produced in woodwork was often 'a variation on what was required' because they hadn't really understood the instructions. The teacher confided to me that the Iraqi student Ranid also had a language problem – he didn't listen. I had observed but did not say that several other students seemed to have the same language problem.

As a postscript to this lesson, in an excerpt from the Cantonese interview, John said that Woodwork was possibly his favourite subject. He could pass the practical work, but added, 'If it is in the form of a written exam, I must be failed.' The interviewer queried this.

D:	Why do you think you must be failed?
J:	It's because he doesn't teach in the class.
D:	What does he do if he doesn't teach in class?
J:	Just doing the wood work.
D:	But what can he test in the exam. He can only test what he has taught.
J:	We have workbooks. He didn't teach but we need to finish the workbook by ourselves. Usually, I copy from others.
D:	Do you think it's the teacher's fault if you fail in the exam?
J:	In fact, I don't understand the whole workbook. (C. Int. p. 8)

Having students complete theory workbooks by themselves entails a critical set of assumptions on the part of the teacher. It assumes a high level of literate practice and motivation from the students involved. It also assumes a command of the concepts, content and language used in the text. It leaves students such as John very little option but to 'copy from others'. Not understanding 'the whole workbook' was yet another instance where John was an outsider to the discourse. He did not blame the teacher, although I secretly did.

I had observed John closely in both ESL and mainstream contexts. In the ESL lesson, the Hong Kong boys had set up a little Chinese corner of resistance, remaining detached from the content and purpose of the lesson, bamboozled by the language of the text, and often engaged in presumably humorous asides to each other in Cantonese. Whether the teacher was working with inaccessible material, or whether the boys found her unintimidating and so ignored her repeated requests to listen and respond, the outcome was that the English used was minimal. In the Woodwork lesson I observed, he neither used, nor was called on to use, any English at all, apart from listening to the teacher. And in the mainstream classes, by John's own account, the English spoken was largely unintelligible. Classroom contexts are one thing at school. During breaks between lessons, a different range of social and linguistic practices may be played out. I now turn to some of these.

Where the Boys Are

Sandford and its neighbouring suburbs have substantial ethnic Chinese communities, and these students had previously travelled a long way to get to Newnham. On entering the high school ESL unit, they returned to their 'own patch', a high school with a large visible group of Chinese-speaking students. John had already told me he was looking forward to starting at high school, because 'Sandford have more ESL teacher can speak Chinese and Cantonese. It's very easy to know what they say'. My first thought was that he was still very dependent on and expecting first language support. Later, I thought more about his second statement, 'It's very easy to know what they say'. I thought that knowing what people are saying is indeed a very basic need, tied to power relationships within any interactional context, and to memberships and a sense of self. We know that as John moved beyond the boundaries of the ESL class, his expectations were not met, and that in fact, he often did not know what people were saying. He was able to set up a Cantonese counter-script as it were, which operated both within the ESL and lunch time contexts.

I first visited John soon after he started at Sandford High. Although it was early days, I asked him about friends.

J:	Friends, mm, many Newnham student in, come here. At lunch time we with them to have lunch, to talk, something.
R:	And what nationalities are these students?
J:	I (can't) understood
R:	Um, do they come from, these people who speak, friends who speak Chinese?
J:	Yeah, they speak Chinese, Chinese
R:	So lunch time is speaking Cantonese?
J:	Chinese
R:	Chinese
J:	Yeah
R:	And, um morning tea?
J:	Morning tea ((*unsure*))
R:	Same?
J:	Same
R:	So there are many students who speak Chinese

J: Yeah, in there, yeah, many many can speak Cantonese or
              Chinese
R: And you speak Cantonese and Mandarin
J: No, Chinese and Cantonese   (Int. 14.2.97)

At this point John's membership in the lunch time context was understandably an extension of the group of friends and acquaintances he'd established at
Newnham. The Newnham programme continued to act as a small flag around
which ex-students rallied. However, the group John is referring to was also
defined by its use of one of two Chinese languages. He was bilingual in these
languages, and explained the difference to me.

R: What, what is the difference between Chinese and [Cantonese
J: [Different. Er, Cantonese is (1.0) just use in Hong Kong but
              Chinese is use in (2.0) Taiwan, China, (2.0) er is not same the
              language.   (Int. 14.2.97)

This was the only overlap in any of our talks. He knew about this, and jumped
in. He later told the Cantonese interviewer that there were many more Mandarin speakers than Cantonese speakers, which meant for much of the time he
was operating in his second language.

D: I can see many Chinese students here. You said to Miss Miller
              last time that you speak to Cantonese students only. Is it the
              same now?
J: And Taiwanese. There are much more Taiwanese than Can-
              tonese here. There are only three or four Cantonese.
D: Do you also speak to Taiwanese or just to those Cantonese stu-
              dents?
J: Both.   (C.Int. p. 8)

This was four months on, and the phenomenon of Chinese friendship
groups and language use described by John was, on my visits to the school, an
inescapable feature of the lunch time scene. He had not mentioned gender,
but, as with many Anglo-Australian groups, gender segregation seemed the
norm. Under Block 2 on one occasion I counted 24 Chinese-speaking boys,
sitting around, playing cards, eating and talking. The card players had several
onlookers. I hovered, and eavesdropped. They looked like older students,
around Years 10–12. There were no girls, no Anglo-Australians or other ESL
students in the area. Younger Asian students, predominantly boys, were
playing handball on courts between buildings nearby.

To some extent, the grounds and buildings of Sandford seemed mapped
out in patterns of language use and ethnic groupings. On each visit the
older Chinese boys were under Block 2, which contained the main ESL

office and classrooms. By contrast, in the case of a younger student from the original cohort, a Cambodian boy, I observed quite different patterns of membership and language use during lunch time at Sandford. He was one of the young handballers, who were predominantly Asian boys, but from very heterogeneous ethnic and linguistic backgrounds. I recognised students from Vietnam, Cambodia, Taiwan and the Philippines. As a matter of pragmatic necessity, their lingua franca was English (and handball).

John was older, and he was totally surrounded by speakers of his L1 and L2. He often looked unhappy and taciturn. The Cantonese interviewer also commented to me on this, and wrote on the transcript that he seemed 'lonely and withdrawn from others'. If this was the case, he was not alone. At one Sandford ESL staff meeting I attended, the issue was raised of one Year 10 Taiwanese boy who came very late every day to school. He lived with his older sister, his parents remaining in Taiwan, and wanted the Chinese teacher aide to give him a wake-up call every morning. He had told her he didn't want to be in Australia, or at the school. Truanting amongst the Taiwanese boys was also a serious problem according to the ESL coordinator, taking large amounts of teacher and teacher aide time. By chance, this problem also emerged in the Cantonese interview with John, in the following way.

D: I find that there are also some Chinese teachers here.
J: Two only.
D: Do they teach you?
J: They don't teach.
D: They don't teach? Who are they?
J: They don't teach. They work in the ESL classroom.
D: What do they do?
J: They take records, contact our parents by telephone, keep an eye on those who run away from school.   (C. Int. p. 4)

The Chinese aide's role in John's perception was more about surveillance than liaison – keeping records, contacting parents (always bad news), and tracking 'those who run away from school'. John never did this, but he maintained a social distance between himself and other non-Chinese speaking students of the school.

Staying separate, wanting to leave

In the course of the Cantonese interview, the interviewer, David, tried to construct John as a student who was lucky to have so much access to English speakers, and who was well on the way to successful integration at Sandford. John set up a counter representation almost straight away, as shown in this excerpt from the start of the interview, where David raises the issue of getting used to life in Australia.

D: It's maybe easier for you to get used to it because you have talked to Australians here every day for eight months. In fact, I am still not really used to the life here although I have been here for more than one year. My English may be poorer than you.

J: No, it will not. I don't speak English. ((answers in soft voice))

D: You don't speak English? Is it because there are many Chinese students here?

J: There are many Chinese here. (C.Int. p. 1)

John's claim that he doesn't speak English is ambiguous. It may refer to his self-evaluation of his proficiency in English, to his preferred practice not to speak English, or both. John continued to resist David's discourse of integration, maintaining his sense of otherness and social distance.

D: If you had a chance to speak to the students in Newnham as an old student, what would you say to introduce this school to them, so that they can also integrate into this school as you have?

J: I would not go in for giving such an introduction.

D: You wouldn't? Don't you want to help them?

J: Choose someone else but not me.

D: ((laughs)) What about if there are some Newnham students who had come here already?

J: Such students are many here.

D: As an older student, would you encourage them to integrate into the school? I found that you are not alone. I saw your friends in the playground. So what can you suggest to the new Newnham students in this school?

J: We have our own groups. Taiwanese will group together. The same to those who come from Hong Kong and other countries. We play with our group members. Usually, the Chinese like to sit in the canteen during lunch and recess.

D: Mm.. and you go into your group.

J: Yes, I do

D: Will you join the Australian groups.

J: I still cannot integrate into their groups.

If we look just at John's turns, we see a systematic rejection of David's propositions. Five cases in point are underlined in the text. Read together, they constitute a powerful rejection of the interviewer's standpoint. John is not being what David wants him to be, is not saying what David is leading him to say. In terms of his word-deed-value combinations, John is enacting his identity here in a way that establishes distance from certain groups (ex-Newnham students as a blanket category; and Australian groups), and proximity to others ('our own groups', with Taiwan and Hong Kong mentioned specifically).

David did not give up on this, but returned later to the topic of friends and language use. John had just been reiterating that he never spoke English outside of a classroom.

D: Can you tell me more about your friends? Who are they?

J: Taiwanese.

D: Do they face the same problem as you have? I mean do they also have a language problem in communicating with other Australians? So that you go together.

J: Just like foreign people when they go to Hong Kong, they will also group themselves with the same race and language.

D: Mm. But do you want to break the ice between you and the Australians.

J: Whatever's natural.

D: Will you actively approach them or just wait for them.

J: I will do it if it is necessary.

D: But at least you are prepared to do that.

J: No. Only when there is something I don't understand, I have to ask them. Otherwise, I don't think it is necessary to communicate with them.   (C.Int. p. 8)

The same pattern of opposing discourses shown in the last excerpt is evident here. It is noteworthy that in answer to the first question, he does not name or describe any friends, but provides a category – Taiwanese. Note that John is constructed here as someone with a language problem. However, John's analogy of foreigners in Hong Kong, whom he claims also segregate themselves from the dominant groups, is revealing. He attributes the grouping, and the distance, to 'race and language'. And he minimises David's proposal of 'breaking the ice with Australians' to bare functional necessities, outside of which there is no need to speak English. Overall, he represents communication with English speakers as unwarranted. He later specifies that, in fact, he does not want to stay in Australia, and longs to return to Hong Kong. This is not, as David suggests later, because Hong Kong is more attractive, but, as John puts it, 'there is nothing attractive here'. Towards the end of the interview, he confided to David that the one 'exciting thing' here was driving the family's cars, which had been bought 'for future use'. This was of course illegal, as he was under age and had no licence. John claimed that driving illegally was the only positive aspect of his life here.

In September 1997, Sandford's ESL coordinator informed me that John had left the country with his mother and sisters very suddenly. On discovering that her husband had a mistress in Hong Kong, she had 'packed up the four children and left at very short notice'. This was in August, and the mother had sent a simple note to the school, saying they were returning to Hong Kong. The coordinator added that there was anecdotal evidence of high divorce rates in Hong Kong and Taiwan as a result of the common practice of separated families such as John's. Ironically, she also said that in the stress of the moment, John was reluctant to return. He had become close to his friends here, and she said that they 'derived strength from each other'.

Tina and John: A Summary

The issues I have raised in relation to these two students throw light on social identity as it is enacted through particular contexts, memberships, and discursive practices. They also reveal schools as sites of competing constructions of identity, counter discourses, inclusion and exclusion. The stories of Tina and John have much in common, yet there are some important differences.

Tina and John were of similar ages and backgrounds. Their families were business migrants and in both cases the fathers were absentees, remaining in the home country to maintain business interests. Both students expressed the desire to return to their countries, and identified strongly, socially and linguistically, with their first language groups, although John was bilingual in Cantonese and Mandarin. Both had established themselves as part of these groups at Newnham, and then attended ESL units and high schools where there were large numbers of the L1 group. Although their schools were on different sides of town, the Chinese students in both sites congregated under the ESL block, physically separate, and visibly and audibly different from other mainstream groups who spoke English and other languages. I regularly observed Tina and John 'doing identity in Chinese', a physical representation of Tina's sense that all her friends were from the same place, and that everywhere she went was Taiwanese. It is also worthy of note that both resisted discourses of integration, John in a very overt way during the Cantonese interview.

In tandem with these representations went some resistance to using English, to the point where both students claimed it was unnecessary to use English outside of the classroom. There are several ways to understand these students' choices to remain largely within their own language groups, and to resist speaking English. First, they both had limited proficiency in English, which meant that on occasions when they had spoken, they had frequently been misunderstood. Over many months, they found this discouraging, and perceived only slight or no improvement in their spoken English. It is widely understood that practice in a language is critical to language acquisition (Savignon, 1991), so Tina and John's very limited use of English outside (and indeed within) the classroom prolonged their limited proficiency, and slowed their progress. I suspected that my talks with these students possibly represented their most sustained interactions with an English speaker in the time I knew them. Second, even in contexts of so-called natural language acquisition, people often are ambivalent in their desire to learn and practice the target language, based on their investment in the new language (Norton Peirce, 1995). Tina and John did not have a strong investment in using English, although this began to change for Tina in some of her mainstream Year 9 classes. Further, rather than be subordinated or disempowered by English, the majority language of the school, they remained within a substantial linguistic minority, where their first (and for John, second) language was dominant. Outsiders to the majority discourse, they positioned themselves as insiders to Chinese discourses, and in both schools they had the numbers to do it.

This raises a third issue, namely the reality of the problem of natural language acquisition, for example English in an English-speaking country (Spolsky, 1989). In schools where substantial linguistic minorities exist, 'natural' acquisition may be subverted by sheer weight of numbers. It is unnatural to expect large homogeneous groups of speakers to interact spontaneously in the L2 outside of formal classrooms (Beardsmore, 1993). Although Beardsmore's study was in the context of Canadian immersion programmes, the same conditions obtain in some schools here, where classroom use of the language is effectively the *only* use of the language. In the case of John, I increasingly felt that the situation most analogous to his experience was that of the EFL (English as a foreign language) student. Outside of the classroom, he had virtually no interaction in English, no communication with English speakers, at school or in the community. Learning English in Hong Kong or in Australia was effectively the same for him, more an EFL than an ESL situation. It should be added that John was not responsible for his exit to high school from the Newnham intensive programme, before he was really ready. We can also raise questions about the suitability of some of the texts he was studying at high school, and the lack of language support and overt teaching in his mainstream subjects.

We might also question whether the use of Chinese and avoidance of English represents a choice at all, or if the conditions presented by the *fait accompli* of an instantly recognisable group of first language speakers, meant that subverting the social and linguistic norms of either of these high schools would have required an extraordinary effort of will. In other words, on arriving at Sandford, for example, John immediately recognised his group – the Taiwanese and the students from Hong Kong – all congregating under Block 2. This was a preexisting site in which members shared ethnic backgrounds, cultural understandings and language. What is more, many were former students of Newnham, which meant that recognition of former friends and acquaintances was commonplace. To bypass this highly visible and recognisable group would have meant entering unknown sites, establishing new memberships and using a language in which Tina and John were not at all confident. For some students, this must seem an insurmountable prospect, and we can surmise that being 15 or 16 years old makes it even more difficult. Bourdieu (1993) reminds us that the essence of communication lies more in the social conditions of possibility of communication than in the communication *per se*. The conditions obtaining at Sandford and Taylor meant that the prevailing form of linguistic capital most readily available to and usable by these students was Chinese.

A fourth dimension may be added to this consideration of language and representations of identity by Schumann's (1986) 'Acculturation model' of language acquisition. This too assumes the notion of a target language, but sets up conditions whereby social distance between the speakers of the target language and those who are acquiring that language represents the degree and ease of acquisition. Both Tina and John positioned themselves within a 'dominant' minority, which was socially and linguistically very cohesive and showed a 'degree of enclosure' by close physical association within the institution. Tina felt that her family might leave Australia, so there were limits to her intended length of residence. John had no idea his stay in Australia would end so abruptly, but spoke of going back to Hong Kong. According to Schumann's model therefore, these students maintained through their memberships, social practices and language use a considerable social distance between themselves and English speakers at school and within the community. This model ties in with the notion of identity established across categories of likeness and difference – identification with some, and differentiation from others. Through social categorisation and comparison, individuals recognise themselves as members of particular groups, and outsiders to other groups (Tajfel, 1981). However, more recent social constructions of identity have emphasised the effects of social relations and institutions on group memberships and identity. Wexler (1992) argues that for marginalised groups, processes of in-group identification may represent elements of defensive compensation created as a response to a lack of viable social relations in schools. In other words, if you can't establish meaningful relations with members of the mainstream discourses, you will use other means to represent who you are, within your group and to others – and you will remain at the margins. In the case of Tina and her friends, I am suggesting that the lack of viable communicative interactions with English-speaking students meant that the only chance these students had of 'being somebody', to use Wexler's term, was to be somebody in the Chinese group.

Bourdieu (1993: 68) stresses that there is 'a micro-economics and a macro-economics of linguistic products'. While the Chinese-speaking students in the micro-contexts under Block 2 and under C Block are defending their own value and their own capital, in the macro context of the schools overall, their linguistic products are valued quite differently. For example, while Chinese is valued highly in the Chinese language classes (Tina got an A), it is elsewhere represented by teachers as a problem and a barrier to learning. It is also not viable on the wider social linguistic market of the school.

In spite of some points of convergence, there were clear differences between the situations of Tina and John. First, because Tina lived a long way from her Chinese friends, she went out a lot, to the city, to Chinatown, and in fact to the Chinese suburbs where John lived. This meant she had a broader perspective on the city and its people than did John, who said he never went anywhere. Second, unlike John, she had represented herself as 'other' in very explicit ways, but although she was still with Chinese-speaking friends in her out-of-class time, as the months passed there was evidence that she placed a decreasing emphasis on her otherness. The third and most significant difference in my view, concerns her more successful integration into the mainstream, in terms of her participation in groupwork ('doing things with Australians'), and academic success on assignments and exams. This was a gradual and progressive emergence into main-stream roles, accompanied by an increasing awareness that using English to achieve these roles was possible. In her diary, she expressed increasing confidence as a result.

The periods of data collection on Tina and John, 14 months and 7 months respectively, represent only brief fragments of time in the lives of these students, especially in terms of language acquisition and representations of identity. Hall (1996: 4) suggests that identity is about processes of 'becoming rather than being: not "who we are" or "where we came from", so much as what we might become, how we have been represented and how that bears on how we might represent ourselves'. Representations of identity for Tina and John were for some months firmly fixed on 'where they had come from', but in the case of Tina, there were insights into the changes wrought by her movement into the mainstream, and a sense of her becoming something and someone other than the person she had defined as a 'black hair'. The oral group tasks, for example, provided a common goal for her and her Australian peers to negotiate language and content and to achieve. This was a shared and validating experience. In Gee's (1996) terms, Tina engaged in a new social group which also constituted, for her, a new learning context and which used the language of the mainstream, English. In this way she was able to enact the identity of a mainstream student, and to be heard as such by her peers and the teacher. Students who find themselves in a new country, but surrounded by speakers of their first language, must actively meet the challenge to move beyond the sites and memberships of first language use. It is this movement which enables the project of becoming, along with language practice and acquisition, the possibility of success in mainstream academic contexts, and the discovery that in spite of language differences, people share many things. However, in staking out and inhabiting particular linguistic territory, for some students there is little chance of establishing new common ground.

Chapter 5

Milena: Being Friends with Everyone

Introduction

Sixteen-year-old Milena arrived in Australia with her mother, father and 12-year-old sister, Tanya on 21 September 1996. The family, along with her aunt, two cousins and grandmother had left Bosnia to escape the war, moving from Sarajevo to Belgrade in 1991, when Milena was 11 years old. Both of her parents worked in Bosnia as economists. In 1994, the families fled to Denmark as refugees, leaving Milena's father behind to fight in the war. For two years he could seldom be contacted. They stayed for almost three years in Copenhagen, during which time Milena attended high school, learned Danish and acquired close friends. She continued her music studies in piano, and also started to learn English at school. After two years, to the family's immense relief, the father joined them in Copenhagen. Milena said her family moved to Australia 'to start a new life', and specifically because of the possibilities of citizenship and work in Australia. Permanent residency status is extremely difficult to achieve in Denmark, whereas this is granted to approved migrants and refugees in Australia. Milena's mother spoke four languages, including English, and her father three. On arrival, Milena was bilingual in Bosnian and Danish, and had some knowledge of English. She thus already possessed substantial cultural and symbolic capital (see Chapter 2).

Within three weeks of arriving in Australia, Milena and Tanya enrolled in the intensive Newnham reception programme, on 8 October. Her aunt and cousins had arrived one month prior, and helped Milena's family to settle in. The cousins already attended Newnham. Both families lived in outer suburbs, and initially the children had to travel for well over an hour each way by train to the school. In Milena's class at Newnham, nine of the 17 students were from Bosnia. Milena exited the programme after just 10 weeks, her teachers satisfied that in terms of her social adjustment and English proficiency, she was ready for the move to the high school ESL unit. Milena, her sister and cousins wanted to go to Markwell High School, although they had heard it was hard to get into, due to large student numbers. They knew that many migrant students, including many Bosnians, attended the school. Milena's only concern, apart from not getting in, was that she would have to wear a school uniform. She was used to wearing short skirts, heeled shoes and make-up. She told me that she found all uniforms ugly, but that Markwell's at least was 'the nicest you can find'. One of Milena's outside interests was fashion design. She was also a prolific letter writer (to her friends in Bosnia and Denmark), loved drawing, listening to music, being with her friends, and talking.

In this chapter I begin with a drama lesson which encapsulated four analytic themes related to identity in Milena's story. These themes were: agency; language competence and language learning; social networking; and confidence and collaboration. I then discuss each of these themes at length. The following note on Markwell High School provides some contextual background for the lesson and the development of the four themes.

Multicultural Markwell High

Markwell High is a large city school of over 1800 students which prides itself on being a school of 51 nations, that is, with students from 51 countries and a vast range of ethnic and language backgrounds. The principal told me that over 30% of the students were from non-English speaking backgrounds. The school had an ESL unit for students who had exited Newnham, but many other NESB students were actually born in Australia or had arrived when very young. The school is in what the principal described as a solid middle class area, is well resourced in terms of sporting and cultural facilities, materials and technology, and also features a centre for artistic development in dance and the performing arts. Some of the more predominant ethnic groups in the school include Bosnians and Serbs, Vietnamese, Chinese, Taiwanese and students from Hong Kong, Filipinos, Koreans, Indians and Pakistanis, Polynesians and Greeks. The principal described this diversity as 'a fantastic resource' but stressed that it also placed extra demands on teachers, particularly in terms of language and cultural issues. He added that staff numbers of 108 mainstream teachers and five ESL staff were not really adequate to cope with these problems. It had been calculated that while the school received funding for 115 ESL students, 227 students urgently needing support were identified by staff.

The school represents itself as ethnically and culturally diverse. Signs and photos in Markwell High's administration foyer draw attention to its visibly and culturally diverse population. Chinese, Japanese, German and Russian were taught at the school, and numerous practices reinforced the school as a bastion of multiculturalism. The school diary proclaimed, 'Markwell is proud of the diverse background of its students from Australia and from many overseas countries. This blend of cultures gives Markwell a unique opportunity to learn from others.' The diary also listed Chinese, Muslim, Jewish, Greek Orthodox, Hindu and Christian religious festivals on the Year Planner, while daily school notices included announcements for Muslim students of a weekly *Jummah Salah* or prayer meeting. In May, a Multicultural Week was celebrated at the school, which featured a multicultural food festival, a writing competition (translations required when not written in English), poster and badge design competition and a concert in school time for the entire school community. Form notices in the week prior to the Multicultural Week concert urged students to 'Enter the spirit of multicultural Markwell'.

Milena's drama class

Prior to my arrival at Milena's Year 11 mainstream drama class, she had seen the teacher and requested that I be introduced as an interested observer of the class (rather than someone interested in Milena). This was to ensure she was not singled out or embarrassed in front of her peers, and that her membership of the group was not compromised. She told the teacher that she did not want to be 'looked at'. The teacher complied, and I noted Milena's initiative in taking charge of a situation she might otherwise have been uncomfortable with. She knew that my gaze was directed at ESL students, and I came to realise that this was not how she perceived or represented herself.

The task for the lesson was to work in groups on improvising a scene in which a group of teenage boys goes into a café, and one of them touches a waitress in an unsolicited and unwelcome way. The students had only seven to eight minutes to devise their improvisation, and then were to present it to the class. During the preparation time I talked to the teacher and observed groups working. Milena was talking happily in her group, which comprised one boy and seven girls, as they constructed the scene. A member of this class for four months, Milena seemed comfortable and accepted, and although not a major protagonist in this improvisation, took her part as one of the sexist youths confidently. It was almost unnerving to watch the degree of authenticity with which some of the girls portrayed young sexist male behaviour. The improvisations were full of youth language and slang. Through the process of their enactments, the students constructed and reflected on the prevailing attitudes, values, actions and responses of young people, in the face of issues such as sexual harassment, gender conflict, rights and resistance.

Milena's teacher told me that she was a very good drama student, who had also elected to take the extension drama subject, Theatre Arts. She said Milena was excellent in discussion, had very good ideas and had fitted in well with the group. Any mention of Milena's English proficiency was notably missing, but she stressed that Milena had been helped in the class by a Bosnian boy, Milenko, who was an extrovert, popular and extremely confident. The teacher commented on the physical attractiveness of both students, adding that they always did pair work together, often discussing the concepts in Bosnian, as well as in English.

After the lesson, I went up to Milena when most others had left. I said it seemed a nice class, and she agreed, adding 'everyone was friendly, everyone talked, there is no hate', before hurrying off to her next lesson. Later she told me that by 'no hate' she did not mean racial hatred, but the tensions and bitchiness which sometimes characterise interaction in adolescent groups. I reflected that the drama class seemed a very positive environment to facilitate the integration of an ESL student. It must be stressed that by this stage Milena spoke very fluent but accented English. The atmosphere of this drama room was accepting, 'talky', interactive and seemed non-threatening. The lesson addressed contemporary youth issues in contemporary youth language. Yet there was another aspect arising from this observation, one which concerned me as researcher, and Milena as someone I had categorised as an ESL student. She had been in Australia only six months at this point. I was aware of a certain tension between my representation of her, and the way she projected herself as a mainstream student. Although she had started out in my cohort from Newnham as part of the category 'ESL students', this was now challenged by her self-representation and identity choices. As she hurried off to rejoin her next mainstream class I felt left behind in more ways than one.

Within the micro-context of this drama lesson I identified four broad thematic strands which I note in Table 5.1 and will develop as central to Milena's language and identity work. The drama lesson illustrated ways in

Table 5.1

Theme	*Example*
Agency	Milena's initiative in setting up my introduction.
Language competence	Her participation in the improvisation, and bilingual discussions with Milenko.
Social networking	Her friendly acknowledgment and inteactions with class members.
Confidence	Her group participation and performance in front of the class, and her ability to talk to the teacher privately.

which the acquisition and use of spoken English was related to self-representation and social identity. Milena was audible to others, heard and acknowledged as a speaker of English, and able to participate productively in a mainstream context. She was able to represent herself, build relationships, and work with peers confidently, all of which provided the underlying conditions for her ongoing English language development and continuing identity work. In the next section I examine the four themes listed above more closely, using data from Milena's own accounts.

Four Analytic Strands in Language Use and Identity

To understand the relationship of agency, language competence, social networking and confidence to identity, it is useful to return to Bourdieu's (1991) notion of the *linguistic habitus*. To summarise some of the critical points raised in Chapter 2, we should note that the *linguistic habitus:*

- is a set of dispositions acquired through speaking in different contexts;
- is generative and transposable to other social fields;
- determines the value that linguistic products receive in social fields;
- enables social interactions and participation in culturally valued practices;
- is realised through legitimation by the hearer;
- is related to power and other forms of symbolic capital.

In these terms, acquisition of the dominant language (and its discursive practices) must be seen as enabling and empowering for minority language speakers. And since identity is constructed and represented through language use (Hall, 1996; Norton Peirce, 1995), the acquisition of English is vital for the renegotiation of identity in new social contexts. The four themes of agency, language competence, networking and confidence are all related to discursive resources, and to the construction of identity and its use as a resource, and all four are related to the notion of power. Furthermore, these themes are not discrete, but closely interlinked. That is, for example, agency is broadly to do with having your 'word-deed-value combinations' recognised, or legitimacy in Gee's (1996) terms, but also with sociolinguistic and strategic language competence, along with having the confidence to initiate and participate in agentive moves and social interactions.

Agency

Giroux (1992) argues that radical theories of subjectivities have erased any notion of viable human agency, failing to provide a sense of:

> how people actually take up particular subject positions, what individ-
> uals and groups are privileged in having access to particular positions,
> and what conditions are that make it possible for some groups to take
> up, live, and speak particular discourses. (Giroux, 1992: 207)

Extrapolating from Giroux's statement, we can say that agency is a social
phenomenon which refers to ways in which some people are able to take a
standpoint, to show initiative even where there may be an asymmetry of
power relations, and to use discursive resources to represent themselves
and to influence situations to their own advantage. It is about using access
to discourses and all this represents (see Norton & Toohey, 2001). My data
provide numerous examples of Milena's agency in these terms, along with
insights into how she operated and some of the conditions which made it
possible.

On leaving Newnham, 16-year-old Milena was bound for a Year 10
grouping in the ESL unit of her new high school. Although most mainstream Year 10 students are 15 years old, both the Newnham and Markwell
High teachers felt that given her level of English, she would need to start at
Year 10. In their eyes, and indeed in mine, she was still an ESL kid after all.
When I arrived at the school just two weeks into the new school year,
Milena was neither in the ESL unit nor in Year 10. I asked her how she had
come to be placed in mainstream Year 11. Our talks were always in English,
with no interpreter.

> Um, I should actually be in (.) Year 10. But because of my age, er, I asked
> Mrs Parditch *(the ESL coordinator)* if I may, er (.) move to Year 11.
> Because I really think (1.0) this Year 10 is easy for me. And er many of
> my friends are Year 11, many Bosnians *(inaudible)*. So it's like, easier to
> be with them (.) they can help me finding something, an', I just, and my
> parents think that, er, it's, 11, grade 11, no that grade 10 is too easy for
> me, so, I'm (.) I'm (.) I choose English, Maths B, Theatre Arts, Drama,
> Music and Biology. And (.) it's not hard, at all. Just sometimes in Music
> (.) I find a bit difficult because I don't know, do all, all the words, but I
> know them in Bosnian, so they just bit different.   (Interview 2, p. 1)

In this excerpt, Milena reveals an analytic standpoint, enunciating five
grounds which constituted her case for a change of year level, presumably all
of which she used with Mrs Parditch. These included her age (objectively a relatively minor one year difference), the 'easiness' of the work in Year 10, the
presence of her friends in Year 11 (former Newnham students), the fact that
her Bosnian friends could help her with the work, and parental support for the
move. Mrs Parditch commented to me briefly on the change when I raised it
with her later, saying she was not entirely happy with it, that she didn't think

Milena was ready and that a lot of Bosnian students think they are better than they actually are. She gave me that resigned-when-students-get-their-own-way look. What can you do? A new ESL student had tackled the ESL coordinator in her new high school on a previously taken decision, and prevailed.

Mrs Parditch was working with the same framework of categories I had started with – Milena as a Bosnian ESL student. Anecdotal evidence among teachers was also that although Bosnian students were often highly verbal and confident, their strengths in oral English were often not reflected in academic work which demanded a high level of written skills. Milena's English, both spoken and written, was deemed good enough for her to go straight to the mainstream, except for the subject English itself, which she did in the ESL unit, but she had self-selected her year level, promoting herself by one year.

Milena extended her account later in the interview, as shown in the following interchange. (R = myself as researcher; M = Milena)

R: Do you , do you feel as if you belong (.) to the mainstream bunch of kids or do you feel different?

M: Erm, I feel as if I belong, but when I was in grade ten, first week, oh all the kids, they were only kids. I came first day into my form meeting, and some small guys and girls, and I, and I said to myself, 'I'm out of here. I can't be in grade 10.' Then I went to Mrs Parditch and said 'Please please please please' and she talked to my Mum, 'please please please' (1.0) and I moved (laughs).

R: Lucky it worked.   (Interview 2, p. 4)

This is an account of how Milena negotiates identity, but at the same time, the account reveals her agency, as she constructs for me the process of getting your own way with teachers, and displays her levels of competence. It was as if she had recreated the ruse, inviting my complicity. I did not disappoint, rounding off her anecdote with 'Lucky it worked'. In fact, I felt that luck was not really a factor, but more to do with her linguistic and cultural capital (see Chapter 2). In this account, she had spent one week in Year 10, greeting with disdain and virtual disbelief the notion that she could ever belong to this group of 'small guys and girls' who were 'only kids'. Her response was summed up in her use of the youth vernacular 'I'm out of here'.

Students dislike some of their classes every day of the week – but not many go to the authorities to effect a change. Milena went straight to the co-ordinator, then brought in reinforcements in the form of her mother, an apparently irresistible combination. What conditions made the initiative possible? First, it is hard to ignore her linguistic and strategic competence in English, epitomised by her use of persuasive devices and skill in argumentation. Her arguments to me were succinct and aptly phrased, and clearly she had used more than 'please, please, please' to convince Mrs Parditch. Second, her parent had called the school and supported the move. Milena's mother spoke four languages fluently, and the appeal was made in fluent English. Milena and her mother were therefore heard by the institutional representative, using the dominant discourse to argue their case. This was a hearable representation acknowledged as such by the school, an instance of where Milena's linguistic capital was legitimised and accorded value (see Chapter 2). Bourdieu (1984) stresses that the speaker must achieve his / her desired effect in order to get the 'pay off' or value accorded by the listener. He also suggests that prevailing within the linguistic market is less about grammaticality than knowing what is socially required and acceptable. However, I would argue that for second language speakers, getting the right pay-off is indeed contingent on a certain level of competence in the dominant language, and I would include grammaticality in this. Milena could not have achieved her aim through an interpreter. In Gee's terms she also had to sound right in English.

In addition to the above example of agency, I observed an instance in which Milena challenged her English teacher during one lesson. In the weeks preceding the school's Multicultural Week, many students were meeting to rehearse their concert items. Milena's English teacher was responsible for the 'former Yugoslav' groups. At the start of the lesson, Milena raised her hand (this was to be a public statement) and asked if the Bosnian and Serbian groups were supposed to practise together, because she didn't think this was right. She was in fact hinting at tensions which were emerging in the school between Bosnian Serbs and Bosnian Muslims. The teacher reassured her that the groups would rehearse separately, but added, 'It's supposed to be a Multicultural Day, not a war!' Milena had made her point, and in a very public way. Milena claimed she made a habit of participating actively in class, as shown in this interview fragment,

> I'm getting better, and I try to talk in class as much as I can. I mean the teacher asks I try to answer as much as I can and sometimes I can't, but then I just shut up , and that's another thing.   (Interview 3, p. 3)

So she consciously contributed, and was heard by both her teachers and her peers. Once again, answering class questions is a public display of language and social competence. Unlike Milena, Tina and John (see Chapter 4) found this extremely difficult to do. Neither ever asked or volunteered to answer a question in the lessons I observed. One of John's teachers said he hadn't 'uttered a peep' in five weeks. Although they did not have the same level of spoken skills in English as Milena, they also had less symbolic capital – less access to native speakers, less parental support for their learning of English, a more restricted social circle, fewer experiences of success in using English at school and more dependence on their L1 groups. Both Tina and John had said they were unwilling to risk entering the linguistic market. People didn't understand them, or value what they had to offer.

In choosing her subjects, Milena drew on the cultural capital she had arrived with, but also exercised a considered choice. Her subjects were (parallel) English, Maths B, Theatre Arts, Drama, Music and Biology. She had learned piano for many years, and studied music and drama in Denmark, where the family had lived for three years after leaving Bosnia as refugees, before migrating to Australia. She told me of her love for these subjects and added,

> I wanted to choose <u>art</u>, but I have biology because I want to have (.) some education of (.) of <u>life</u>, you know. I want to know something about life. And I (.) my Mum can teach me to draw if I don't know something, so it's not, not, I mean, yeah.   (Interview 2, p. 3)

Knowing something of Milena's background, it occurred to me that Milena had seen more of life than most 16 year olds. She had lived in three countries and spoke three languages. But she had a strong sense of what she wanted, and the resources to achieve whatever this might be, including asking for assistance.

On one occasion, Milena had said, 'if I need some help I just ask.' She had done this on several occasions in our talks, when I used vocabulary she didn't know. Two examples were as follows:

Example A

R:	And what about the size of this place? Do you find that (.) daunting?
M:	(2.0) What's 'daunting'?
R:	Daunting um, it bothers you, puts you off, it worries you
M:	Oh (.) I don't know. I been in a big school in Bosnia, really big school and then in in, in a small school in Denmark. So I'm in a big school again. ((soft laugh)) (Interview 2, p. 3)

Example B

M:	My sister panics but she's just grade 8. She wants to have best marks in class
R:	She's competitive
M:	Pardon?
R:	She's competitive
M:	What's that?

R: Oh (.) she wants to compete with the others

M: Yeah! She wants to have best marks, she wants to be like the <u>greatest</u>   (Interview 3, p. 4)

These examples of asking for meaning look like textbook language learning strategies, which will be discussed in more detail in the next section. However, they also reveal a competent agent able to successfully maintain the flow of conversation by asking for meaning, apprehending a given meaning and incorporating it smoothly into her next turn by using paraphrase. While I may be overattributing the category of 'conscious language learner' to Milena here, I also saw these moves in conversation as part of the way she represented herself in speaking, part of how she 'did' conversation.

In her interactions with me, Milena was unfailingly polite and cooperative, yet at the same time assertive and independent. To negotiate and confirm times that I would visit her at school, I phoned her, and then checked with the ESL coordinator. Milena always negotiated a time which would suit her best. For example, on one occasion, she asked very politely if she might consult her timetable when I suggested Period 1. She fetched it and then explained she was preparing a Drama exam in that period with a partner. She said Period 3 would suit her best as it was Maths, and her teacher was going to be absent. She apologised if this was not suitable and asked if it would be alright. This was a high level of strategic discourse, in which she communicated and justified her preferences, establishing through her competence a symmetry of power relations. During this visit, we spoke about the diary I was asking students to write and I stressed she could staple shut any private sections. Milena countered that she might instead write personal sections in Danish, which she knew I was unable to read. She had specific reasons for wanting to write in Danish, which I will outline in the following section on language use. Her ultimate expression of agency was in fact to choose not to write in the diary at all. She explained in her only page of writing:

> *The real reason why I really don't feel like writing into this diary is because I know it is going to be published and a 'Diary' is just to private, for me, to be published. I see my diary as alive person, and I would never let anybody but my 2–3 closest friends which are like sisters to me, read it.*

I had not said my study would be published, yet rather than explain the concept of a doctoral thesis, I had initially told students I was studying and writing a kind of book. I was aware that Milena was not writing for some time after receiving the diary. She told me on the phone that she had a friend from Denmark visiting, and was extremely busy. She then had exams and assignments and was even busier. The reasons why she chose not to write interested me less than the decision *per se*. Here was a student who felt she was her own agent, able to represent to teachers (and researchers) her own needs, priorities and interests. She was also resisting my categorisation of her as research subject, ESL student, or indeed compliant pupil in the face of teacher pressure, all through the medium of English. She was too busy being herself to write a diary for somebody else.

The final example of her agency occurred during an interview about half way through the school year. Milena was concerned about being legitimately absent from class to talk to me, as shown in the following excerpt.

M: Are you going to write any note and see at the office?
R: We'll make a note for your next lesson. What's your next lesson?
M: Mm biology. I don't need a note for next lesson. Just if, there's one thing (.) I think you need to go to office, or ring them and say that I've been here, because they probably mark me away. And I might get in trouble.
R: When is the roll marked, every lesson?
M: Yeah
R: OK we'll ring up the office.   (Interview 3, p. 5)

Her opening use of the interrogative and her injunction for me to act in, 'I think you need to go to office' placed me in a particular position. I did not view these exchanges as a student telling me what to do, but felt a clear obligation to respond. The coordinator was well aware of our talk, as we were using her office, but Milena was a mainstream student who had to obey mainstream attendance protocols. Her explanation of the procedure and consequences if it was not followed were very clear. She negotiated in this excerpt that I take some responsibility for following the procedure. And I responded to the degree of authority she was able to convey.

In this section I have outlined ways in which Milena was able to take up particular positions and represent her own interests. She did this from the start of the year when she literally upgraded herself. Similarly, by taking a stand on separate rehearsals for Bosnians and Serbs, participating actively in class discussions in English and Drama, negotiating with me over suitable times for visiting the school and ways she would write (and then not write) her diary, Milena was able to represent herself and her own position in the school, as well as in relation to me. It is simply unthinkable that a student with limited English proficiency could have made these particular moves. I have suggested that an important condition that made such a realisation possible was her linguistic and strategic competence in English, evident in the interview excerpts, in the examples where she sought and responded to new meanings, and in the ease of the conversational flow. I turn now to the domain of language competence and aspects of language acquisition.

Language competence and language learning strategies

In Chapter 2, I mentioned Canale's (1983) model of communicative competence, and its subsequent validation and refinement by Celce-Murcia *et al.* (1995), as outlined in that chapter. Clearly all learners do not have access to the same resources in the process of acquiring discourse competence, linguistic competence, actional competence, sociocultural competence and strategic competence. Nor do they approach language learning in the same way. In addition to Celce-Murcia *et al.*'s valuable conceptualisation of communicative competence, Cook (1993) and O'Malley and Chamot (1990) have outlined cognitive and metacognitive strategies used by effective language learners. This work is from an individualist and cognitivist standpoint rather than a sociocultural perspective, focusing on an idealised 'good language learner', rather than on the ways in which language use is socially defined and determined. However Cook's checklist of learning strategies provides a key to discerning and understanding particular discursive resources, and is therefore useful for analysing some aspects of spoken and written discourse. Furthermore, cognitive strategies such as independent use of reference sources, note-taking skills, deductive application of L2 rules, using key words, contextualisation and inferencing are vitally linked to the acquisition of school English, and success on academic tasks.

With these key SLA principles in mind, I now turn to Milena's accounts of acquiring English and using it at school. Recall that she had acquired spoken and written Danish in her three years in Denmark, where she had also started learning English at school. Judging from Milena's use of English after just a few months in Australia, my intuition was that her Danish would have been quite accomplished. Having outlined types of language competence, I begin with an area in which Milena perceived she was less than competent. It should be added that as interpretive categories, notions of competence are generally attributed to the language user, rather than being consciously understood or acknowledged by him/her.

'I find my grammar big problem'

After Milena had completed one semester in high school, I asked her if she had any particular problems.

M: Yeah, I have, OK, I put love problems aside. I have, I have problems with school about my subjects and language.

There's a big language problem but I just try not think about it at all. I just take dictionary, find a word and try to learn it. And I talk to my parents (.) they help me but, I have such problems.

R: You're saying a big language problem. *((having spoken at length with Milena on many occasions, I was disbelieving.))*

M: Not <u>huge</u>, but in biology we do so many things and I can't understand sometimes and sometimes I really can't be bothered taking dictionary and all that. Same in music. But I just do the best I can.   (Interview 3, p. 6)

Despite the tantalising opening turn, the focus here was on difficulties Milena perceived and was experiencing in English. Her 'big language problem', which she mitigated to 'not huge' in her second turn, seemed to amount to a question of lexis in her view, further evidenced by her idea that a dictionary was the solution. She was also able to use her parents as a resource. Even at the start of the year, she had made a similar comment relating to vocabulary, saying, 'Just sometimes in Music (.) I find a bit difficult because I don't know, do all, all the words, but I know them in Bosnian, so they just <u>bit</u> different'. She perceived that 'all the words' were the problem. It is significant that Milena found vocabulary a problem in Music and Biology, both of which contain specialised technical terminologies, that is, vocabulary that people would not readily encounter in everyday life.

When I asked her further about the language problem, Milena raised something quite different from the question of unfamiliar lexis, as shown in the following exchange.

R: Is it understanding what you hear or is it writing English that's hard, or both?

M: Both. Sometimes sometimes talking sometimes writing (.) it depends. It's when we need to write, like assignment, report and then sometimes it's really hard. But I just look at the books and try to copy (.) try to put sentences in different way. I don't want teacher to know that, like I copy from the book but everybody does it, you know. And sometimes it's really hard, I don't know, I can't explain that.

R: Talking doesn't seem to be a problem, when you say talking's the problem:

M: It's not a big problem but my grammar is. I find my grammar big problem.

R: That's more for writing though isn't it [than

M: [And for talking as well I think, is it?

R: Well have people said you talk with [terrible grammar?

M: [No. (laughs) No.
R: 'Cause the grammar of speaking's very different, from the grammar of writing.
M: Oh OK
R: You know, cos we go OK and we say things, you know an' repeat ourselves, I'm not talking like I write, you know what I mean?
M: Yeah   (Interview 3, p. 6)

In terms of Celce-Murcia *et al.*'s (1995) model of communicative competence (see Chapter 2), I was explicitly using and referring to elements of actional, strategic and sociocultural competence, as distinct from linguistic and discourse features so necessary in written forms. Milena mentioned first talking and then focused particularly on writing as a particular area of concern. Her comments on assignments and reports, and the need to read and paraphrase reference texts in the writing process, threw light on what was perhaps her major preoccupation. She identified what students are told to do and what she knew to be necessary for her assignments, namely writing sentences 'in different way', or paraphrasing. She understood that copying from books, even though 'everybody does it', was not ideal and needed to be concealed. She then identified grammar as 'the big problem'. I recalled that even at Newnham, she had told me that grammar and verb tenses were what she still really had to learn. At this point I was unable to resist reverting to my teacher identity, drawing her attention to the difference between speaking and writing, and trying to illustrate this for her with my last turn.

There are three main points to be made in regard to the excerpts above. First, from Milena's own account, vocabulary and grammar (specifically sentence construction) were her major difficulties in English. In the communicative competence model these belong firmly in the domain of grammatical and discourse competence, encompassing mastery of the language code in terms of vocabulary, word and sentence formation, spelling, semantics and cohesion. Second, in the writing of reports and assignments, these grammatical skills are the primary resources which students must be able to draw on, as Milena realised. To me, her comment 'sometimes it's really hard, I don't know, I can't explain that' needed no further explanation. Writing any form of institutional genre (from Science report to thesis) is indeed 'really hard'. Her evaluation of the writing process was both succinct and eloquent. In these terms, Milena did not have a language problem, but a school language problem, with grammatical competence being the language competence most valued and rewarded on the school linguistic market. Ironically, at the end of Year 11, Milena failed Maths and Biology, whereas she received Cs for English, Music and Drama, subjects which require more extended, cohesive, written text as a part of their assessment. The Maths teacher commented that she was trying hard, and that language was 'the problem'.

The third point relates merely to highlighting the fact that Milena was not consciously aware of the very high levels of language competence she displayed in other areas, or rather she did not acknowledge them. For example, the sociolinguistic and strategic aspects of her discourse, as evidenced in our spoken interactions, and in the episode where she convinced the school to change her year level, were very competently realised. As her interlocutor, I perceived only minor grammatical anomalies in Milena's talk, yet was often struck with her very accomplished use of a number of discursive strategies and resources, as well as her understanding of *how* to go about acquiring another language.

'That's how I learned Danish, so I'm using that way to learn English'

Milena was trilingual. She spoke Bosnian at home, mostly Bosnian and English with her friends, Danish occasionally with her sister and other friends, and used English in class and for assignments. She also wrote a personal diary in Danish, and letters up to 20 pages long in Bosnian and Danish to her friends overseas. She switched languages depending on social context and the first language of her interlocutors or readers, but also consciously used certain strategies to learn and maintain her second and third languages. Some of the language learning strategies mentioned by Cook (1993) include self-management of the conditions for learning, using resources such as dictionaries and textbooks independently, translation, transfer from previous language knowledge, inferencing and asking for clarification. I gave examples above where Milena sought clarification of the meanings for 'daunted' and 'competitive'. From my first interactions with Milena I realised that she did many of the things suggested by Cook.

To begin this section, I present three transcript excerpts: one from a focus group at Newnham; one from early in the high school year; and one five months later. They focus primarily on Milena's maintenance of Danish, her second language, but provide insights into her language practices generally and also into her metalinguistic awareness.

Excerpt 1: Focus group 1A (after 10 weeks in Australia)

Me:	What are some good ways to learn a language?
A:	Read books.
S:	Speak with Australian friends
M:	That's how I learned Danish, so I'm using that way to learn

English. I speak a lot in English (1.0) just read something and translate, take a book and a dictionary.

Excerpt 2: Interview 2 (after 5 months)

R: And what about socially, on the weekends, and [..

M: [Oh: half half. I'm like sometimes with (.) er Bosnians sometimes with Danish, sometimes with Australians I mean, I speak like mostly English and Bosnian, it depends

R: Are you still speaking Danish sometimes?

M: Yeah, with my sister. And I write my diary in Danish because I don't want to forget Danish and I want my friends to read it when they come, because one (.) one of my friends coming here to visit me about (.) maybe about fifteen months or something

R: Um, we wondered last time why you speak Danish with your sister.

M: Er I don't want to forget Danish. It's, erm it's very important for me to speak Danish (.) because (.) I have my best friends in Denmark (2.0) and er I love them I really do, so …

Excerpt 3: Interview 3 (after 10 months)

M: OK. First of all I have my own diary, and it is in Danish and the reason why I write in Danish is because (.) first of all I don't want anyone to read it, except my parents and my sister can speak Danish but, they never check it and, uh, second of all I want one of my friends from Denmark (.) to be able to read it. And my friend from Denmark will come the eighteenth of June so I want her to (.) to be able to read (.) it's easier for her to read in Danish than in English and um, third thing is I didn't wanta forget Danish. It's a good opportunity to remember it (.) for<u>ever</u>! (laughs) Yeah.

In the first excerpt, Milena explains that she transfers strategies which were clearly successful in learning Danish, to English – namely, speaking with others, reading, translating and using a dictionary. She told me that she did these last three quite independently of school work, in her own time. In the second excerpt, she provides the contexts of her use of the three languages, first in speaking, then in writing, contexts in which her language practices are shaped primarily by her social relationships. In this excerpt, she explains her writing in Danish as a language maintenance strategy, but also because

Danish is the language of her 'best friends', and so it provides a concrete link and a symbolic attachment to these friends.

My question as to why she would use Danish with her sister was a reference to an earlier discussion, in which Milena and other Newnham students had dismissed as a nonsense the suggestion that they practise speaking English with each other, that is with friends from the same language group, or family members, so as to learn more quickly. ESL teachers often exhort students to speak English 'amongst themselves'. Milena had said, 'Here it's just so weird you know (.) to speak other languages with your family.' From the students, I understood it was limiting and embarrassing to attempt to communicate using the artifice of a still shaky second language with members of your first language group. Beardsmore (1993) reminds us that it is unrealistic to expect homogeneous L1 speaking peers to engage in self-initiated interaction in L2 outside the formal classroom. Although Milena had labelled it 'weird', she used Danish with her sister mainly to retain her fluency – an example where a conscious language strategy overrode the norms of a sociocultural context.

In the final excerpt, five months later, she expands further on her maintenance of Danish. This is presented as a formal argument in which she enunciates three reasons for writing her diary in Danish, introduced by the formal markers, 'first of all', 'second of all', and 'third thing'. The first reason is to do with excluding anyone but her best friends from reading it. Recall that Milena chose not to write in the journal I gave her, because for her, a diary is like a live person, and the content is far too intimate to be revealed to outsiders. Second, her diary was written with a specific reader in mind, namely her close Danish friend, and third, she reiterates the importance of not forgetting Danish. This reason is tantamount to a conscious cognitive strategy regarding language use. It is tied to social practices and specific social goals, but it is at the same time a knowing and instrumental act.

We can note several things from these three excerpts. The first is a simple but significant linguistic point, namely the length and complexity of turn. As the months progress, Milena's turns are progressively longer and also more syntactically complex. In addition, she has acquired certain sociocultural norms such as the ubiquitous adolescent 'like', and uses 'wanta' rather than 'want to' by the third excerpt. Her reiteration and paraphrase show increasing strategic competence, and the cohesive elements noticeably missing from the first excerpt are there in the other two. The second point to note is that Milena understands that languages can be used to include and to exclude others, as with her diary. Milena developed particular strategies which accelerated and enriched her language acquisition and use because for her languages are primarily about establishing and maintaining social relationships. The brief excerpts used above contain seven direct references to 'friends' and three to her family. Friendships in particular were a key to her language development and use over time.

Language, social networking and self

> Talk is social action: people achieve identities, realities, social order and social relationships through talk.   (Baker, 1997: 132)

Milena's trilingualism was important in her relationships and in her sense of identity. In his book on modernity and self-identity, Giddens (1991) suggests that all human experience is mediated through socialisation, and particularly through the acquisition of language, although he is not writing with SLA in mind. His work provides a useful conceptual vocabulary for thinking about identity, difference and power. Giddens writes of the 'reflexive project of self', which is enacted against a background of multiple choices, and consists in sustaining 'coherent, yet continually revised, biographical narratives' (p. 5). A vital element of the multiple choices available to Milena in her biographical narrative was language, as evidenced in the following summary of the life and language contexts she had experienced (see Table 5.2).

Giddens views self-identity as a trajectory across different institutional settings, categorically resisting the simplistic notion of multiple identities in changing contexts, and suggesting instead that the individual 'incorporates elements from different settings into an integrated narrative' (p. 190). Milena's 'integrated narrative' included a self operating routinely in three language domains, and reflecting a diversity of social interactions, experiences and friendships, and the choices she had about these. Her peer relations at school were very important.

Wexler (1992) concluded in his studies on identity in schools that for students, school life revolves around the everyday project of establishing a social identity, with peer groups playing a vital role, as havens of emotional support. He writes, 'The peer network isn't just the place where you reinforce your image or where you communicate. It is a social structure which is integral to self construction' (p. 134). For ESL students, peer networks

Table 5.2

Country	At home	School (in class)	Socially
Bosnia	Bosnian	Bosnian, German	Bosnian
Denmark	Bosnian	Danish, English	Danish
Australia	Bosnian, Danish	English	Bosnian, English, Danish

often take on a particular self-affirmatory significance, as shown in Ryan's (1997) study of patterns of peer association in culturally diverse schools. Many ESL students I have observed in schools tend to associate according to what Ryan terms 'the basis of heritage' (p. 40), while others are able to move more fluidly between groups. Within all peer groups, repertoires of language, speech and action play key roles (Wexler, 1992). As with many teenage girls, Milena's friends meant perhaps more than anything else to her, although her friendship groups changed over time. It is useful to look now at the changes in Milena's friendship groups, and the ways in which Milena chose to be represented in this context.

A trajectory across peer groups

In her first months in Australia, Milena told me on several occasions that her best friends were in Denmark, where she had spent three critical teenage years, between 12 and 15 years of age. They were emotionally difficult times, with her father absent and often uncontactable in the war in Bosnia for two of these years. The bonds between Milena and her Danish friends were great, surviving Milena's migration to Australia. It is worth noting that such strong and intimate relationships were dependent on the use of a common language, Danish, which Milena acquired quickly. In the on-arrival programme at Newnham, Milena encountered other Bosnian students, but did not establish firm friendships with them. On moving to Markwell High, she met many more, as shown in the following interview excerpt.

M: I'm mostly with Bosnians Oh, I have never been with Bosnians so much since I left Bosnia. But there's a girl from my country, from Sarajevo, that our fathers worked together before, so we're like, very close to each other because of that, and our fathers know from a long long time ago, so, an' it's just (.) we trust each other, and (.) we're very close to each other.

R: You told me when you're with Bosnians it would be stupid to speak English, so you're speaking a lot of Bosnian now?

M: Yeah. Yes, some. sometimes we do say something in English, but (.) erm like, I speak Bosnian a lot, and when I came to Australia and start (.) started to have Bosnian friends, I found out that I <u>forget</u> some of the Bosnian words, and I forget my own language, because in Denmark I spoke Bosnian only with my family, and so (1.0) sometimes I really like to speak Bosnian a little bit but sometimes I would rather speak another language much more.   (Interview 2, p. 2)

The concentration of Bosnian students in Markwell High was not coincidental, but had to do with Australia's migration policy on refugees during the war in former Yugoslavia, and with the effective social networks often established by refugee groups, whereby a school is identified as desirable and actively sought out by a particular group. The link to the Bosnian girl whose father had worked with Milena was a historical one, characterised, in Milena's account, by a sense of closeness and trust. They went back a long way, in time, and to their home town, Sarajevo.

The second half of the excerpt deals with her predominant use at this time of the Bosnian language at school. Her comment that she was forgetting her first language after three years in Denmark was telling. There is a price to be paid by language minorities in the integration process in a new country, namely the attrition of the first language, known as language shift or language loss, due to subtractive bilingualism (Clyne, 1998). Giddens (1991: 7) offers us the insight that 'In general, whether in personal life or in broader social milieux, processes of reappropriation and empowerment intertwine with expropriation and loss'. For Milena, moving to Markwell High provided a temporary reprieve in her partial loss of the Bosnian language. School provided a ready-made peer group, which provided links both to her past and to her first language, as well as a measure of security in a time of transition. But Milena made it clear that she was not bound exclusively to this group. She had social and linguistic skills which allowed her to move more fluidly between groups than many other students I had met.

Markwell High had almost 1800 students. In the face of such a large institution, some newly arrived ESL students understandably retreat to the relative safety of the ESL unit or first language group. After only two weeks in this school, Milena looked happy and unfazed by the size or complexity of the school. I asked how she went about meeting people in such a big place. She replied,

> How do I meet them? Oh, first erm (.) my friend she's half Danish and half New Zealand, er, I met her when I came to Australia and she wasn't in this school. She was in another Catholic school. And then erm (.) we came together and she knew some people and I knew some people. So we introduced our, our friends to each other and stuff, to like meet. And then the ones that I know they introduced me to other, then I talked to everyone and if I need some help I just ask, and they ask for me, and (.) just like that. (Interview 2, p. 1)

She made it sound simple. I felt instinctively that it was not so easy for many ESL students to establish social networks in a new school, and over the years had observed students who experienced much difficulty in feeling accepted, and being integrated. Tina and John were cases in point. What conditions made it seem so easy for Milena? First, her New Zealand (half Maori) friend spoke

English (and very little Danish), which meant Milena effectively had a native English speaker with whom she could interact and meet others. Second, as a confident speaker of English, Milena was unafraid to ask for help. She could ask, be heard, be understood, and would understand the response. That is, her social skills, together with her language skills, enabled her to move across linguistic and ethnic boundaries. And these areas were mutually reinforcing.

To further illustrate this point, here is another interchange, in which Milena hints that her friendship groups were evolving, and less bound to the 'best friends' in Denmark.

R: So (1.0) it's not just the learning English but it's all the other things you can be involved in because you speak English.

M: Yeah that's the key (.) of it, is just be friends with everyone. Not just for me, not just for people from Bosnia? but everyone, with Asian, all the Europeans, and Americans everyone, Aussies. That's what I do. My really <u>close</u> friends, one of them is half Danish half New Zealand, half Maori and I speak English with her? because she can't really speak Danish. And other friends are from, like India, and all Asians and um, I have Bosnian friends, a lot of them as well, but I don't spend much time with them? once a week or something.

R: Mm hm

M: Yeah so that's how I learn.   (Interview 3, p. 2)

In my first turn, I was trying to draw attention to what interested me specifically about Milena's ability to use English so fluently. This is not what Milena picked up on in her response. Rather than 'all the other things you can be involved in', she talked about all the other people she was involved with. The coda in her last turn, 'So that's how I learn', may partially have been for my benefit as researcher and teacher, but also seemed a statement of fact in light of what I knew about her. This excerpt, several months after the one about being primarily with Bosnians, reveals a shift towards a much broader group of friends, encompassing a range of ethnic, language and cultural backgrounds. Apart from the Bosnians she saw 'once a week or something', she clearly used English with the six other categories mentioned – Asians, Europeans, Americans, Aussies, the Danish Maori, and Indians. The continuing trajectory reflected the sequential changes in her self-representation, and the shifts in her sense of identity that these representations may indicate.

Just be friends with everyone

Milena's strategy indicated in 'just be friends with everyone', struck me in some ways as a very tall order. How is this achieved, and what conditions make it possible? She had reiterated on several occasions what worked for her. In the following interview excerpt, I open with a 'hypothetical' question.

R:　　　　Imagine if a new kid came to Markwell from Newnham, and they said 'Milena look after this kid' and you had to give them advice about how to fit in quickly, how to um, you know be a good student (.) how to fit into Markwell. What would you say to them?

M:　　　　I would just say, try to be friends with everyone and smile all the time (.) be happy and talk to everyone, and I don't know (.) just a person just needs to be nice to everyone and then people are nice to them.

R:　　　　Yeah

M:　　　　and er, and everybody needs to make friends of their own like I make friends myself, and er I find friends that are the same as I am, they have same interests in music, in clothes, in guys and all that. So just to find somebody who looks like them, not looks like them but could have same interests as them, and, just to be nice to everyone.　　(Interview 3, p. 8)

Being friends, smiling, being happy, talking, being nice – Milena had indisputably experienced success with this formula. Yet I found this an idealised and somewhat naive version of how people get on. Milena was beautiful (even the female drama teacher had mentioned this). She had a beautiful smile, a solid grasp of a range of discourses in English and a great deal of confidence, all of which allowed her to find and attract others who shared her interests in music, clothes and guys. She had never personally experienced, for example, the kind of racist incident she recounted to me about one of her friends, a Pakistani, to whom a white Australian student had said, 'Why don't you go and wash your face? It's all black. And all your hair is so oily'. She had also heard about but not seen incidents involving racially motivated fights in the school, as shown in the following excerpt.

But sometimes I've heard that there were some fights against Chinese and Vietnamese, but I don't know it's just something small it's not really important. I don't, my friends they don't really care because we're all black and white and we don't care about people who are racist, we just don't think about them. Cos we don't wanna worry ourselves because of other people, you know what I mean?　　(Interview 3, p. 7)

This was a positive view, and underscored Milena's sense of equity and tolerance in a group where racial distinctions were simply not made. However, clearly for some students who were black or Asian, the option of 'just being nice to everyone' was not always available. Milena's evaluation that the issue was 'just something small it's not really important' was a product of her own very positive experiences in a variety of cultural and linguistic settings. As Rampton (1995: 16) reminds us, 'People's social evaluations and classifications are shaped through experiences of interaction'. The resources of smiling, talking, being happy and being nice were available to Milena, who looked like the dominant white majority, as well as being beautiful, and who spoke the dominant language fluently, with a Yugoslav accent that was positively received. I could join with Norton and Toohey (2001: 318), who write, 'We wonder what data we would have collected had Eva and Julie not been blond and white-skinned, slim, able-bodied, well-dressed, and attractive to Western eyes'.

Five girls, walking, having fun

Schumann's (1986) 'Acculturation model' of language acquisition suggests that acquisition depends on the degree to which the speaker acculturates to the target group. While it is not possible to argue directly from this model to a multicultural, multilingual environment such as Markwell High, Milena's identification and constant interaction with English-speaking groups played a powerful role in her learning and use of English, as she herself acknowledged. It was a reciprocal relationship in which language use and social networking were mutually facilitated and developed. It must also be added that Milena's best friends were what she described as 'very much multicultural'. After some months, her three best friends at school came from Pakistan, Iran and Venezuela, using English as their lingua franca.

In social terms, it is significant that the English speaking friendships Milena established at school were not contained or limited to within the school site, but extended to weekends and other time outside of school. She explained that she and her friends went to the city, swimming, ice-skating, or stayed at home, sewing or doing homework together. Milena had taught herself to sew and was helping friends to make garments at her house, which I saw as another area of her expertise or capital perceived to be of value by others. Furthermore, in this way, English became a 'home language', as well as Bosnian. We get a sense of this in one descriptive writing task Milena wrote in her parallel English class. In this piece, she described an outing with her friends.

> A Friday night. Streets full of happy people. No free seats in restaurants or on the street chairs. Few bottles broken on the ground. People singing. Stars are shinning. Five girls, walking, having fun. I remember good laughs that we had. We were in such a good moods, happy, as if

we so ((saw)) Mr Bean doing some of his dumb things. I remember plenty of food that we ate at Sizzlers. We were so full that our stomachs were big and hard as watermelons. I remember all the hot guys walking down the streets and holding their gorgous girlfriends by hands.

Milena has clearly incorporated aspects of the genre suggested by her teacher, including sensory imagery, similes and descriptive detail which creates an almost film-like quality. The teacher had corrected grammatical elements of the text such as 'shinning', 'so,' 'a good moods' and 'gorgous'. The tone of the piece is confident. We see 'girl power', girls in control, complicit in the project of 'having fun' – the shaping of an image of identity so important to self-construction (Wexler, 1992).

It is also worth recalling the suggestion that who you are, who you want to be, and who you go out with is part of an ongoing reflexive social process (McRobbie, 1996). Milena was able to engage with this process in English, her third language. 'Going out' in English was for her a part of life. Milena also had a series of English-speaking boyfriends, with whom she talked constantly. Just as the school represents a formal linguistic market in Bourdieu's terms, in which there are symbolic benefits for those whose primary discourse approximates school English, we can see that effective social networks in the target language provide another linguistic field or market, in which one of the symbolic benefits is a developing confidence and sense of self, as well as enhanced acquisition of the primary discourse. A knowledge of discourses and genres were the linguistic resources which allowed Milena to take up a range of subject positions, in a confident and empowering way. In the final section of this chapter, I explore further the notion of confidence.

Confidence and collaboration

'I mean everything is new and everything is normal'.   (Int. 2, p. 4)

On arrival in high school, Milena's agency was shown in a number of ways, including negotiating her own year level, and through her social networking and relationships, she had continued to develop confidence and to expand her network. When plans for the Bosnian singing group at the Multicultural Concert fell through, Milena told me that she was hoping to do the lambada with a group of South Americans instead! Here was the antithesis of a shrinking violet, and I secretly marvelled at her secure sense of self. For most of us, switching from singing in our first language to doing the lambada would not be an obvious move. In this section I elaborate on the notions of confidence and collaboration in discourse, and their links to the themes discussed so far in this chapter.

The changes involved in moving from the Newnham reception programme to high school were often problematic for students (see Miller, 1999). Milena summarised some of these changes quite succinctly on my first visit to Markwell High.

R: So, compared with Newnham how have things changed?
M: They changed a lot. New friends, new school (.) erm, new teachers, new(.) erm, I mean everything is new (.) and everything is (.) normal. Because in Newnham we were, it wasn't like a normal class we were like, some people 20 years old and 14 years old in the same class. But here we're like 15 and 16 in one in one grade, so it's more normal. I mean it's a real school.   (Int. 1, p. 4)

In addition to drawing attention to the homogeneity of age groups in year levels at Markwell High, which she saw as a function of normality, and 'real school', Milena here draws an interesting and unusual parallel between what is 'new' and what is 'normal'. She has new friends, a new school and new teachers, and whereas we might expect a period of adjustment and reticence for most students, her repetition in 'everything is new, and everything is normal' reveals a remarkably self-possessed and confident position in the face of multiple transformations in the new environment.

It is worth noting that although Markwell was a new school for her, she had been in very big schools before. Furthermore, in Bourdieu's terms, she had arrived with sufficient cultural and linguistic capital to assert herself, and to negotiate certain boundaries. Confidence was a critical part of this process. Very quickly, she had positioned herself as a mainstream student, rather than an ESL student.

She contrasted this situation with the experience of her male cousin Alex who had arrived at the same time at Markwell High. Alex, aged 15, was one year younger than Milena.

R: . . . And what about Alex? He's.
M: Oh: poor Alex, he's in grade nine.
R: Alex doesn't seem as happy as you
M: No, um he's in grade <u>nine</u> (.) and he's in ESL I think most of his time. And I think that he wants to move to grade ten because (.) I know that year nine's (.) too easy for him. <u>I</u> know because he's really clever, he's my cousin and I know him. And um (2.0), I think Mrs Parditch said that she needs to (.) see his

> English, how is it and stuff, but (.) he's good, I think he'll go, so I hope (.) he moves to grade ten.
>
> **R:** He doesn't look like a grade nine
>
> **M:** No! He's too <u>old</u> to be grade [nine
>
> **R:** [He's mature
>
> **M:** [Yeah   (Int. 2, p. 4)

In this text we hear her as a confident speaker, and the degree of collaboration in the conversation is part of this confidence. Milena positions herself as a mainstream student and commentator on those just behind her. Alex was 'in ESL . . . most of his time', whereas she was outside in the mainstream. He was still subject to Mrs Parditch's decision on his proficiency, whereas she had brought weight to bear to change one of Mrs Parditch's decisions. As Alex's cousin, she suggests that she knows him better, and that he is 'clever' and also too old to be in Year 9. Here Milena uses the language of expressing opinions, using the verbs 'I think', and 'I know' three times each. Note also the conversational collaboration in the last four lines. She agrees with me that Alex doesn't look like a Year 9 student, and adds further evidence as to why he doesn't look the part. The overlaps in the last three lines reinforce the collaborative nature of this part of the talk. Some months later, we were again talking about Alex. In this talk, I perceived a continuing refinement of her conversational competence, and her ability to collaborate in talk. In notes related to the 'feel' of this later interview, I wrote,

> Milena was very relaxed and happy, smiling a great deal, and speaking fluently and naturally. Apart from her light Bosnian accent, and omission of the odd article, she spoke like a very competent bilingual . . . I was not aware of modifying my own talk in any way during this interview.

It was a situation of complete comfort for me as both speaker and hearer. I could not avoid the contrast between her communicative competence and openness as we talked, and the lack of these when I spoke to Alex. The interview had been in fact a long rambling chat, ranging over numerous topics and with some very extended turns by Milena. In the following excerpt I tell her that I am having difficulty relating as comfortably to Alex, and also attempt to ascribe this to a gender difference. This rather rash assumption is less important than the way the topic was taken up in the conversation.

R: (Alex) doesn't talk to me as much as you do but then, that's boys.

M: Yeah (laughs) I don't know (.) I always talk so much. (laughs) I always talk a lot.

R: I think girls talk more than guys do you think?

M: Probably, maybe cause they're more open.
R: Yeah. The girls are? *((confirming the reference for 'they'))*
M: Yeah
R: Boys don't like to reveal too much
M: Feelings and all that
R: Yeah, they like to keep their distance sometimes
M: Yeah. Sometimes I keep it in myself, all feelings and all that
            There is always, I need to talk to my friends, so that's why I
            keep diary, so that I can write everything in it.   (Int. 3, p. 10)

Although we orientate slightly differently to the topic, there are five examples of 'yeah' in this excerpt, showing a high degree of collaboration in the talk. In her first turn she agrees with my opening, but uses the mitigating 'I don't know', and switches the focus from the general to her own case. In my next turn I return to the generalisation about gender differences in conversation, which Milena conditionally agrees with, as shown by her use of 'probably'. She then ascribes a possible cause to the difference, the fact that girls are more 'open'. In my next turn, I generalise the problem in terms of 'Boys don't like to reveal too much', to which Milena adds 'Feelings and all that'. This was smooth conversational work.

Although later appalled at my own consistently gender biased position in this talk, and the relentless way I sought agreement with this position, I was impressed with Milena's strategic competence in seeming to agree, while providing the counterpoint of her own experience. In both her first and final turns, she deflects my generalisations with personal accounts. For example, having said that boys tend to withhold feelings, and listening to my suggestion that this was about establishing distance, she stated in her final turn that she also chose to keep feelings 'in herself' sometimes. Her final comment reveals the contradictory position of her need to express her intimate thoughts and feelings with her friends, hence her use of a diary.

Milena's confidence was something I could hear and observe. It was her confidence in language use, as revealed in the cadence of our conversation, and it was in the comfort of our social interactions. I did not have to do my 'ESL teacher identity' in any overt way in these interactions. That is, although I asked questions and made comments, I was under no pressure to come up with another question because the participant's turns were minimal, unclear or simply dried up. In my interactions with her, I was aware of a powerful interrelationship between her competence in spoken English, her social and cultural capital, and the social conditions which had enabled her language acquisition. In terms of the model of communicative competence outlined by Celce-Murcia *et al.* (1995), Milena displayed high levels of sociocultural competence, discourse competence, linguistic competence, strategic competence and actional competence. But in addition, her spoken discourse was 'acceptable' to her teachers, to me and to her peers. Bourdieu (1993: 79) points out that such acceptability 'presupposes the conformity of words not only to the immanent rules of the language, but also to the intuitively grasped rules that are immanent in a 'situation', or rather a certain linguistic market. This leads Bourdieu to replace the term linguistic competence with *linguistic capital*, a notion that incorporates both the idea of value or profit assigned to spoken discourse (and thus to the speaker), and the critical role of the hearer who assigns this value. Where does this leave Milena and the other students in this study? For all students acquiring a language, it seems reasonable to assume a powerful symbiotic relationship between access to linguistic markets where their attempts to speak the target language are valued, and the ongoing development of language competence. I will expand this argument in the final chapter.

At the end of Milena's first year at Markwell High, we had a long involved phone conversation, in which I heard her as a bilingual speaker, a fellow speaker of English. At one point she said, 'Just a second, my Mum wants me. Can you hold on a second please?' This simple statement and request reflects much of what I have discussed in this chapter. I perceived once again her initiative in taking control of the discourse, the competence of her language use, the careful managing of her social relationships, and her confident collaboration in this situation.

Summary

Through her agency, language competence, social networking and confidence, I have suggested that Milena possessed resources which were acknowledged and valued within the school and other fields. The data provide a sense of how Milena took up particular subject positions, and the conditions which made this possible. She had sufficient symbolic and linguistic capital to influence people and events around her, and to allow her fluidity of movement across sites. She was able to seek help, to negotiate changes and outcomes and to take initiatives in class, with the administration, with her friends and with me. She was able to use a discourse of justification and collaboration which involved high levels of strategic and sociolinguistic competence. Being heard, being audible, being accepted – these were key elements in her negotiation of identity. Although she perceived and indeed experienced certain difficulties in the grammar and lexical demands of school English, her metalinguistic awareness of language acquisition led her to use a number of specific language learning strategies. These included asking for help, answering in class, speaking in a range of social contexts, using textbooks and dictionaries independently and actively maintaining her first and second languages.

Socially Milena was in a strong position to *acquire* as well as learn English, her third language. Gee (1996) makes a clear distinction between acquisition and learning, emphasising that acquisition through enculturation is a more powerful process than overt learning (see also Krashen, 1981; Schumann, 1986). Milena's social networks provided ample opportunity to use English in natural settings and in numerous face-to-face interactions. As she moved across ethnic and linguistic boundaries, her language and social development were mutually reinforcing. In other words, her repertoires of speech, language and action continually fed in to her developing confidence and a stronger sense of her social membership and identity. In a number of instances she resisted the category of NESB or ESL student, aligning herself with mainstream students in general.

Successfully enacting a range of subject positions through discourse is an empowering phenomenon. Not only was Milena able to represent herself through speaking English, she was able to be heard as a legitimate mainstream student and user of the primary discourse. Returning finally to the notion of speaking as representation, we hear her – we hear who she is. And we gain insight into the means she has at her disposal to make herself heard and to define herself as an active participant in the world (McLaren, 1994), both within and beyond school.

Chapter 6

Nora and Alicia: Speaking with the Foreigners

Introduction

All speakers represent their identities through language use, and in previous chapters we have seen that linguistic minority speakers position themselves and are positioned through the ways they speak and are heard by majority language speakers. Those who sound different may be silenced, or censured before their message is heard (Lippi-Green, 1997). Some students, like Milena, arrive with substantial cultural and symbolic capital, and acquire mainstream discourses to a point where they are well received, linguistically and socially within a short time span. In this chapter I look closely at speaking in school contexts, the construction of ESL students by teachers, and the ways linguistic capital is differentially valued in schools. I introduce Nora and Alicia, both from the People's Republic of China, whose story is a trajectory across several schools, three languages, and numerous contexts and social memberships. They arrived in Australia two years apart, from different backgrounds and speaking different languages. This did not prevent their becoming firm friends, to the extent that 12 months after I met them, they were at their third school, but still sitting together in class. I have chosen to write about them together in this chapter, partly because of the importance of the role of friendship in the construction of identity and in language use, but also because Nora and Alicia represent a dyad in the data in terms of their school contexts, and social memberships, and the fact that I often talked to them together. The chapter is not therefore organised around individual students, but around the central theme of speaking – 'speaking up' at school, access to and relations with native speakers, oral presentations in mainstream classrooms, speaking with peers, the ways students and teachers construct each other, and the possibility of using English outside of school.

Although this book draws primarily on spoken data, voice is of course also represented through writing. In Chapter 1, I outlined a rationale for including student diaries in this study, and sections of this chapter are based on narrative accounts from Nora's diary. They provide important insights into her identity, positioning by mainstream discourses, social relationships and and language learning. Before moving to the data and discussion, I provide brief biographical notes on the two girls.

Nora

Nora, an only child, arrived in Australia from Shanghai with her mother on 4 May 1996, to be reunited with Nora's father, who had moved to Australia six years earlier. Nora was 13 years old, and said her father had come to Australia 'to learn English' and to find work in restaurants. Nora was overjoyed to see her father, who had phoned her every week for six years, but she was impatient to start school, and to start learning English. I asked how long she stayed at home on arrival. 'Twenty-five days' was the lightning response. By the end of May she was enrolled at Newnham, and placed in the beginners class. She had studied written English in Shanghai (one lesson a week for almost three years), but she spoke virtually no English on arrival.

Over the six years in Australia, Nora's father had established a network of friends and business associates, managing a series of successful noodle bars, and finally buying one in a suburban location in 1997. Both Nora's mother and Nora worked there on weekends and during holidays. From Nora's accounts, and when I visited the noodle bar, they seemed a very close family. Nora once bemoaned to me (with her inimitable smile) that she was a 'free worker', that is, an unpaid worker in the noodle bar, where she worked for up to 15 hours some weekends.

Alicia

Alicia was 11 when she left Guangzhou for Australia, arriving with her widowed mother and her 13-year-old sister in December 1994. The circumstances were quite traumatic, as her mother had been persuaded to move to Australia to help, and marry, a family friend. Alicia and her sister were enrolled in a primary school. Alicia's teacher wrote in a report that Alicia spoke no English at all on arrival, and became distressed easily at school, particularly when it was decided her sister was too old for primary school, and was sent to Newnham. The stepfather had what Alicia described to me as 'a brain problem', and within a year of the marriage, had become abusive. Alicia's mother moved out with the two girls.

Alicia had completed Year 6, and half of Year 7 at primary school, when she was referred to Newnham. She started there in August 1996, and shortly after met Nora, who had arrived there almost three months earlier. By this time, Alicia's sister had gone through an ESL unit and was in a mainstream high school near their home. Alicia's mother worked in a friend's restaurant, and the family lived with these friends, who were all Chinese. As a native of Guangzhou, Alicia's first language was Cantonese, and her second language, which she had studied at school, was Mandarin. Nora told me that Alicia understood and spoke Mandarin quite well. What I remember from my first meeting with Alicia is that she had one of the softest voices I had ever heard.

Nora and Alicia exited the Newnham programme at the same time, starting at the Taylor High School ESL unit in late January, at the start of the 1997 school year. Both were interviewed in Mandarin, as well as in English. In this chapter, 'M. Int.' following interview excerpts refers to the translated Mandarin interview, which was conducted and translated by F, while R denotes myself as researcher in the English interviews.

Speaking Out at School

The underlying theoretical position of this volume is that language use shapes social identities, contexts and relations. The micro-contexts of schools have been described as 'borderlands crisscrossed with a variety of languages, experiences and voices' (Giroux, 1990: 109), in which the social relations and identities are in a constant state of flux. Gumperz and Hymes (1986) note that the presence of two languages in a community is compatible with a variety of underlying social relationships. At Taylor High, there are many more than two languages within the student community, and students such as Nora and Alicia each functioned in two or three language domains. These domains were not symmetrical in terms of fluency, proficiency or confidence, and nor were the domains equally valued by the school.

Speaking up

In a context of second (or third) language acquisition, speaking audibly and without anxiety is an enormous challenge for most students. Reticence in speaking, particularly in the early stages, is a natural and very common phenomenon and may manifest as silence, minimal responses or extreme soft spokenness (Tsui, 1996). As I observed Alicia and Nora's classes, there were frequent admonitions from the teachers, such as 'Alicia, I need to hear', 'Could you speak up a bit', or 'Can you repeat that a bit louder'. I heard one mainstream student call out 'Can't hear!' as Alicia delivered an oral presentation, and I had transcripts with many turns marked 'inaudible'.

In my first talk with the girls at the start of the Taylor High school year, audibility (in terms of volume) was a problem compounding the difficulty they were having in talking to me in English. This was a difficulty for all of us. Tina, whose case study is reported in Chapter 4, was also present in one group interview. In my notes on the interview, I wrote,

> (The girls) arrived, all smiles. The aide said, 'They're very pleased to see you.' As we walked to the library, they chatted away in Mandarin. Lots of smiling. The talk was characterised by lots of giggling, hands over mouths and silences at the start (not uncomfortable). Continued to break into Mandarin. They seemed to need permission from each other to speak in English. When I asked a question at times, there was silence, the girls seeming not to know how to take up the turn at the start.

I was struck with what Giroux (1990) would call the limits of my own voice. Unable to speak either Mandarin or Cantonese, I was seriously limited in what I could say, what I could have them hear and understand. The early interviews were hard work for us all. They had spoken little English during the six week holiday, and I was very aware of modifying my own talk, speaking more slowly, with more pause and repetition, and with a simplified syntax and lexicon. It was classic foreigner talk (Lightbown & Spada, 1999). In classrooms, their teachers would continue over many months to urge them to 'Speak up!' Ironically, when they went to the mainstream in a new high school nine months later, one of their first comments to me was that the teachers constantly asked for quiet. In Nora's words, 'The social science teacher shouts "quiet please" all the time. About five times in one minute she says "quiet please".'

Speaking with the foreigners

Multilingual schools, as sites criss-crossed with a diversity of competing languages and voices, are complex environments, where second language acquisition and use do not take place as a smooth continuum. There are no neat boxes which define or confine language practices. Students are moving constantly across languages, sites and social memberships, mixing languages, learning languages, resisting languages, tentatively testing them out, and then reverting to more familiar linguistic and social territory (see Miller, 1999, 2000). I have described language use as a process of representation, closely tied identity formation. Recall that identity is represented or enacted through a three-way simultaneous interaction between a social language, social membership, and a particular context (Gee, 1996). For example, the intensive reception programme at Newnham offers a particular environment where membership is by definition constructed as being from elsewhere, speaking languages other than English and being a learner of English. Some continuity of context is afforded by the high school ESL unit, but one critical difference in the move to high school entails the presence of large numbers of monolingual English speakers, along with what Heller (1994: 4) has called 'the silent acceptance of the hegemony of English'. Before looking at the girls' language use at high school, we return briefly to the conditions for learning and speaking English offered at Newnham.

In the following interview excerpt, from my first talk with Nora when she was still a student at Newnham, she talks about speaking English in class with her teacher and fellow NESB students. Nora had been at Newnham for six months at the time of this talk.

N: The teacher is kind and er (1.0) student is (5.0) we English is (.) to <u>nearly</u> (.) we speak English is nearly, not very well.

R: So you speak a kind of English, not correct English? What do you mean? Tell me again.

N: The students speak English not well. So I don't need to speak English very (.) be careful.

R: You don't need to?

N: I don't afraid (3.0) mistake.

R: You make mistakes. (2.0) Does everybody make mistakes?

N: Yes

R: So the students don't speak English very well. Tell me again, how that affects you.

N: Um, I don't need to speak English very well (.) to afraid mistakes

R: Are you ever afraid of making mistakes?
           (3.0)

N: Mm, to shopping, afraid ((*very soft*)).

In her opening turn, Nora uses 'nearly' as synonymous with 'not very well', to describe the students' levels of proficiency and fluency in English. Although I felt I understood, I spoke as if I didn't, and my turns in this excerpt are requests for verification. I am still unsure why I did this, except to ensure that I 'got it right', that is, I really wanted to hear and understand her. My formulation of 'correct English' in my first turn now seems singularly inappropriate, yet I was trying to paraphrase Nora's turn with a word she would understand. In her second turn, it is interesting that she transforms 'we speak English is nearly, not very well' to a more standard 'the students speak English not well'. It's as if we see language processing in action here from one turn to the next, acquisition and negotiation of meaning captured as they occur. Similarly, with prompts she extends, 'So I don't need to speak English very be careful' to an explanation that freedom from the need to speak carefully is more a freedom from fear of making mistakes while she speaks. In her ESL class at Newnham, Nora claims she doesn't need to be afraid of making mistakes. Everybody makes them, and is expected to make them. There is no pressure to speak perfectly. The context of shopping provides an anxiety-inducing contrast, a place to be afraid. This, as we see later, changes for Nora with time, practice and experience.

On moving to high school, Nora was still in an ESL class, with 14 students, eight of whom spoke Mandarin and three Cantonese. Taylor High had close to 800 students, including 30% from language backgrounds other than English. I have suggested that any shift in context may entail a shift in social memberships and language use. What changes were initiated by Nora's shift to high school? The 'foreigners' in the title of this section were not Nora's classmates at Newnham or in the ESL class. In the excerpt below, she tells us who the 'foreigners' were.

F: Do you get to talk with Australian kids?
N: Yeah, at mainstream, they are all foreigners, so I speak English
            to them.   (M. Int. p. 2)

The word 'foreigners' recurred frequently in Nora's discourse – both in speaking and in writing. I found it endearing that the tables were turned in this quintessentially Chinese perspective, in which all those not from the middle kingdom, were outsiders, foreigners. Other examples of her usage of the category 'foreigners' are found below:

(1) because my dad has a shop, I work there, I have to talk with the foreigners,
     it is in English.   (M. Int. p. 2)
(2) it is bit troublesome to talk with foreigners   (M. Int. p. 5)
(3) Last time a foreigner written a science report, she copied my other class-
     mate   (Diary, 17.6.97)

In the last comment, by 'classmate', Nora meant a Chinese-speaking ESL classmate. Clearly Nora had a sense of contexts in which English was mandated, including the shop and her mainstream classes, even though speaking English could be 'troublesome'.

During the Chinese interview, she had said, 'If I say something, then definitely it is very clear if it is in Chinese, but in English, it is not so clear. Sometimes, when I say something in English, I myself don't know what I am saying.' She seemed aware that if at times she herself was not sure what she was saying in English, the listener might well also be flummoxed. This was a problem, but it was coupled in Nora's case with a very pragmatic view of language use, as shown by this comment:

F: You said just now that when you arrived here, you didn't
            speak much, now you can talk a lot, is that because your lan-
            guage has improved?

N: That is one aspect. Another aspect, you're <u>here</u>, you have to speak. (M. Int. p. 4)

This is a competent representation by Nora of the interviewer's suggestion, and of her own position. If foreigners are beside you in a mainstream class, you have to speak English to them. Improving spoken English makes this increasingly possible, but for Nora, the notion that 'you're <u>here</u>, you have to speak' is a critical one. The words 'here' and 'speak' used in F's question were taken up by Nora. Whether 'here' means Australia or school or just a new place, we see that she acknowledges the *need* to speak, which in this excerpt refers to 'speak English'. This was a strategic response which implicated both social and linguistic considerations. As Norton (1995: 17) suggests, 'If learners invest in a second language, they do so with the understanding that they will acquire a wider range of symbolic and material resources, which will in turn increase the value of their cultural capital'.

Nora spoke Shanghainese and Mandarin, while Alicia spoke Cantonese and Mandarin. The tension between knowing that you can say things a lot more clearly in your first (or second) language than in your third language, English, and knowing that you *need* to speak the third language, is at the heart of the process of language acquisition, and at the heart of the expression of social identity. Nora's understanding that she needed to use English in mainstream contexts was an understanding that she needed to be heard and understood in these contexts. Yet opportunities to speak to other students were not automatically afforded the girls by mainstream classes. For example, when I asked Alicia when she talked to Australian students, the following interchange occurred.

A: In the classroom, sometimes. Sometimes we are doing an assignment in the same group, then English is used.
F: Do you get a lot of such kind of chances?
A: It is OK. Sometimes, a foreign kid sits besides me, then I'll talk to her.
F: So you mean if by chance, you'll speak to them in English?
A: Yeah. (M. Int p. 3)

Although Alicia doesn't directly answer the first question, the modality 'sometimes' occurs three times in this brief excerpt. That is, she speaks English sometimes, during group work, or if a 'foreign kid' sits next to her. My own observation was that ESL students very often sat alone, or together. This meant that access to native speakers and opportunities to practise speaking English in classrooms was quite a haphazard process. What was happening outside the classrooms? What languages were used, and which social memberships were used to construct identity? What were the possibilities of making a new 'Australian' friend at lunch time?

Speaking with friends

Before leaving Newnham, Nora had expressed her fervent hope that she would find new English speaking friends at Taylor High (see Chapter 3). This was what she was looking forward to most, but it proved far from straightforward. In this section I want to look at the linguistic complexity within the Chinese-speaking groups, at the problem of forging new friendships outside of that group, and finally at a dispute between Nora and Alicia which throws light on the power of language to exclude or include others.

Taylor High School, like a number of high schools with ESL units I had visited, had a building which contained the ESL unit and staffroom, and under which there was clear Chinese-speaking territory, where students were visibly and audibly enacting their Chineseness, their 'otherness'. Alicia told me that even students who had been at the school for several years, and spoke 'good English', often chose to remain within this site, speaking Mandarin or Cantonese, the language of 'after class'. Nora and Alicia, as best friends, were invariably in this group, often with other friends, including Tina (see Chapter 4), who was Taiwanese, and Winnie from Hong Kong. Nora and Alicia described the intricacies of the linguistic negotiation occurring within this group, which struck me as a version of the *language crossing* described by Rampton (1995). Alicia had commented to me once about lunchtimes, 'We who speak Mandarin are together'. It wasn't that simple. For example, Winnie spoke Cantonese but no Mandarin; Nora spoke Shanghainese and Mandarin, but no Cantonese; Alicia spoke Cantonese and Mandarin as a second language, and so provided the necessary 'link'. In effect the girls were negotiating constantly in two languages. Alicia and Winnie communicated in Cantonese, and although Nora did not speak Cantonese, she was beginning to understand some. Winnie would speak Cantonese very slowly to her, Winnie's own version of foreigner talk, and Alicia would follow up with some translation in Mandarin. Sometimes they laughed at each other's attempts to speak the second language. Alicia told an anecdote of a time she'd said a word in Mandarin and even after many times, Nora did not understand. Finally Nora asked her to write it down. 'I thought I got it right', said Alicia, 'I think how you say it, I think how to translate it, then Nora and Winnie laugh when we worked it out.' For some ESL students, such as Milena, this intense linguistic negotiation also occurred between the L1 and English, but English speakers need to be present. At Taylor High, it was unusual to see Anglo or English-speaking students mixing with the Chinese groups. Groups of Vietnamese students similarly kept to themselves. There seemed to be very little 'ethnic cross-ing', with language use tied simultaneously to ethnic boundary formation and relations of power (Heller, 1994). It also seemed ironic that Nora's Can-tonese was possibly improving more than her English at school.

Finding new friends

About a month after they had started at Taylor High, I talked to the girls about finding new friends. The following extract is from a group interview with Nora, Alicia and Tina.

R:	Alicia? Do you have new friends at Taylor?
A:	Nora
N:	Other Nora
A:	Yeah (.) we got two Noras in our class
R:	Oh, another Nora, a new Nora
	((giggles, possibly at the alliteration))
R:	And (.) where is she from?
A:	(inaudible) *((I make a guess that the other Nora is not Chinese))*
R:	Mm hm. (.) So you have to speak English (.) with her
A:	Yep
R:	And um, so you have new friends Tina, at Taylor High?
T:	No
R:	You stay with your old ESL group
T:	Ah all my friends (.) they come from Newnham so (.) I knew them already
R:	Yeah, OK. Have you met any Australian students at Taylor
All:	No
R:	In sport, when you play tennis (.) are there Australian kids there too?
A:	No (Int. 23.2.97)

The 'new Nora' was an ESL student from former Yugoslavia, and as Tina indi-cated, the girls drew all their friends from the ESL pool at this stage. Tennis, it emerged one afternoon I spent observing sports groups, was also a refuge for ESL and former ESL students, predominantly Taiwanese and Vietnamese. In four of my turns, I ask the girls if they have established new friendships. Apart from new Nora, there were three instances of a resounding 'No', an unequivo-cal response.

Five months later, this had not really changed, although the girls were now in some mainstream subjects. Asked if she now had Australian friends, Nora commented 'Sure, have some friends, but no good friends.' The Chinese interviewer picked up this point again later.

F: Do you have any difficulty to make friends with your Aussie classmates? From what you've said, you did not mention the Aussies.

N: Good friends? Yeah. If I say something, then definitely it is very clear if it is in Chinese, but in English, it is not so clear. Sometimes, when I say something in English, I myself don't know what I am saying.

F: So you mean that when you say a sentence, you are not quite sure if you've expressed what you want to mean.

N: Yes. So, it is bit troublesome to talk with foreigners.

Nora's primary point here is that clear communication is needed to make friends, and this is not yet possible for her in English. To make friends, you need a shared language, to be sure that your intended meanings are conveyed to your listener, that you are heard as you wish to be heard. It is significant here that when asked about friendships, Nora talks about language, and the need to speak clearly. Her comment that her meaning was 'very clear if it is in Chinese' helped explain why her best friends were Chinese speakers. Alicia also tied language use to friendship groups, as shown below.

F: Some kids who came to Australia from other countries feel after a while they start to speak English, and to lose their first language, what do you think?

A: Probably not, because I also have so many friends.

F: You mean Chinese speakers?

A: Yeah, we use Chinese so often, we won't forget it. Sometimes, I will write letters.   (M. Int. p. 5)

The languages of friendship were Chinese languages, and friendships established at Newnham had proven particularly durable for these girls, continuing into the ESL unit and beyond.

As it transpired, friendships from Alicia's life in China were in fact becoming more precarious. She wrote in her diary,

> *I may write a litter soon for my best friend in China. Sometime I miss her, I haven't write to her a long time. Sometime I don't know what to write. I don't think I will write later, because I don't know what to write.*   (Diary, 16.6.97)

There is a sense here that she had less and less to share with her friends from the past. It may be that time has eroded her understanding of how to represent herself and her present experiences to her former friend. She has nothing to say, nothing to write. They spoke the same language, but their lives had seriously diverged. By contrast, her friendship with Nora was intensely lived on a daily basis, a friendship which included time spent travelling to and from school, time in class, time at lunch, outings, along with the bickering and fights that teenage girls are sometimes renowned for. This friendship became a focus in Nora's diary.

'These week Alicia and me always quarreled'

Nora depicted in her diary the vagaries of her friendships (particularly with Alicia) and family life in great detail, often with precision and poignancy. One of several disagreements with Alicia is described below, including a blow-by-blow description of who said what, and Nora's analysis of the incident. This representation of the conflict is in English, with me in mind as reader, whereas of course the actual dispute took place in Mandarin. Some of the anomalies in the text arise from Nora's use of Mandarin structures. However, the text provides us with several important insights. Keep in mind that she had only been in Australia for about a year when she wrote this.

> *16–7–97*
>
> *These week Alicia and me always quarreled. I don't know why! In Monday we have two times to quarreled, and yesterday, too. I'm not angry. And this morning in the train, we talked about money (last times Alicia borrowed from me $3.) She asked change: I said, 'I don't have change,' and I told her, 'Why you every time let the people to feel awkward?' Then Alicia started to unhappy. In this times I found the five dollars change, she said: 'Who eles said I always let the people to feel awkward? See, you got the change.' I said: 'If I'm not have any change?' 'I can think about other idea, but know you had change!' Her face like very angry. I said: 'I just told you, if you can, don't let the people to feel awkward!' 'I'm not, that very easy things to do!' That means I'm stupid people. I'm just think that this things to change the money is a unconvenient things. Then I said something back to her. After that, we don't speak to each other. But Alicia had an advantageous position. She can use her first language to speak to Hong Kong people! I can't. So I didn't said any thing today.*

Here is a written text about spoken interaction. From Nora's description, we see and hear this argument very clearly. With very few changes, it could be a soap opera script. The direct speech breathes life into the argument, which could be arranged script-like as follows:

((Alicia asks for change))

Nora: I don't have change. Why you every time let the people to feel awkward?

((Alicia looks unhappy; Nora finds $5 change))

Alicia: Who eles said I always let the people to feel awkward? See, you got the change.

Nora:	If I'm not have any change?
Alicia:	I can think about other idea, but know you had change!
Nora:	I just told you, if you can, don't let the people to feel awkward!
Alicia:	I'm not, that very easy things to do!

This arrangement of the text shows the amount of reported speech used in this one entry, and also Nora's sense of the drama in everyday interactions. Hutchby and Wooffitt (1998) suggest that reported speech is often used to convey revelation, response and resolution, and to explicate the participant's orientation to the unfolding of the interaction. They also refer to reported speech as 'active voicing', which is sometimes used 'to warrant the factual status of claims and undermine the possibility of sceptical responses' (p. 226). In this sense, Nora's formulation of the utterances as reported talk could be seen as her appeal to the reader to see things her way, or to protect her stake.

Nora begins the diary entry with the abstract or theme, 'This week Alicia and me always quarreled.' She then exemplifies this by reference to arguments on Monday, and the day before. Emotions continue to figure quite strongly throughout the piece, as she intersperses reported speech with the emotional reactions of Alicia and with commentary on her own actions. These appear almost like stage directions supporting the script. She provides a rationale to Alicia for her irritation, namely that it makes 'people feel awkward'. After the argument, they lapse into silence. It transpires as an inequitable silence, in which Alicia has the 'advantageous position' of using her first language to disbar Nora from other social interaction. Here we have an instance of the precarious interdependence of membership and language use, with language used as a weapon to exclude.

Alicia's use of Cantonese was an effective silencing device, as shown by Nora's final comment that she did not say anything that day. This must be interpreted as 'not anything in Chinese', for at the end of this day's entry, Nora writes that in fact she temporarily became a member of another group, using English.

> *today I with some people they from another country, we all talking English. I think I will with they all the times, because, if I with Alicia, maybe we wil quarrel again, and I with them I can have more time to learn English.*

It is worth noting that the group she found to speak English with were not mainstream Australian students, but other ESL peers, 'from another country'. The three elements of Gee's (1996) notion of enacting identity are there: European ESL (or non-Chinese) school *context*, English *language*, *membership* of the European ESL group. Nora sees the linguistic advantage in staying with this group, but in fact, she does not choose to do so. As with so many girlhood squabbles, Nora and Alicia's fight did not last long. A week later,

Nora wrote (her electronic dictionary firmly in hand), 'Eve(ry) day, Alicia and I had a little bit mitigated.' The lesson was a salutary one however – demonstrating the use of language as an exclusionary practice, in this instance by a bilingual Chinese friend. Within the broader context of the social space of school, the English-speaking and Chinese-speaking groups were mutually excluding. However, in terms of the relative weightings assigned to linguistic capital, English was clearly dominant (Bourdieu, 1991). And the Chinese speakers were a minority not just in numbers but also in terms of power (Mey, 1985).

The diary entry above was the first of several of Nora's diary entries that I use in this chapter. Those interested in language acquisition will see much of interest in Nora's text, and we can reasonably assume that writing regularly and at length in her diary was helpful in her English language development. However, I am aware that such a text has no currency within the official discourse of school English. What kind of *voice* is represented in a diary? I feel I know Nora well from her many anecdotes, yet I am the only hearer as she constructs her identity on the page. Privy to her thoughts, her feelings, her stories in English, I am able to access her representation of self and others. Her teachers would not have these insights. Her fellow students would not know the characters and stories which Nora represents in writing, but would have great difficulty in conveying orally, as she writes more fluently than she speaks. For the same reason, this diary was a valuable resource for me as researcher.

Friendships played a vital role in the daily lives of these girls. After nine months at Taylor High, Alicia wrote in her diary of her sadness at leaving her school friends behind, as she left for Karfeld High.

> *I was sad to lave Taylor. I miss my friends. I really miss my friend. At the last leson, I was hope the time can be a little slow, because I don't want to lave so fast. I want to stay a bit more time with my friend. After today, we all don't know when we can see each others again.* (Diary, 19.9.97)

Luckily, Alicia was in fact leaving with Nora, whom she had once described as 'her best friend in Australia'. At Karfeld High they were placed in a mainstream Year 8 class, but continued to visit an ESL teacher three lessons a week for help with assignments. Karfield High was a school with a predominantly white Anglo-Saxon population, and only a handful of Chinese speakers. Nora and Alicia stayed cautiously together for a few months, but sometimes in the mainstream they had no choice but to speak English, and in a very visible and public way. I am referring to oral presentations, which are standard in school subjects such as English, Geography, Science and Social Science. 'Orals' as students call them, are contexts where students must speak up, speak English, and speak in front of the whole class. For these reasons alone, they can be difficult for students from other language backgrounds, who feel exposed and vulnerable in the face of such attention.

Doing orals

Delivering oral presentations in front of the class is an integral part of the curriculum in many subjects, and ESL teachers try to forearm their students with some experiences of what is for many an unfamiliar genre at school. Before looking at the mainstream context, it is worth noting that practice in oral presentations was also part of the Newnham programme. But in Nora's terms, speaking English in class at Newnham was facilitated by two conditions. First, she said that no one spoke English perfectly, and secondly, because everyone was a language learner, people were unafraid of making mistakes. However, there is a marked difference between answering a question or speaking informally in class, and the stress of speaking in front of a group in the sustained and structured way implied by the oral presentation genre. The latter is nerve-racking for most ESL students, including Nora. She wrote the following in her Newnham class diary.

> *Today we had lecture about 'book talk.' I very worried. In front of the students and teachers I very nervous. Before I stayed home recite from memory to my father. That's very fluent. But at critical moment I all the forget. So I got C+. I very feel unwell.   (Class diary 29.11.96)*

What makes her nervous is in part the thought of being physically in front of the students and teachers, who are watching and listening. Her practice run, recited by heart to her father was 'very fluent', but how well she describes the real thing – 'at critical moment I all the forget'. And once again, a judgement is made in the most concrete, confining and defining way. She took this personally, that is, *she*, not her talk, got C+.

Nora had once commented that 'writing orals' was one of the most difficult types of assignments. Just as she had written her book report oral at Newnham and memorised it, this was also the accepted strategy for orals at high school. It was standard practice for all students, except many did not learn their presentations by heart, but simply read them out aloud. At Karfield High, I observed both Alicia and Nora doing oral presentations in their mainstream English class. For the English oral in question, they had to invent a product and devise the marketing strategy for it. Nora had invented a chair which performed magical transformations, such as putting hair on bald people, and making students more intelligent. Alicia had also worked on a chair idea, basically a 'water-bed chair'. They had written their scripts in full and shown these to the ESL teacher. Here is what the teacher said to me about Nora's.

When she showed me her script I thought oh my god where do I start? If I fix it and make it perfect it's no longer theirs, but we took the most glaringly obvious expressions, we talked about how to express various bits. Even though their language was, you know, what are they trying to say here? (.) they had all the right features of adverts. They understand what they're supposed to do, and some of the subtleties of what they're trying to produce and it's the language that's their biggest problem.   (Talk with ESL teacher, 25.11.97)

As mentioned before, although the task is an oral, current practice for students is that the text is first drafted in written form, and in full. This creates anomalies for all students in regard to the nature of spoken discourse as opposed to, say, an essay, but places particular pressure on ESL students, who must show mastery of standard grammatical forms in the written draft. The oral is in essence another written task, an uncomfortable fusion of oral and literate practice. In other words, the expository talk is a contrived situation in which students must sound like a book (Baker & Freebody, 1993; Gee, 1996). Alicia and Nora were both placed in Year 8, the first year of high school, but there was no concession to the fact that developing the marketing strategy for an imaginary product, complete with visual aid, was quite a demanding task. Nor was there any acknowledgment that these girls were operating in their third language. In fact, while the teacher stated that the girls understood the generic features of advertisements ('they had all the right features of adverts'), their use of language (English) was constructed as 'their biggest problem'. The teacher's impulse was to appropriate their idiosyncratic discourse, and to 'fix it and make it perfect'. This is not a critique of the teacher, as she too is subject to the exigencies of current practice.

In the lesson at which the oral presentations were made, two Anglo-Australian boys volunteered to do theirs first. Each came to stand at the front of the class and each read, with an unwavering flat delivery, the entire talk from palm cards. There was desultory applause at the end of each talk. The teacher then asked Alicia, but Nora said she'd go first. Her voice was soft but she could be heard with effort. She had memorised most of her script, and Alicia stood beside her with Nora's 'visual aid' completely covering her (Alice's) face. It was a drawing of the miraculous chair, which Nora called a 'sofa'. Nora giggled at times, but got through it quite confidently. The students were listening, and it occurred to me it was possibly the first time they had heard her voice, although she had been in the class for two months. Overall, it was not loud enough for students to actively participate as listeners, but the class was attentive and applauded at the end. Alicia was next. She read her script in a tiny voice. The teacher asked her within 30 seconds to speak louder, but the volume didn't really change.

The students were basically quiet, but unable to hear. One boy near me called out, 'Can't hear'. Alicia continued reading, her lips moving, almost soundlessly. Students knew it was over when she moved to sit down, and there was brief applause.

The doing of 'orals' raises several issues for these and other ESL students. They were, as Nora described, 'critical moments' in a number of senses. They entailed the stress of standing very visibly in front of the class, being observed and listened to in a way that was unfamiliar, by class members who, due to limited interaction within and outside the class, were also unfamiliar. There were judgements made on what was heard, and presumably on what was inaudible, informally by students, and formally by the teacher. Finally, the accepted practice of doing orals incorporated a full written script, and even when students used palm cards, the cards basically contained every word of the talk. To illustrate this point further, here is a typical example of an oral task for Year 11 from the school.

> You have been working undercover as a private investigator on the scene of the Shakespearian play you have studied. You have been commissioned to examine incidents of deception and their consequences. You are not to read your talk, however it is *compulsory* for all students to submit a transcript of their oral to the teacher before they present their address. In order to speak for 3–4 minutes your transcript will need to be 500–600 words.

This makes the oral an intrinsically written exercise, subject to the same stringent grammatical criteria as formal written text. Thus even as Nora and Alicia's ESL teacher recognised in the girls' written drafts the requisite elements of the advertising genre implied by the task, she thought, 'Oh my god where do I start?' Although an oral task, linguistically it was a high level cognitive academic task (Cummins, 1984). It is pertinent at this point to consider other representations of these students by teachers, along with some of the ways in which Nora and Alicia perceived they were represented.

The Teachers' View: Working on the Language

The girls often spoke of their teachers at Newnham, Taylor and at their new high school, Karfeld High, as 'nice' or 'kind', although Alicia had commented tactfully that one of their Karfield teachers was 'the opposite of nice'. Nora had characterised Australian teachers as 'more relaxed than Chinese teachers', adding that they were not 'as fiercely strict as the Chinese. And in class we don't need to sit up straight'. In this section I look briefly at how the girls were represented by some of their teachers. I had collected numerous school reports in which the girls were described as 'nice', 'good students' and 'hard working'. Some written reports included comments on language proficiency as well. For example, after 18 months of primary school, Alicia's ESL teacher wrote,

> Alicia seems to understand the various maths concepts well, but still has difficulty with problem solving as the language demands are great ... She is motivated but lacks the English to achieve at a Year 7 level ... Alicia's ESL support has focused on language demands within the Year 7 curriculum. I don't really feel she has mastered any language demands yet.

The assumptions in such a comment are that mastery learning is intrinsic to the curriculum and that ongoing comparisons of ESL learners with native English speakers underlie teacher judgements. Alicia's Newnham teacher wrote that while she understood classroom instructions, 'her writing has lots of spelling mistakes. Also her reading needs improvement'. As students move closer to mainstream integration, the risks of being increasingly represented as 'lacking' in English also increase, although we have known for many years that it takes up to five years to achieve academic parity with native speakers (Collier, 1989).

I have already considered the account by Karfeld's ESL teacher of the girls' oral scripts, which depicted 'language' as 'their biggest problem'. It is worth adding that on starting at Karfeld High, the girls were placed into a Japanese language class, their fourth language and one they had never studied. Although students in Year 8 usually study a language other than English, this seemed to me rather pointless for Nora and Alicia, who already operated in three languages. In fact Nora was also acquiring some understanding of Cantonese through her friends, in addition to Shanghainese, Mandarin and English.

When I first met the ESL teacher at Karfeld, her opening gambit was as follows:

> If anything the girls are a tiny bit too independent, handing in things I haven't seen, that they haven't run by me. They've got the ideas on the whole, but need to work on the language.   (25.11.97)

In representing the girls as 'a tiny bit too independent', the teacher here is representing herself as arbiter of 'the language', that is, of 'proper English'. She is the legitimate gatekeeper of assignments, which must be 'run by her' prior to being submitted to mainstream teachers. While this was almost certainly motivated by a desire to support the girls, it seemed to me rather positive that the girls had submitted their work directly to the class teacher, along with other students. The ESL teacher continued,

In English they had to work on a media folio, and write a news article based on a fairy tale. They had no more trouble than anyone else understanding the structure of the news article.

Just as they had grasped the generic features of the advertising task for the oral, the girls had understood and replicated appropriate features in their news articles. What was the result? How were they assessed? Their mainstream English teacher said she couldn't work out how to give Nora's news story a mark. The same teacher had said to me that the girls' writing was 'difficult, all back to front and twisted' and that she found it 'hard to mark that stuff'. The ESL teacher concluded that Nora writes 'very strange sentences', adding, 'The bits I'd gone through were relatively error-free'. The focus of both these teachers is clearly on form, rather than on meeting the criteria of the genre, or on meaning. To illustrate this point further, and to continue the notion of teacher representation of students, as perceived through Nora's eyes, I now look at some more of her diary entries, in which she writes about some of her teachers at Taylor High. Nora's spelling, punctuation and paragraph structure are reproduced as they appear in the diary. The first extract concerns a class test, and the second is about teacher responses to Asian and other students. Both pieces are about equity.

'A very bad mark'

Assessment for many ESL students is fraught with *angst*. In the following narrative from Nora's diary, she tells of the ignominy of failing a test in the ESL class, recounting what is for her one of the central conundrums of life at school.

> *Today is a bad day.*
>
> *In this morning my Phone teacher gave back to us 'News test.' I got a very very very VERY BAD bad mark. D+. I never got this mark before. <u>Maybe</u> I'm bad, But I don't think I'm bad like that! I think this test was not quite equitable, because I'm lose two lessons on a week. ~~Lask~~ Last Thursday I'm not in the class, and on Friday the teacher told us we have a test. I asked teacher: 'Can I get that paper about News?' Teacher said she don't got any one left. So I can't have a good mark. (Maybe it isn't real reason.)*
>
> *This afternoon when I came home, I very heartbroken. I'm cried, long time, then I wrote a letter to my Phone teacher. I told she what I'm fell. Why I haven't got a good mark, and I said willing getting better. I want my Phone teacher can give me one more chance to look at me.*
>
> *I ~~like~~ think tomorrow will getting better. Every thing will getting better.*   (Diary, 11.6.97)

Nora calls her 'form teacher' her 'phone teacher.' This is one of those high frequency school organisation words, like 'mainstream' and 'assignment' that are rarely spelled out, and yet are quite idiosyncratic. Words such as 'form class' and 'form teacher' vary from school to school, have no currency outside of school contexts, and represent a semantic variation of 'form' that is not common. Such words are part of the culturally assumed knowledge of students, and clearly need to be made explicit to ESL students.

If we look at the structure of this piece, we see the characteristic opening abstract, followed by a complication, elaboration of events and her affective response to these, then a resolution and philosophical coda. Nora adopts an analytic standpoint, offering a critical reading of the episode. She makes a reasoned argument that the test, and the teacher, had not been 'equitable', providing two reasons for the claim, namely that she had missed two lessons and that she was denied access to the primary resource for the test. In her second stanza, she describes her emotional response to the episode – there are tears, catharsis, and resolution as she describes her pragmatic and empowering response in the form of a letter to her teacher. She specifies three elements included in the letter , namely her feelings, her account of the result, and an assertion of her willingness to improve. She also provides the rationale for writing to the teacher, whom she wants to have 'one more chance to look at me'. That is, one more chance to be considered as something/someone other than a D+. The level of self-representation in this text is powerful, and the reader has clear insight into how it affected Nora and how she responded.

This excerpt also provides an example of Nora's agency at work. Her letter was unusual, in that I have seen many students receive bad marks on tests, and heard many complain, but have never seen or received such a representation in writing. Nora has attempted to represent herself via an official school discourse, a letter to the teacher. In language terms, this was a very authentic, communicative and instrumental use of English. It is also likely that she would have had difficulty representing herself as cogently through speaking. Nora completes her diary entry with a cultural aphorism, a message of hope that everything would get better. In response to her letter, Nora later told me the teacher had said not to worry, and that the test didn't really count for much. But how was she to know this? Knowing what counts to whom is part of the problem here.

'All the teachers are not equitable'

In this journal entry, Nora presents what she perceives as inequitable treatment from the mainstream science teacher. While I point out elements of structure and second language features in the text, it should be understood that the focus of the analysis is discourse, and not errors or interlanguage. A detailed analysis is provided to advance the notion that such texts constitute a powerful resource for representation, and also a way to apprehend the voices of ESL students. I would argue that they are not only deserving of detailed analysis but constitute a powerful means for language learning. In addition, such texts allow space for students to theorise their own identities and their experiences (Baker, 1982).

> *17–6–97*
>
> *Oh! I very to be out of luck!*
>
> *From this morning, when I caught the bus, I'm discovered my bus ticket was finished and I forgot to change the bus ticket, so I paid for that bus, and that driver was very ferocious. I don't like he, I don't want see he again.*
>
> *In the first period I very carefully listen to the teacher . . . Teacher let us do some work, I done very well (I think) A person she copied at me, when I readed it out, teacher said 'good'. She didn't said anything ((else)). But that people copied at me, she readed it out, My teacher Yelled: 'Excellent! That was excellent!' And said many good words of she. I'm very set ((sad/upset)). I thinks the teacher was very equitable, she just like foreigners, and every she always think the foreigners are getting better. Foreigners are best! For example: last time a foreigner written a science report, she copied my other classmate, when she gave this one to the teacher, somethings were wrong, but the teacher still mark she's right, and gave her full mark. My classmate got lower marks than that foreigner. so I think all the teachers are not equitable.*
>
> *In this afternoon, a foreigner just asked me somethings about that video. When I answered her, teacher said 'Nora, shout up!' I very unhappy all the day.*
>
> *Before the Tina told me some thing about the teachers likes the foreigners. I don't believe she, now I realize that. I just don't know why the teachers always likes fornigner, they always like white skin, gold hairs?*
>
> *In world was cares never equitable, not equitable at the all.*

In this journal entry we recognise immediately some features typical of narrative structure, as suggested by Labov (1972), including the opening statement of the general theme, orientation to the events and description of the events themselves, the inclusion of one or more complications, followed by a resolution of sorts and a coda. The abstract of Nora's story is 'Oh! I very to be out of luck!' This contains both Chinese word order and unconjugated verb form. In the first three paragraphs she then describes four incidents which are instances of the bad luck theme. The fourth paragraph contains her moral evaluation of the instances described, in which she concludes teachers are guilty of discriminating against Asian students. The final line constitutes the coda to the narrative. In spite of its anomalous syntax, it conveys the clear message that the world is not a fair place. This is a structure very typical of

Nora's entries in the journal. The final coda is a common feature in her writing, in which she seems to draw on a discourse of cultural aphorisms in order to provide philosophical commentary on what she is experiencing. A Chinese teacher also suggested to me that the concluding homily is a generic feature of many texts presented to primary students in Chinese schools. A story is followed by a moral, and Nora is therefore drawing on this cultural resource to conclude her narrative.

The first paragraph contains the bus incident, in which she recounts the driver's anger when Nora's ticket was found to be out of date. In the second she depicts two categories of students who are the protagonists in two episodes from her science class. The categories are represented on the one hand by 'a person', 'foreigners' and 'white skin, gold hairs', and on the other hand by Nora herself, as shown in the use of the first person pronoun, and 'my classmate', by which we should understand ESL classmate. That is, she sets up a dichotomy within the class, opposing mainstream Australian students with ESL students. She then argues that the teacher discriminates in favour of the former group, who in both incidents have plagiarised work from ESL students. She narrates the story of the girl who copied from her, and then conveys the teacher's comment on the their respective efforts – 'good' to Nora, and a yelled 'excellent' to the plagiariser.

It is possible that the teacher said only 'good' to Nora because Nora's response was hard to hear, but note the contrast Nora makes between this understated comment and the yelled 'excellent'. Note also that switching the verb from 'said' to 'yelled' is a sophisticated rhetorical device, which contributes to the contrast. She then summarises what she sees as the teacher's predilection for Australian students, and concludes this with the formulation, 'Foreigners are best', a construction she attributes to the teacher. She then proposes a further example of an analogous incident of the teacher's favourable evaluation of work plagiarised from an ESL student. In this instance, she depicts the discrimination not in terms of an oral comment, but in terms of marks, lower for her ESL classmate than for 'that foreigner'.

In this text Nora constructs her day of 'bad luck' chronologically, as indexed by the adverbial time phrases which begin each paragraph. In the third paragraph we are privy to an afternoon incident when she was told by the teacher to 'shut up', ironically misspelt by Nora as 'Shout up!' In the final paragraph Nora relates the gist of talks with her Taiwanese friend Tina, who had been talking to Nora about discriminatory practices by teachers, such as preferring blond-haired students (see also Chapter 4). Clearly at this time, in Nora's representation at least, 'foreigners' and ESL students are seen, heard, and evaluated differently by teachers in her classes. Whether teachers treat English-speaking and ESL students equitably or not cannot be judged from the evidence of Nora's journal. It is noteworthy, however, that as she represents others, she is also reflexively representing herself within the marginalised group.

The text reveals a number of other features very typical of Nora's diary writing, which extended to over 7500 words in a three-month period. First, there is evidence of her use of her electronic dictionary for vocabulary such as 'ferocious', 'equitable' and 'realize'. The use of the term 'foreigners' speaks also to her sense of identity as Chinese, and her membership of the category which is not 'white skin, gold hairs'. Second, Nora heightens the impact of her narrative by including reported speech three times, on each occasion to convey the teacher's voice. Third, although there are numerous grammatical errors in the text, and certainly inconsistencies in the grammar and spelling, they do not impede meaning, apart perhaps from the word 'set' used for 'upset / sad'. Fourth, there is a dramatic quality to the writing, enhanced by the conscious injection of Nora's emotional responses to the events she is describing. Within the narrative, she develops an argument, to which there is a moral conclusion, namely that the world is not equitable. Who could argue with her?

As someone who taught mainstream English for many years, I can see why a teacher might find this writing a little strange, but have seen many texts written by native English speakers with fewer grammatical anomalies, but far fewer points of interest. The example above is admittedly a personalised diary genre, not a news article or 'approved' academic text. However, the demonstrable quality of the writing suggests that the English teacher's rejection of Nora's school task writing as unmarkable, and 'back to front and twisted' is open to question. Just prior to this comment the teacher had railed against other students she described to me as 'dickheads who do no work, but were the first to complain when they get a D'. I wondered what was worse – getting a D or being assessed as unmarkable. Embedded in her evaluations lies the ideological workings attached to any discourse, that is, the way it is valued, interpreted and received (Fairclough & Wodak, 1997). I would also argue that narrative diary or journal writing should have a legitimate place within the mainstream curriculum, as it opens up to students the possibility of building a complex self-portrait while honing genre-specific and other language skills. Schiffrin (1996) suggests that the ability of narrative to express and situate experience as text 'provides a resource for the display of self and identity' (p. 167). She demonstrates how narrative is used to reveal aspects of the narrators' 'agentive and epistemic selves', their positioning within social contexts and their display of social identity. Such arguments suggest that journal writing merits an explicit presence in the curriculum. It extends to students the opportunity to develop their skills in a non-threatening format, recognises that the negotiation of identity is fundamental to educational success, could open up opportunities for dialogue with teachers and other students and thus as a strategy sits well with the notion of transformative pedagogy described by Cummins in *Language, Power and Pedagogy* (2000).

Whether teachers treat English speaking and ESL students inequitably, as both Tina and Nora suggested, is not the primary issue here, but should be seen as a concern. The fact that teachers expect unreasonably high levels of grammatical accuracy from students who have been here, in Nora's case, for less than two years, defies what we know about the time needed by many students to acquire academic proficiency in another language (Collier, 1989; Cummins, 2000; Cummins & Swain, 1986). Negative comparisons with mainstream students are felt keenly by ESL students. Nora and Alicia both felt that they were having difficulty competing, as shown by Nora's story above, and by the following interview excerpt from Alicia.

A: Mm I'm scared that I can't catch up↑ in that high school, in Karfeld↑ (.) where my sister is
R: Why
A: My sister is hard to catch up too. She come here and then go Taylor, I mean Karfeld. It's real (.) she said it's really hard to catch up
R: So (.) what will help you to catch up
A: oh (.) donnow ((laughs))   (28.2.97)

Alicia's insight about the difficulty of catching up was via her sister. There is no doubt that the challenge of competing with users of the dominant discourse is very real. Yet it seems that teacher representations of such students and their work have a serious influence on a student's ability to catch up, and on the way the student perceives that ability. In addition, while placing Nora and Alicia into Japanese might be seen as normal by the school, since all Year 8s studied either Japanese or German, it constituted a complete negation of the extraordinary language skills the girls already possessed, and challenges they already faced in acquiring English. It also disadvantaged them by placing them in the last three months of a one year subject they had never studied, time which perhaps could have been spent developing skills judged to be 'lacking' by their other teachers.

In the final section of this chapter, I want to return to the theme of speaking, and other ways that students can find a voice. So far I have discussed the role of language use in representing social identity and in building social memberships within school contexts. I turn now to sites outside of the school, which open to some students new possibilities for language practice and for the negotiation of identity. Nora had once pragmatically concluded that, 'you're here – you have to speak'. Unlike students such as John and her friend Tina (Chapter 4), she found new contexts and ways to speak.

Nora in the Noodle Bar

Over the course of her first six months in high school, I perceived that Nora made much progress in spoken English, as evidenced in our increasingly fluent and comfortable conversations, where hearing became less conscious and talk more spontaneous. This was perhaps less due to the classroom learning and social interaction, where she, like Alicia, spoke a lot of Chinese, than to her out-of-school opportunities, which scaffolded her developing confidence and competence in English. Asked when she actually used English, she said, 'because my dad has a shop. I work there. I have to talk with the foreigners – it is in English'. At the start of the year, I had asked her to describe her work in her father's noodle bar. My question as to whether she answered the phone brought gales of disbelieving laughter, followed by 'Oh no, my father and another girl do that'. By mid-year she was taking phone orders, and could scarcely remember a time when she had not done so. In the following exchange from the interview in Mandarin, she recounts a recent incident in the noodle bar.

F: Can you tell me something about working in the noodle bar?
N: Nothing new, very boring, every time, just repeating the same sentences. If it is very busy, then it is very troublesome. For example, last Saturday, all of a sudden we had a lot of customers, after they ordered, my dad was too busy to cope, he is the cook, he was not able to cook that fast, then many customers were not happy. It is very troublesome in such situation.
F: Do they need you to explain to the customers?
N: I did, I said sorry to them, we were so busy. But some of them still not happy.   (M. Int. p. 3)

It seems likely that even 'just repeating the same sentences' may have given her a great boost in confidence. It was practice in an authentic context in which outcomes depended on her ability to understand and to communicate. In addition, in the social context of the noodle bar, she had a dual legitimacy, as a member of the Chinese owner's family and as a worker, serving customers in English. Even if her utterances did not range far beyond the noodle menu, they were of necessity heard and understood. Having her language use validated in this way, to the point where she was able to apologise on behalf of her father to a group of disaffected and impatient customers, is evidence of the linguistic capital she had accrued in the space of a few months.

Going shopping

The noodle bar was only one of several sites where Nora used English regularly. For example, her family had friends whose children were Australian born Chinese, and not proficient speakers of Mandarin. This meant that she was using English in social contexts outside of school and work. She also pointed out that one of her favourite pastimes, shopping, was part of the process of using, and we can also infer *learning* English. She linked this phenomenon to the location of the shops.

N: unless you go to Chinatown, you need to speak English every-
            where else. This forces you to speak English.
F: What do you feel about your English now, compared to when
            you arrived?
N: Much better.
F: So, you have more courage [to
N: [dare to talk with the foreigners.
F: When you just came
N: When I just came, eh, I didn't know. Once I said a sentence, I
            always felt this sentence was not right. Now, my English is
            much better, I don't think this way any more.   (M. Int. p. 4)

Nora draws attention here to her understanding that being 'forced' to speak English is a vital part of the acquisition process. The excerpt provides insight into her developing sense of confidence and progress over time, culminating in her courage to 'dare to talk with the foreigners.' In her final turn, we see echoes of Krashen's (1978) notion of *the language monitor*, the self-editing, self-censoring mechanism which indicates to language learners whether an utterance is right or not.

After their first year in high school, Nora, Alicia, Tina and I went on an outing to a large shopping complex. I watched as Nora went up to the Shiseido make-up counter in an up-market department store, to seek information about and to price a particular product. I made a mental note of the cultural and indeed linguistic capital needed to do this. The girls were also fascinated by the animals in a pet shop window, but it was Nora who went in to the owner, and got all the details on one pedigreed puppy on display. She came back and reported the details, especially the outrageous price, to us. Later the girls headed off to see the movie, *Titanic*. I found the session times in a newspaper for them, but it was in a city cinema they had not been to before, and they had to catch a train. Alicia had me explain, then repeat all the necessary directions and landmarks, taking control of 'getting them there'. Using English to take control in such contexts is once again an empowering phenomenon, involving levels of participation which are simply unavailable to those who don't yet 'dare to talk with the foreigners'. Once again I was struck with the negotiation and language processing we engaged in, and I wondered who else was doing this with them, particularly with Tina.

Nora calls for help

The corollary of Nora's view that 'you have to speak' is that 'you have to be heard.' Although being heard in English at school still seemed difficult, the girls were able to do this in other contexts. I was also aware that possibly I was for both Nora and Alicia the exception to the rule, the sympathetic and interested Australian listener. Early in the second year at Karfeld High, Nora rang me to seek help with a homework sheet, which was to be the basis for a test the next day. She explained the problem, and asked if I had time. The subject was Business Principles, and the topic was the three levels of government in Australia. The sheet was a cloze exercise for which no list of words had been provided.

She read the sentences out to me, replacing the blanks with 'the word' or 'something'. I deduced from context that the first words were 'federal', 'state' and 'local', and provided the names of the leaders of these levels of government, which were also needed. I was a little surprised that she did not know the name of the Australian Prime Minister. The sheet went on to sentences about statutory authorities and marketing boards, the promotion of primary produce, and other issues of government funding and jurisdiction. Half way through it, Nora asked, 'How do you know all this?' I tried to explain that much of it was general knowledge that I got from my own schooling or reading the papers. At the same time I knew that perhaps a majority of students would have a great deal of trouble with this sheet. I told her it would be difficult for many students. Nora explained that the teacher had not given answers to the sheet and that she couldn't find any answers in the text book. She had thought the subject Business Principles would be something like Maths, but it was full of reading and she did not understand 'any of the words'.

This phone call raised two issues for me. First, as Nora entered Year 9, the academic demands of the work had clearly intensified linguistically and culturally, and there seemed to be no recognition by this teacher that Nora would need more support than had been offered in this instance. Second, the phone call *per se* was evidence of Nora's initiative, agency and increasing communicative competence in English. In these terms, I felt certain it could not have taken place even six months earlier. Although we were focused on the sheet, with her reading and repeating sentences to me, and me speculating on possible answers, giving her instructions, and asking questions, it was a 45 minute conversation, our longest and most symmetrical in turns. At the end, she asked about finding a tutor for science and English, asked when I was coming to visit her and Alicia again, and finally invited me to dinner, adding her mother would like to cook for me. I found her very easy to understand and felt certain that her part-time job had helped her English and her confidence considerably.

Summary

In this chapter, we have followed the journeys of Nora and Alicia across three schools – from the intensive reception centre, to Taylor High's ESL unit and then into mainstream Year 8 at Karfeld High. Although the convenient 'ESL' label was attached to the girls in each of these sites, we have seen that Alicia was learning English as a third language, and Nora was learning it as a fourth language, if we count her social acquisition of Cantonese. Both Norton (1997) and Gibbons (1991) draw attention to the inappropriateness of attaching labels such as ESL, LEP or NESB (non-English speaking background) to students, labels which reinforce notions of English language deficiency and undervalue the linguistic capital of these students. Labelling Nora and her language as Chinese, for example, dissembles the fact that while acquiring English, she speaks the dialect of Shanghai, as well as Mandarin and also has a passable aural understanding of Cantonese. Reified ethnicities and institutional labelling also do little to help us understand the dynamic interplay of language and social identity within schools (Leung *et al.*, 1997; Thesen, 1997).

Alicia and Nora are examples of students expanding their social and speaking resources over time and in different sites, gradually developing their repertoire of discourses, enabling them to move across sites. For both girls, it is important to recognise within this process the competing influences of the ethnic Chinese language groups and the demands of the official discourses of school English. The Chinese-speaking students exhibited what Rampton (1995) would call an extremely strong in-group affiliation. The cohesion of this group, in which identity was visibly and aurally enacted as Chinese, and in which important social relations were established, hinged on the use of Mandarin and Cantonese as shared languages. Using Rampton's reconceptualised terminology for native speaker competence, I would suggest that in the case of Alicia and Nora (and indeed their Chinese peer group) there was an extraordinary synchronicity, or overlap, between their *language expertise, language affiliation* and *language inheritance* (see Chapter 2). The power of such a combination of expertise, affiliation and inheritance meant that becoming audible in English at school was an ongoing challenge for Alicia and Nora. Contexts outside of school gave them some access to practising

English. Both were inveterate shoppers, but Nora also had the contexts of the noodle bar and social occasions with English speaking family friends in which to use English. This accounted in part for what I saw as her development of increasing confidence and agency in communicating in English, both of which meant she was more audible to majority language speakers.

Nora pointed out that at Newnham, speaking English in class was made easier by the fact that everyone was in the learning-English boat, and she was unafraid to speak there. Newnham therefore provided its students with a risk-free and stress-free environment for language learning (Trueba, 1989). Taylor High's tightly knit group of ethnic Chinese students meant that the predominant languages used by students, both in and outside of classes were Mandarin and Cantonese. On moving into mainstream classes, students were asked to do sustained formal oral presentations in English on a range of topic areas. The orals raised a number of issues for Alicia and Nora. First, they were very anxious about them. As Chinese speakers, they were basically inaudible to mainstream hearers in the school. Suddenly they were highly visible, at the front of the room, expected to speak so that all could hear, and in a highly structured way. Nora described this as 'the critical moment', which was not only linguistically and emotionally demanding, but also officially assessable. It was a moment in which their (in)audibility was on display, particularly for Alice, whose oral no one could hear. It was a small crisis of self-representation in a mainstream context, in which they were visibly and 'audibly' inaudible. Finally, the so-called 'oral' had to be written first, and so was subject to all the exigencies of formal written English.

As the girls progressed into the mainstream at Karfeld, it became increasingly apparent that the demands of school English would prove immensely difficult. The mainstream is all about marks, alluded to by two of the Karfeld teachers in their statements on the girls' writing – 'Oh my god where do I start' and 'it's all back to front and twisted, I don't know how to mark that stuff'. Nora's phone call for help on what was for her an utterly incomprehensible worksheet on government instrumentalities was another case in point – the test was the next day. The representation of these students by teachers as language deficient is both wrong and a serious risk. Such a representation by teachers is based partly on a misconception of the differences between basic communicative skills and academic work, and a failure to appreciate the time needed to master cognitively demanding genres (see Cummins, 1992). Bourdieu (1984) reminds us that any theory of language competence must take into account the social conditions which make the competence possible, or otherwise. In practice, the school did not provide the conditions where frequent interactions between native speakers and ESL students were facilitated, where ESL students were sufficiently well supported in the mainstream, and where English language acquisition could flourish. In addition, it seriously undervalued the cultural and linguistic capital of these students, not to mention their achievements in English language acquisition in a short time span. Understanding the critical nexus between the negotiation of identity and language acquisition would help teachers and schools to transform their practices in a way that would benefit all language minority students (see Cummins, 2000).

Another dimension of this chapter has been the use of language as an inclusionary and exclusionary device. Numerous examples of the latter emerged in the data. For example, I was excluded from interactions between the girls or in class which were in Mandarin; Nora was excluded socially when Alicia switched to Cantonese with the Hong Kong students; many of the ESL students were excluded from the broader school community by the ethnic divisions evident in the seating arrangements at lunch time; Nora and Alicia's written English was excluded by teachers from the range of possible, markable discourses; and Nora's diary in particular may be seen as an inadmissible genre in school. Giroux (1992: 205) reminds us of the imperative to work towards learning that goes beyond knowledge acquisition to an appreciation of cultural practices 'that offer students a sense of identity, place, and hope'. Assigning higher values to texts that more truly reflect students' identities would be a start. Giroux's proposal of *border pedagogy* seems a fitting conclusion for the story of Nora and Alicia, a conclusion which offers a pathway to a sense of place, hope and identity:

> ... border pedagogy suggests not simply opening diverse cultural histories and spaces to students, it also means understanding how fragile identity is as it moves into borderlands crisscrossed with a variety of languages, experiences, and voices. There are no unified subjects here, only students whose voices and experiences intermingle with the weight of particular histories that will not fit into the master narrative of a monolithic culture. (Giroux, 1992: 209)

This chapter has provided some insights into the complexities of identity and language use of two quiet girls who worked hard to gain a voice within the mainstream. We have seen that the classroom is only one place in many where 'languages, experiences and voices' mingle, albeit the only one where teachers usually see and hear their students. Asking who is (in)audible within the class, who speaks, and how they are heard are important questions, and a necessary prerequisite to opening up to students the diverse spaces suggested by Giroux. Read in this light, the classroom becomes a context where particular forms of language use need not be constructed as 'the problem', but as intrinsic to a more diverse heteroglossic approach to language and literacy. The classroom thus becomes a public sphere in which linguistic minority students can begin to acquire the saying-doing-being-valuing-believing combinations, which will allow them to become legitimate and valued members of dominant mainstream groups (Gee, 1996).

Chapter 7

Audibility and Institutional Deafness

Aussie kids rule

*On Thursday afternoon as I was travelling
into the city by tram, a large group of
students from one of Melbourne's exclusive
eastern suburbs schools got on. Although,
judging by their faces, they were all of
southeast Asian heritage, a smile came to
my face when I heard the distinctive Aussie
twang of their accents.*

*They dumped their bags in the corridor,
and sat together in a huge group, feet up on
the seats, talking loudly about the footy and
who was "getting with" whom, liberally
sprinkling their every utterance with swear
words. When one of them alighted, they
yelled out happily to him: "Seeya faggot!"*

*It certainly warmed my heart to see how
these youngsters had so readily taken on
and been embraced by our Australian way
of life. Good onya, true blue!*

Ralph Saubern
Northcote, Victoria

(*The Weekend Australian*, 19–20 May, 2002, p. 20)

This letter to the editor in a recent national newspaper highlights some of the
key issues in this book, namely audibility, difference and the representation of
identity. The clear contrast in the opening paragraph of this letter is between
the students' Asian appearance ('judging by their faces'), and their Aussie
accents, which not only reassured but brought a smile to the face of the over-
hearer. The students are constructed through their reported demeanour and

169

discourse as Asian Aussie larrikins, 'embraced' by Australian culture, and hearable as 'true blue', meaning 'authentic' or 'mainstream'. Recall the comment from one student in Chapter 2:

> If your English is as fluent as Australian students, the Australian students do not really see you that much differently. I saw them talking to those Asian students whose English is good in the same way as they would to other Australian students.

Ralph Sauber's letter depicts other Asian students 'whose English is good', students who were not seen as different. Or rather who were seen only momentarily as different – until they opened their mouths. At this point the Aussie twang and classic topics of Aussie discourse emerged (the footy and sexual gossip), along with the inevitable adolescent swearing and slang. The experience 'warmed the heart' of the observer, who wrote about it with no trace of irony. The phrase 'onya' means 'good on you', or 'well done!' Saubern's initial assessment (and he uses the term 'judgement') of the students' Asian appearance, was an assessment of these students as 'other'. It was dispelled as he recognised the mainstream discourse of Australian adolescents.

The findings in the cases presented here support the notion that if you *sound* alike, you are not *seen* as different. At school, 'good English' frames you as acceptable, a potential speaking partner and legitimate social member. Some minority speakers understand very well that how you sound affects how you are seen and heard, where you can go, whom you can speak or be with, how you are treated, and how you can influence events and those around you. My point is that discrimination by majority language speakers may be on the basis of audible rather than, or as well as, visible differences. This is not to discount the realities of racist practices on the basis of visible difference, and it would be an analytical error to diminish the importance of appearance in many interactions. Many studies have provided powerful descriptions of the childhood experience of such discrimination (see for example Tyagi (1996) and Johnson-Powell (1996)). However, I wish to provide a more nuanced view of the social and linguistic minefield which some immigrant students encounter as they learn and speak English in school contexts. Before taking up the main themes in the case studies, I wish to comment briefly on the cases themselves, and the questions they pose as to interpretation.

The Case Studies: Alternative Readings

The participants speak and I record and selectively re-present their voices . . . I hear their voices in my ears, and I speak my words, condi-

tioned by my place in historical social movement and by the language
and analytical resources available to me. (Wexler, 1992: 2)

I began this series of case studies trying to explore and to understand the
relationship between acquiring English as a second language and social
identity, taking as a basic theoretical standpoint that identities are discursively constructed and negotiated in social contexts through social
memberships. In case study, the metaphor of the researcher as 'primary
research instrument' has often been used (Glesne & Peshkin, 1992;
Merriam, 1988). It is a metaphor that does not do justice to the multifaceted,
intellectual, subjective and reflective nature of the job. And as in all qualitative research, the cases do not provide any neat and tidy contours for a trim
table in the final chapter, no deft linear argument leading ineluctably to an
uncontestable conclusion. Wexler's careful qualification of the researcher's
role above reminds us that any one reading of a social situation is simply
that, and that conflicting, even contradictory positions are inevitable when
seeking to analyse and interpret complex social phenomena. Through the
data chapters I have represented second language acquisition and use as a
move towards self-representation. The voices I had in my ears were those
of Tina, John, Nora, Alicia and Milena.

How was it that Milena moved so quickly into the discourses of English,
meeting new friends, settling into the mainstream, and resisting the ESL
epithet, while Tina, Nora, Alicia and John struggled for a long time and
with varying degrees of success to learn English, and to become members
of mainstream social groups? There is clearly a range of interpretive positions and explanations. Let us look at three of them briefly. First, through a
traditional SLA lens I could identify a range of individual language
learning factors to do with motivation: 'good language learner' strategies,
prior learning, psychological make-up, aptitude and intelligence. I could
argue that Milena consciously applied techniques which had already
helped her to learn Danish; she was more extroverted and gregarious than
the other students; she had a stronger metalinguistic awareness; and she
was more motivated to compete with mainstream students. However, this
view is not only oversimplified and incompatible with the theoretical
position I established in Chapter 2 and have maintained throughout this
book, it ignores complex ideological issues of social context, power and
identity negotiation. Milena had other forms of capital on which she could
draw, such as physical attractiveness, a language background in which
many forms were cognate with English, multilingual parents, an extensive
network of friends and family, and access to opportunities to practise and
to use English.

A second position could be based on social rather than linguistic practices, drawing attention to the fact that all of the Asian students had problems, while the white European student did not. One might suggest that the Asian students' limited access to practice with English speakers reflected subtle racist practices which excluded them from mainstream discourses on the basis of visible difference, or even that the Chinese speakers excluded themselves, preferring to mix in their first language groups. Many years of observation in high schools suggests to me that this interpretation must carry some weight, and as stated above, visible difference cannot be discounted. However, the problem is that Asian students are not a linguistically or culturally homogeneous category. Lippi-Green (1997) points out that dumping all Asians in one basket is a resort to racist stereotypes which is as misleading as it is expedient. Asian Australians are an extremely diverse group, and while discrimination based on visible difference may well be part of the picture, socially and linguistically the story is more complex.

I wish to propose a third reading of these case studies which involves a complex combination of both linguistic and social factors, including access to interactions with English speakers and what I have termed audibility. Further, a sociocultural framing of language acquisition and use, such as that I outlined in Chapter 2, does not preclude a consideration of important notions derived from SLA theory, such as communicative competence. The contribution of this study is that it places communicative competence in a broader social and institutional context, linking the ways students speak to the ways they are heard and the possibilities and conditions which enable or constrain the representation of their identities in social groups. The key questions I posed in the first chapter were:

(1) How do linguistic minority students in the early stages of language acquisition represent themselves to other students and teachers?
(2) How are they heard and represented?
(3) What conditions at school facilitate or constrain the acquisition of spoken English by recently arrived NESB students?

The data chapters present quite divergent stories and accounts which provide different images and representations of language use and identity. These students' stories show that there are diverse modalities of displacement, difference, inclusion and exclusion, and that the homogeneity of NESB or ESL students as a category is as misplaced as that applied to any group of students. Rather than claiming generalisable truths, the following discussion is aimed at tying theoretical concerns to actual encounters with the mostly subordinated voices of these students, and at a re-theorisation of the conditions surrounding their language use and self-representation. There are three main sections in this chapter. They focus on the role of speaking in the representation of identity; the role of discourse in discrimination; and the institutional practices implicated in the marginalisation of linguistic minority students.

Ways of Speaking, Ways of Hearing

The cases in this study show that the complex practical activity of speaking is a critical tool of self-representation. Speaking constructs aspects of our identities, but requires the collaboration of the listener, who must not only hear, but as Bourdieu points out, must also believe. In terms of the authority and power which derive from the differential uptake of the linguistic habitus in different social fields or sites of exchange (Bourdieu, 1991), it seems clear that we cannot view the competence of the speaker in isolation from the linguistic market, language in isolation from social practices, speaking in isolation from hearing. Mey (1985: 240) suggested that 'one's highest priority in speaking a foreign language should be to make oneself understood; sounding right is definitely a subordinate goal'. Few would question the importance of intelligibility in any communication, but for migrant students struggling to learn and to speak English in Australia, _sounding right_ makes you more acceptable to speakers of the dominant discourse, as shown in Ralph Saubern's letter above. Although my intuition is that the speakers he heard on the tram were more likely Australian born Chinese ('ABC's) than recently arrived immigrants, the point about the acceptance of a discourse which sounds audibly mainstream stands. This is not an apology for an assimilationist position, which I do not support, but rather a description _of how things are_ in the everyday lived experience of those who may look and/or sound different.

Hymes (1996) claims that there is something primary about speaking, in that it shapes the speaker, and is a surrogate for all communicative modes. He writes, 'Diversity and inequality are not manifest in matters of representation alone: they are manifest in _what it means to speak_, to write (or hear or read), at all' (p. 36, emphasis added). Hymes' concern is with 'ways of speaking', which 'comprise _speech styles_, on the one hand, and _contexts of discourse_, on the other, together with _relations of appropriateness_ obtaining between styles and contexts' (p. 33). But unlike Gee (1996), Hymes does not build social memberships and identities into the equation, nor does he provide any insight that the conditions or production and reception are also part of the text. This seems essential since speech is a social activity in a sense that writing is not (Spolsky, 1998). Cazden (1993), in a comparison of the theoretical constructs of Hymes and Bakhtin, also suggests that in regard to linguistically diverse communities, Hymes provides images of peaceful and painless coexistence, whereas Bakhtin highlights 'the complexities of finding a voice, of being communicatively competent, in heteroglossic speech situations where voices (and the roles they express in the social structure) are felt by the speaker or writer to be in conflict' (p. 203).

In a social account of language use we have to allow for the roles of contexts, social memberships, speakers and hearers. Recall Bourdieu's (1991) stress on the acceptability of any utterance on the linguistic market, with schools specified as formal linguistic markets with symbolic benefits for those whose discourse approximates school English. From much of the evidence in this study, we can see that on the linguistic market of schools there are ways of hearing, and that some ESL teachers, mainstream teachers, Anglo peers, NESB peers and L1 peers hear differently from others. Some are more willing and/or able to assume what Lippi-Green (1997: 71) calls 'the communicative burden'. It is incumbent on schools to make this explicit to their communities, both as an awareness and as a strategy for learning to share the burden more equitably in everyday practices.

The question of who is heard and how, and who is acknowledged and thereby legitimated as a speaker of English is an important one throughout this study. The practical activity of speaking English is a move towards representation and recognition in mainstream contexts; it enables the Greek poet komninos [*sic*] to shout 'Hey Aus tra lia! look at me! whether you like it or not i am one of you'. In Bourdieu's terms speaking English moves the speaker into a dominant linguistic market, where value can be accrued and a set of discursive practices which comprise the linguistic habitus developed. The market also determines the social conditions of the possibility of communication. In Gee's (1996) terms it implicates new social memberships in new contexts, memberships which themselves become new symbolic resources. In regard to second language acquisition and use, Norton Peirce (1995) uses Bourdieu's metaphor of 'capital' to replace the traditional idea of individual motivation with that of *investment*. She writes, 'If learners invest in a second language, they do so with the understanding that they will acquire a wider range of symbolic and material resources, which will in turn increase the value of their cultural capital' (p. 17). She adds that the notion of investment 'presupposes that when learners speak, they are not only exchanging information with target language speakers but they are constantly organising and reorganising a sense of who they are and how they relate to the social world' (p. 18). This view highlights the cumulative effects of language acquisition and its spin-offs in terms of identity representation.

Speaking, Audibility and Representation

Achieving self-representation through speaking a new language requires that the speaker becomes audible to mainstream hearers. This is an extremely complex process, entailing control over the mechanics of production, a knowledge of how discourses work and of social relations in particular contexts. Milena was a student who typified this process, able to represent herself through speaking English, to be heard as a legitimate mainstream student and user of the primary discourse, and able to move across linguistic, social and ethnic boundaries. She was able to engineer a move from Year 10 to Year 11, thereby escaping those she described as 'only kids'. Her orchestrated campaign to change from Year 10 to Year 11 involved talking with her parents and having her mother come up to the school, talking with other students, and representing her case to the ESL co-ordinator. That is, she was able to take up a particular subject position, one of the conditions making this possible being her competence and confidence in spoken English, the symbolic capital she had accrued to invest in her own representation. In addition, one of Milena's prime purposes of language acquisition was to establish and maintain new friendships, which she did in both Danish and English. English was socially significant to her.

Other students had made smaller but nonetheless significant steps in representing and negotiating their identities in English. Although in written form, Nora's letter to the teacher asking 'to be looked at again' after her low test result was a clear instance of self-representation, once again to those in authority and power. It entailed representation as _self-advocacy_, or the self as agent, able to speak and act in the interests of self. I suspect that had Nora been able to do this through speaking rather than a letter, the impact would have been more powerful. Unlike Milena, who got value from her investment, Nora was shortchanged. She was told her marks, and her concern about them, were unimportant. There were other instances of shifts in identity negotiation through the use of English, such as Tina's first participation in mainstream group work, and Nora's part-time job in the noodle bar. These were small moves, but essential in the process of language acquisition and identity work, and they allowed the students to be heard and acknowledged by majority language speakers.

It seems that students are increasingly able to draw on and accumulate representational resources as they expand their communicative competence, and symbolic capital. This entails moving beyond basic referential levels of language use to more strategic and agentive levels. Practice is critical to the development of speaking as a representational resource, but the necessary conditions of audibility and legitimisation by the hearer must also be met. Legitimisation involves being acknowledged as having the right to speak, and having value assigned to what is spoken. For linguistic minority speakers, the move towards self-representation through speaking English is a potentially empowering one. In Figure 7.1, I have tried to convey what I see as the critical aspects of this process, and to sum-

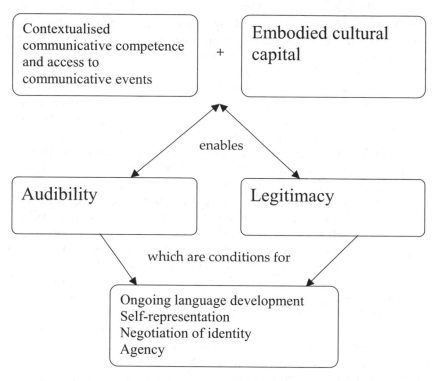

Figure 7.1 The move towards self-representation

marise what I have said so far. Any model is a contingent and somewhat perilous undertaking. My proposal here is merely one way of relating critical elements in a highly complex social process.

Figure 7.1 shows that the move towards representation begins with the acquisition of communicative competence in speaking, incorporating a range of linguistic, phonological, discourse and sociocultural knowledge. In an obvious sense, audibility is tied to intelligibility, and thus a socially contextualised understanding of the notion of communicative competence is necessary to understand the move towards the representation of identity in a new language. If we look at the constitutive elements of communicative competence as proposed by Celce-Murcia *et al.* (1995) (see Chapter 2), it seems as if discourse competence, sociocultural competence, linguistic competence, actional competence and strategic competence develop simultaneously. There are two points to make about this. First, while intuitively one knows that these elements occur in tandem in any successful communication, the model does not suggest that for learners, a threshhold level of linguistic competence may be a necessary precursor to the development of the other competencies. That is, it seems likely that the development of syntax, morphology, phonology, and lexicon must be under way for a speaker to display discursive, strategic, actional and sociocultural competence. In other words, an understanding of the mechanics of production enables a sense of the relation between the social uses of language and discourse patterns in particular spoken contexts. Second, we could add to this model the critical element of access to communicative events which are essential for the learner to practise and to learn (Norton, 2000; Norton & Toohey, 2001; Savignon, 1991). The data in this study seem to suggest that the combination of these two factors, namely emerging linguistic competence and participation in social communicative exchanges was vital in what we could perhaps label 'communicative confidence'.

In addition to communicative competence and access, I have added embodied cultural capital in the first level of the diagram above. This is a tentative position for Bourdieu's concept, which has to do with other forms of capital, such as skills, physical features, ethnicity, qualifications, and economic and social capital (see Carrington & Luke, 1997). Taking this line of argument, namely that there is an interplay between the development of linguistic skills, access to practise and embodied cultural capital, we can see that for some students who are visibly different, their ethnicity may lead to discrimination and insufficient access to the language interactions which are a necessary condition for learning.

In the second level of the diagram, the elements of audibility and legitimacy focus on the hearer, and the complicity needed between speakers and hearers in interaction. This highlights also the power of the hearer to deny and to devalue the competence of the speaker, along with their embodied capital. Lippi-Green's (1997) language subordination model provides ample evidence that accent, for example, may become a 'litmus test for exclusion' (p. 64), and that in rejecting the spoken words and texts of immigrant students, dominant language users are actually rejecting the identities of the speakers. It is important that mainstream students and teachers learn how to listen to students who are acquiring English, and how to hear above the noise of difference – this remains vital for language acquisition, and for language learners to become audible, with the potential empowerment for all participants that this entails. Taking the mainstream headphones off, as it were, will make space for new voices to emerge, and to be shared. Finally, the diagram defines audibility and legitimacy as the conditions which open up the possibility of self-representation, identity negotiation and ongoing language acquisition. Tied to this is the notion of agency, which is critical to the negotiation of identity (Norton & Toohey, 2001).

The students in this study were at different stages in this move towards representation, and the powerful positionings it conferred. They spoke differently; they were heard differently by me and by others; and their spoken discourse in English was assigned differential values at school. Before moving to the school as an institutional site of representation, I return briefly to how difference is constructed through discourse, to what speakers do, and hearers do.

How Difference is Constructed Through Discourse

In the discussion above, I have focused particularly on the joint participation of speaker and hearer in the discourse, and the move towards self-representation. The students themselves were of course hearers of other speakers, and in some instances, were complicit in constructing these speakers, or themselves, as different. In speaking and listening to them, I was also party to this process of identification with some, and differentiation from others.

Discourse is often used to mark social allegiances or distance. For example, Milena constructed herself through her talk as a mainstream student, differentiating herself from ESL students. She orchestrated her own agendas (and mine) through the medium of English, avoiding participation in the overt practices of the research, which she understood was about 'ESL students'. Similar to another Bosnian student, Neta (see Miller, 1999), Milena spoke of her confidence and participation in what these girls saw as socially normal, positioning themselves inside some categories and outside of others. As hearer, I found it increasingly difficult to think of and talk with these students as ESL students, as this wasn't how they represented themselves. In contrast, Tina and John articulated a sense of isolation from mainstream students and thus from vital language interactions, a sense of their own limitations in speaking English, and a close affiliation with their own ethnic and language group.

All of the Asian students had difficulty in being seen and heard as competent speakers of English, and in moving beyond their first language groups within and outside of school. For these students, visible difference may well have been a factor in their 'othering' at school. Carrie, an Australian university student, recently spoke to me of her perception of Asian students at her former high school and at her university. She put it this way:

> You know the Asian students are there, but you don't acknowledge their presence in any way. You look at them as though they're see-through, and they do the same to you. It's not the same if get to know

one of them, or speak to them. But that hardly ever happens, unless they were born here or speak really good English.

There are many issues within this one quote, the most striking perhaps being the idea of being 'see-through'. Carrie's view was that non-acknowledgement was mutual, but perhaps the Anglo students had more choice. May (2001: 40) observes in regard to the tendency of ethnic groups to stay together, 'Individual and collective choices are circumscribed by the ethnic categories available at any given time and place'. Unlike Milena, who was white, May suggests that Asian and black people have only one ethnic choice available to them, and that different ethnic choices available to minority and majority groups 'are a product of *unequal* power relations in the wider society' (p. 41). Added to the physical difference of Asianness for these students was their silence, and silencing in English. However Riggins (1997: 6) reminds us that 'discourses of Otherness are articulated by both dominant majorities and subordinate minorities'. The point is, whether marginalised or self-marginalising or both, these students had insufficient access to communicative events in English. In what ways did these students themselves construct themselves as different? And how were they seen and heard as different by others?

In Nora's diary there are several discursive categories, in which she sets herself apart from others, but there is also evidence that she is excluded by and through discourse in a number of ways. In the first instance, she includes herself in the ESL group, and specifically the Asian group, the one that is not 'white skin, blond hairs', or 'foreigner'. Rightly or wrongly, at one point she perceives that the teacher discriminates on this basis also, favouring the blond hairs, seeing, hearing and evaluating them differently from her and her friends. The original suggestion that 'black hairs' were treated differently came from Tina. It was Tina also who stressed her Taiwaneseness, emphasising that her social memberships, everyday contexts and language use all centred around being Taiwanese. She had been discouraged by the lack of understanding when she tried to speak English and, like John, had virtually given up trying. It was through the discourses and practices of mainstream English and Geography classes that she came to work in English-speaking groups, and to see herself for the first time as part of a team not referenced by her ethnicity or first language.

It has been suggested that the ways members of an ethnic group speak to each other are 'related to their position in society, and how they are spoken to and spoken about by dominant group members' (van Dijk *et al.*, 1997). Categorisation and representation of the Other are therefore subtly shaped by others' representations. The construction of discrimination on the basis of visible difference by Tina and Nora is a case in point. This is how they thought they were seen. Once again, their marginalisation, whether partially self-imposed or imposed by others, had serious consequences for their English language development (Miller, 2000) and therefore for their ability to participate in and to succeed in mainstream society.

Nora offered the example of how she was once excluded from social interaction by Alicia's use of Cantonese, at which point Nora really had nowhere to go. Nora's linguistic exclusion by her friend was an instance of what clearly happens to ESL students every day on a much larger scale – namely their exclusion, intentional or otherwise, from social interactions involving groups of mainstream speakers of English. Several of the students claimed that Anglo-Australian students simply didn't talk to them, which was one way they represented the social order of the school. John and Tina and other students stated that Australian students were not available to them as partners in talk or social interaction, or as friends (see also Miller, 1999, 2000). At the time of writing, more than five years after our first meeting, Nora and Alicia still don't have any English-speaking friends.

The exclusion of Tina, John, Alicia, and Nora from mainstream groups was both socially and linguistically consequential for them. Projecting forward, there are also serious economic consequences. The lack of outside opportunities to use English meant that these students were operating in what was basically a modified EFL or foreign language environment. Savignon (1991) is unequivocal in her claim that language learning results from participation in communicative events. How are students to acquire the majority language if they cannot participate in personal interactions with its speakers at school? This is a problem in many western countries with large numbers of immigrant students. Gumperz (1996) reminds us that for most South Asian migrants in the UK there are few opportunities for direct interaction with native speakers of English, or 'in-depth conversational involvement in the conditions of equality most conducive to learning' (p. 378). This was also the case at several high schools I visited.

What is difficult to resolve is whether the Chinese students in this study stayed together through choice or as a response to what they perceived as imposed marginalisation, or to a *status quo* where segregation was normalised in the social order of the school. Often unable to represent themselves through the use of English, their Chinese identities and language seemed an obvious resource for them to maintain social memberships and to represent their identities. In addition to the purpose of maintaining meaningful social relationships, Goldstein (1997) also argues that students function in their first language for the academic support it provides, whereby students collaboratively work out difficult concepts and monitor both their understanding and their results (see also Cummins, 2000). While this is of obvious benefit to students in many subjects, this study shows that the Asian students had insufficient ongoing English language support to succeed in many mainstream tasks, along with inadequate opportunities to speak with dominant language groups. Because access to mainstream discourses and communicative events is tied to issues of power and dominance, as well as to racialising practices (van Dijk, 1996), it is important to look now at ways in which institutional practices frame linguistic minority groups as different, thereby excluding them from full participation in their education.

Institutional Practices in the Representation and Marginalisation of Linguistic Minority Students

Ideology entails a set of representations, views, practices and discourses that are associated with particular symbolic values, and with differential positions of power within society or any institution (Bourdieu, 1991). In analysing the ideological function of discourse, we need to look at how texts are interpreted and received (Fairclough & Wodak, 1997). This largely has to do with what Bourdieu (1993) has specified as the combined effects of linguistic competence, status, power and values assigned to particular types of texts on the linguistic market. In Bourdieu's terms, 'One of the political effects of the dominant language is this: "He says it so well it must be true"' (p. 66). The manner of discourse thus determines the acceptability of the discourse. As a consequence of this understanding, many discourse analysts posit a hierarchy of meaning, whereby any voice from the dominant group appears to speak true, whereas subordinated voices are heard as partial or distorted accounts (Riggins, 1997). How are high schools implicated in this process?

For several students in this study, the move to high school from the Newnham reception programme was difficult. For these students, high schools were not places where you met new friends as Nora had so fervently hoped, but places where you were physically and socially isolated within the ESL unit; realised you didn't speak properly; had to catch up with the others; felt lost; didn't understand the tests, the texts, or the assemblies; and had to rely on L1 friends for all social interaction. As ESL students within the high school, the students encountered a range of micro-contexts, and systems of values and practices subtly different from those at Newnham, a school purpose-built and organised to cater to the needs of NESB students. Where these students were at the centre of the social field of Newnham, they found themselves in many ways at the margins of the mainstream high schools.

To better understand this, it is useful to look at some of the representations of such students occurring within high schools, representations which are not ideology free, but impose specific positionings on linguistic minority speakers. In what follows, I address three themes related to these positionings. They are: (1) the assumed assimilation to an abstract standard of school English; (2) the practice of devaluing the linguistic resources of NESB students; and (3) the need to move beyond inadequate labels to describe such students.

Competing with fictional norms

In Gee's (1996) analysis of children's oral narratives, he draws strong contrasts between what is deemed appropriate and successful in terms of school language and what is not. There is considerable evidence in the literature that texts valued by school encompass discourses which require students to reproduce 'particular forms of cultural logic and social identity under the guise of the transmission of neutral skills and techniques of authorship' (Luke, 1995–6: 33; see also Heller, 1994). Central to these neutral skills and techniques are expository genres and grammatical accuracy, although as Bourdieu (1993) stresses, grammar determines meaning only partially. The example of Nora's diary text in Chapter 6 is neither 'admissible' nor valued in this sense. In fact at high school, there is little call for the type of text which Nora does best, namely the dramatic and creative narratives which fill her journal, everyday stories which as Gee (1996: 103) suggests 'often make "deep sense" in quite literary ways'. Instead, she finds at school what Rampton (1995) has described as the institutionalisation of 'a fictional norm of perfect monolingual competence against which the abilities of bilinguals are measured'. For linguistic minority students, such competence may be both liberator and weapon.

Rampton (1987) warned of the problems associated with remaining focused on the space between a speaker and his/her grammar, yet this focus seems intrinsic to the experience of ESL students at school, as evidenced by numerous students in the study. Alicia, Tina, and Milena all stated that 'words' were their main problem, with Milena adding that her grammar was also a big problem. Grammar was certainly the underlying concern of Milena's teacher who said Milena 'wasn't as good as she thought she was', and of the teachers of Nora and Alicia, who found their writing 'all back to front, twisted and unmarkable'. 'Oh my god where do I start?' bemoaned another teacher, 'If I fix it and make it perfect it's no longer theirs'. Cummins (2000: 251) also observes that for many teachers, 'it is the ESL student who requires "fixing" through more intensive and extensive ESL instruction', a belief which obviates the need to interrogate broader systemic problems in schools. The mournful threnodic tone adopted by some teachers I met to talk about ESL students' writing seemed quite misplaced as I reread Nora's diary, or Milena's essays. Furthermore, on oral tasks the primary model was invariably the grammar of written English, as found by Carter and McCarthy (1995: 210), in which the spontaneous, interactive and informal elements of speaking were actively discouraged by the insistence on a complete written draft of the talk. Within the formal perspective on language widely attended to in SLA research, Kelly Hall (1995: 210) suggests that 'genres are perceived as ideal models or fixed types of language use, while performances are treated as mere, and usually flawed, instantiations of these idealized models'. This was a problem for all students in this study.

Some teachers of these students seemed to be operating from a position of firm belief in a standard English and its forms, unaware that for these students, who in some cases had been in Australia less than a year, they were raising the linguistic high jump bar to a level the students could never clear. At the same time, some students received inadequate support from mainstream teachers to complete tasks that were set. John was given tests he could not read and workbooks he could not work in. Nora was given no help from the teacher on her government instrumentalities worksheet which was set for homework as a prelude to an in-class test. It has been argued that schools have a moral responsibility to provide conditions which challenge the marginalisation of minority groups (Auerbach, 1995). From a curriculum standpoint, this entails embedding English activities in activities which connect the students to their own linguistic and cultural backgrounds wherever possible, and scaffolding tasks to support learning.

I have tried to provide some insight into the types of texts valued by teachers and schools, and the problems this poses for ESL students. Ongoing language support is one condition needed to redress these problems. But schools also need to validate what students already know and bring to learning. Valuing and validating this knowledge and competence would immediately add to the symbolic capital of these students.

English 1, other languages 0

From Bourdieu it is clear that authority and power derive from the linguistic habitus, and that particular types of symbolic capital are rewarded on the school linguistic market. Alongside the asymmetrical value assigned to various discourses within institutions, in a practical sense, different languages are valued differently (see Miller, in press). In the 1990s in Queensland there was the anomalous situation whereby policy in foreign language education laid enormous stress on the study of Asian languages by Anglo-Australian students, without mentioning the resources, potential and value of the already present native speakers of these languages. In the rhetoric of foreign language education, Asian languages were an economic priority, but on the level of practice, thousands of speakers of Asian languages seemingly accrued no symbolic capital. Native speakers of these 'priority languages' remain unheard in the official discourses of schools, discourses which implicitly equate educational opportunity with English language proficiency, thereby placing the full burden on the immigrant student to adjust to the conditions present in schools.

Although taught in some schools, Mandarin was not part of the foreign language curriculum in Nora and Alicia's school. They were instead put into a Japanese class (shades of Kan and Hank in Chapter 1 – *So are ya Chinese or Japanese?*). It seemed an utter irrelevance to the school that these girls were already multilingual. Nora spoke Mandarin, Shanghainese, and English, and also understood some Cantonese. Alicia spoke Cantonese, Mandarin and English. In other cases, Milena spoke Bosnian, Danish and English. John spoke Cantonese, Mandarin and some English. Several students in this study were already competent bilinguals before they began learning English. In all schools I visited, a degree of lip service was paid to the value of multiculturalism, but at the Markwell High multicultural concert, no language but English was used in presenting the items and representing the diverse body of students. Multiculturalism here was about singing and dancing, but not actually speaking out loud. Recent research stresses that schools need to take the relation between language and identity much more seriously (Cummins, 2000; Norton, 1997; Pavlenko & Blackledge, in press). Schools need to understand that language use is not neutral but implicated in unequal sets of social relations. The ramifications of this extend of course well beyond schools. A key ideological issue here concerns how the students were read and heard by others. Nora's letter was not viewed as out-of-the-ordinary by the teacher, who merely told her not to be concerned about her bad mark, as the test didn't count for much (secret teacher knowledge?). And texts such as those in Nora's diary are not normally affiliated with cultural capital, particularly in the context of school. The denigration of students' writing is implicated in normalising the exclusion of such texts from school discourses. Yet the power of Nora's narratives provides insight into her experience of learning and using English, her experience of school, and her positioning in what she perceives as the social order around her. These deserve to be more widely read and understood, as such autobiographical narratives convey an understanding of the representational resources and contexts of minority students. Such texts and the students' own languages are minority discourses, which are and remain outside of the official discourses of school. For that reason alone they are worthy objects of ongoing analysis and research.

There is a substantial literature using discourse analysis to reveal how certain texts marginalise minority groups, and how discourse is implicated in the production and reproduction of racism. Less often reported are the ways in which the texts of minorities simply lack representation within dominant discourses. When a language is either stigmatised or ignored, this amounts to what Mey (1985: 351) suggests is 'linguistic oppression', which takes place whenever people are 'denied the right to language'. There seems a dual denial which operates in some schools and for some students, in that the first languages of the students have no value or legitimacy, and there is inadequate support in academic work for them to learn 'school English', along with inadequate opportunity for interpersonal social relations for them to improve their communicative and social competences. Instead they are confronted with 'preferred models' of communication, to which they do not have access. Hymes (1996) points out that such preferred forms are shaped by cultural values and social hierarchies, and are inconsistent from one institution to the next. We tolerate, for example, anomalous language forms in certain domains, such as phonetic spelling in advertising, or song lyrics with non-standard grammars. On the linguistic market of schools, such forms have no legitimacy. It is not just English which is privileged, but specific forms and genres of English.

Trueba (1989) makes it clear that schools need to value what linguistic minority students bring with them. He writes,

> Psychological adjustment, cultural integration into the school, acquisition of communicative skills, and academic achievement are critically linked to opportunities given to students for using their previous sociocultural experiences and knowledge. (Trueba, 1989: 183)

This includes their language knowledge, which is critically tied to identity work. As Cummins and Swain (1986) point out, where the first language of the student goes unrecognised, untapped and undeveloped, and where proficiency in English is or remains very limited, identity work in the public arena is at risk. Cummins (1996, 2000) continues to strenuously argue the link between bilingual development and continued development in the L1. While this may not be feasible in many schools, due to the diversity of languages spoken, it is vital to understand that presently within many classrooms, students are often positioned in ways that recast and undercut their intellectual and linguistic resources, and devalue their identities. Cummins (2000) points out that in the face of the linguistic diversity now present in schools, effective instruction must be linked overtly to the negotiation of identity in classrooms, to 'the ways the students view themselves', and to the future options and identity choices for students. This is critical to what he calls 'transformative pedagogy'.

Beyond the limitations of labels

Although schools in Australia and those within them routinely label linguistic minority students as ESL students, it is clear that for many immigrant students, English is in fact their third or fourth language. The term NESB student (non-English speaking background) is also a definition of the student in terms of what they are not, diminishing their linguistic and cultural backgrounds. While these terms are at times useful in a practical sense, neither does justice to the knowledge and social and cultural competences of these students. Pennycook (2001: 145) also observes that labels in the TESOL field generally tend to be 'deeply Othering'. Gibbons' (1991) suggestion that *emergent bilingual* is a more appropriate term than ESL or NESB student amounts to a recognition of this problem. This term ascribes the competence of bilingualism rather than pinpointing what the students may currently be lacking, in spite of being somewhat 'clunky'. Recent definitions of bilingualism stress simply some functional ability in a second language (Spolsky, 1998), without trying to pin down the degree of bilingualism. The term *emergent bilingual* also allows us to envision many Australian students as 'emergent monolinguals', turning the tables, and signalling in a new way the problem of hegemony.

It has also been suggested that labels signal an institutional discourse which is implicated in special pathways or language development courses which 'simultaneously enable and stigmatise learners' (Thesen, 1997: 490). To rename these students as bilingual may well be productive in bringing about a shift in perception which assigns new symbolic capital to these students. That is, there is a need to reinscribe linguistic minority students as competent in a variety of ways, and to place a positive value on these competences. Students such as Alicia and Nora switched between Mandarin and Cantonese, dived into Chinese electronic dictionaries, gave oral presentations and wrote journals in English, and worked hard to succeed in the mainstream. These were in my view extraordinary displays of linguistic competence, deserving of wider acknowledgment within the social, curriculum and pedagogical practices of schools. It is worth noting that recent work on critical or tranformative pedagogy as outlined by Cummins (2000), McLaren (1994) and Pennycook (2001) stresses the fundamental importance of valuing what linguistic minority students bring to class (see also Goldstein, 2003).

Within the institution of school as a social field, the conditions of reception often work against a hearing for minority speakers. Schools must be aware that where English-speaking students do not talk, or even try to talk to linguistic minority students, discriminatory and racialising practices are implicated. It is a case where silence speaks volumes to the acceptance of segregated school communities, and the denial to one group of the right to participate fully. To claim or to accept that Asian students for example marginalise themselves is part of a dominant institutional discourse, as van Dijk (1996: 91) makes clear. He writes,

> One strategy of such dominant discourse is to persuasively define the ethnic status quo as 'natural', 'just', 'inevitable' or even as 'democratic', for instance through denials of discrimination or racism, or by deracialising inequality through redefinitions in terms of class, cultural difference or the special (unique, temporary) consequences of immigrant status.

While students cannot be forced to mix (Ryan, 1997), there are sound reasons for drawing such understandings to the attention of _all_ students, along with an awareness of the consequences of certain groups remaining socially and linguistically unheard and separate in schools. One consequence is of course that _everybody_ loses.

Because even small and apparently inconsequential interactions help trace how the world is socially constructed, and are an index to social and cultural understandings, everyday interactions are part of the _doing_ of social identity (Moerman, 1993). These interactions are essential for the acquisition of discourse and sociocultural rules, and the building of what Kelly Hall (1995: 208) describes as 'interactive resources'. This applies equally to Anglo-Australian students as it does to immigrant students, but linguistic minority speakers need the chance to acquire proficiency and confidence in using English (Norton, 2000; Norton & Toohey, 2001; Sharkey & Layzer, 2000). Second, access to a range of communicative and social roles is access to social power (van Dijk, 1996), its converse being equally true. The effective marginalisation of linguistic minority students poses a risk to all members of the school community, which Cummins (1996) has suggested can only be challenged by the affirmation not of difference, but of diversity, in which the negotiation of identity is a key. This entails a shift in perception in relation to the identity of linguistic minority students. Instead of viewing students who have lived on two continents and speak three languages as having a language problem, Cummins' proposed affirmation of diversity reframes these students as competent and productive members of the school community, which can only benefit from their inclusion as members. Ironically, within _foreign_ language policy and rhetoric in Australia, monolingual students are the problem. But there is a world of difference between rhetoric and practice. Perhaps it is schools as institutions which have the language problem, an inability to listen to or hear varieties of English which lie outside that defined as the valued norm, and to allow language learners the traditional Australian 'fair go'.

Conclusion

While writing this final chapter, I took time out to attend an assembly at Newnham High to mark the exit of two classes moving to high school, and to acknowledge their achievements in the reception programme. The exiting students were to perform a presentation to their teachers and 160 peers, some of whom had just arrived in Australia and at Newnham. The assembly began with a short performance by an Aboriginal community member, who played the didgeridoo and then donated the hand-painted instrument to the school. At Newnham, reconciliation and the study of indigenous peoples are a strong focus in the curriculum. The exiting students then performed, presenting posters of their 'life images' in small groups and pairs, outlining their dreams and aspirations, their problems and strengths. They performed in English, using a microphone, and then summarised the talk in their first languages. I was part of an audience which sat in rapt attention, listening to English, Bosnian, Vietnamese, Mandarin, Tagalog, Indonesian, Samoan and Somali. I was part of an audience which saw and heard this as utterly unremarkable in terms of its linguistic plurality. Here was a performance, and a *hearing* which accorded respect and value to the speaking of many languages. The Newnham assembly finished with a large group of former Yugoslavian students, a united group of Bosnians, Serbs and Croatian students, singing *Twist and Shout* in Bosnian. The audience clapped along.

Social identity, and the integration of language learners with language learning contexts have seldom been on the agenda of researchers working within SLA (Norton Peirce, 1995, Pennycook, 2001). Pennycook suggests that mainstream SLA research 'has had virtually nothing to say about learners as people, or contexts of learning, or the politics of language learning more generally' (p. 144). I have tried through these case studies to portray these students as people within specific school contexts, using both SLA and social theory to analyse the data. I began this chapter talking about acquisition, communicative competence, audibility, identity and representation. I then talked about institutional conditions surrounding the acquisition and use of English, and ways in which English and other languages are heard. The discussion of these conditions constitutes in effect a changed vision of what the 'language acquisition' problem is, and a move into new terrain, marked by the empirical and epistemological understanding that to talk about SLA without talking about identity and representation, is to miss aspects of the utmost salience to the acquisition of discourses in a new language, and to ignore the power of conditions of reception over spoken production.

Norton Peirce, Rampton, Kelly Hall, Pavlenko, Goldstein and others have already moved into this terrain. I have attempted here to relate spoken language acquisition and use to specific social fields and practices, and to represent some of the complexities of this interrelationship through the cases of these immigrant students. The study has been in one sense an attempt to bridge the gap between macro theoretical analyses of language and power, and the micro realisation of some of these theories in interactions with and of immigrant students. Further, I have tried to frame the interrelationship of language user and social field critically, highlighting what could be described as the politics of speaking and hearing.

The theoretical contribution of this study is that an economy of reception within any social field impacts powerfully on the conditions of production for linguistic minority students. The accounts by and phenomena surrounding the students highlight that to be a social user of language is to take part in the shadowy game of dominance and submission, the rules of which are rarely consciously acknowledged or even understood. While some maintain that positions of subordination and dominance for linguistic minority students are not final, and an understanding of identity as an ever evolving and transforming resource would seem to support this, educators need to be cognisant of the fact that diminishing or ignoring the voices of linguistic minority students is essentially a racialising act which denies valuable experiences to all students.

It is important to understand and to acknowledge that speakers are heard differently across a range of social fields, resulting in serious power differentials for those who sound and look different. Institutional practices which are complicit in the inaudibilility or the invisibility of immigrant speakers as they acquire and use English deny these students their simple right to be heard. Hearing and acknowledging these speakers opens up for them the possibilities of self-representation and ongoing identity work in their new schools and communities. For the hearers, the focus on reception opens up a terrain where diversity may be heard as normal and valuable, as at the Newnham concert, where the headphones are off, and responsibility for communication consciously shared.

References

Antaki, C. and Widdicombe, S. (eds) (1998) *Identities in Talk*. London: Sage.

Antaki, C. (1996) Social identities in talk: Speaker's own orientations. *British Journal of Social Psychology* 35, 473–492.

Auerbach, E. (1995) The politics of the ESL classroom: Issues of power in pedagogical choices. In J.W. Tollefson (ed.) *Power and Inequality in Language Education* (pp. 9–33). Cambridge: Cambridge University Press.

Australian Bureau of Statistics (1996) *Migration*. Canberra: ABS.

Baker, C. (1982) The adolescent as theorist: An interpretive view. *Journal of Youth and Adolescence* 11 (3), 167–181.

Baker, C. (1997) Membership categorisation and interview accounts. In D. Silverman (ed.) *Qualitative Research: Theory, Method and Practice* (pp. 130–143). London: Sage.

Baker, C. and Freebody, P. (1993) The crediting of literate competence in classroom talk. *Australian Journal of Language and Literacy* 16, 279–294.

Baker, C. and Luke, A. (eds) (1991) *Towards a Critical Sociology of Reading Pedagogy: Papers of the XII World Congress on Reading*. Amsterdam: John Benjamins.

Beardsmore, H. (1993) European models of bilingual education: Practice, theory and development. *Journal of Multilingual and Multicultural Development* 14, 103–120.

Bottomly, G. (1997) Identification: Ethnicity, gender and culture. *Journal of Intercultural Studies* 18, 41–48.

Bourdieu, P. (1977a) *Outline of a Theory of Practice*. Cambridge: Cambridge University Press.

Bourdieu, P. (1977b) The economics of linguistic exchanges. *Social Science Information* 16, 645–668.

Bourdieu, P. (1984) *Questions de Sociologie*. Paris: Les Editions de Minuit.

Bourdieu, P. (1991) *Language and Symbolic Power*. Oxford: Polity Press.

Bourdieu, P. (1993) *Sociology in Question*. London: Sage.

Brown, H.D. (1987) *Principles of Language Learning and Teaching*. New Jersey: Prentice Hall.

Caldas-Coulthard, C.R. and Coulthard, M. (eds) (1996) *Texts and Practices: Readings in Critical Discourse Analysis*. London: Routledge.

Canale, M. (1983) From communicative competence to communicative language pedagogy. In J. Richards and R. Schmidt (eds) *Language and Communication* (pp. 2–27). London: Longman.

Carrington, V. and Luke, A. (1997) Literacy and Bourdieu's sociological theory: A reframing. *Language and Education* 11, 96–112.

Carter, R. and McCarthy, M. (1995) Grammar and spoken language. *Applied Linguistics* 16, 141–157.

Castles, S., Cope, B., Kalantzis, M. and Morrissey, M. (1992) *Mistaken Identity:*

Multiculturalism and the Demise of Nationalism in Australia (3rd edn). Sydney: Pluto Press.

Cazden, C. (1993) Vygotsky, Hymes, and Bakhtin: From word to utterance and voice. In E. Forman, N. Minick and C.A. Stone (eds) *Contexts for Learning* (pp. 197–212). Oxford: Oxford University Press.

Celce-Murcia, M., Dörnyei, Z. and Thurrell, S. (1995) Communicative competence: A pedagogically motivated model with content specifications. *Issues in Applied Linguistics* 6, 5–35.

Clyne, M. (2003, January) Language and freedom or imprisonment. Plenary session at the Australian Council of TESOL Associations National Conference, Sydney.

Collier, V. (1989) How long? A synthesis of research on academic achievement in a second language. *TESOL Quarterly* 23, 509–531.

Cook, V. (1991) *Second Language Learning and Language Teaching*. London: Edward Arnold.

Cook, V. (1993) *Linguistics and Second Language Acquisition*. New York: St Martin's Press.

Cummins, J. (1984) *Bilingualism and Special Education: Issues in Assessment and Pedagogy*. Clevedon: Multilingual Matters.

Cummins, J. (1992) Language proficiency, bilingualism and academic achievement. In P.A. Richard-Amato and M.A. Snow (eds) *The Multicultural Classroom* (pp. 16–26). New York: Longman.

Cummins, J. (1995) Discursive power in educational policy and practice for culturally diverse students. In D. Corson (ed.) *Discourse and Power in Educational Organisations* (pp. 191–213). Cresskill, NJ: Hampton Press.

Cummins, J. (1996) *Negotiating Identities: Education For Empowerment in a Diverse Society*. Ontario: California Association for Bilingual Education.

Cummins, J. (2000) *Language, Power and Pedagogy: Bilingual Children in the Crossfire*. Clevedon: Multilingual Matters.

Cummins, J. and Swain, M. (1986) *Bilingualism in Education*. London: Longman.

Davies, A. (1991) *The Native Speaker in Applied Linguistics*. Edinburgh: Edinburgh University Press.

Doughty, C. and Williams, J. (1998) *Focus on Form in Second Language Acquisition*. Cambridge: Cambridge University Press.

Drake, S. and Ryan, J. (1994) Narrative and knowing: Inclusive pedagogy in contemporary times. *Curriculum and Teaching* 9, 45–56.

Edelsky, C. (1991) *With Literacy and Justice For All: Rethinking the Social in Language and Education*. London: The Falmer Press.

Ellis, R. (1994) *The Study of Second Language Acquisition*. Oxford: Oxford University Press.

Fairclough, N. and Wodak, R. (1997) Critical Discourse Analysis. In T. van Dijk (ed.) *Discourse as Social Interaction* (pp. 231–257). London: Sage.

Fairclough, N. (1989) *Language and Power*. London: Longman.

Fine, J. (ed.) (1988) *Second Language Discourse: A Textbook of Current Research*. Series Advances in Discourse Processes Vol. XXV. Norwood, NJ: Ablex Publishing Corporation.

Firth, A. and Wagner, J. (1997) On discourse, communication, and (some) fundamental concepts in SLA research. *Modern Language Journal* 81, 285–300.

Firth, A. (1996) The discursive accomplishment of normality: On 'lingua franca' English and conversation analysis. *Journal of Pragmatics* 26, 237–259.

Freebody, P. and Luke, A. (1990) 'Literacies' programs: Debates and demands in cultural context. *Prospect* 5, 7–16.

Freebody, P. (1990, January) Inventing cultural-capitalist distinctions in the assessment of HSC papers: Coping with inflation in an era of 'literacy crisis'. Paper presented at the Inaugural Australian Systemics Conference on Literacy in Social Processes. Deakin University, Geelong.

Freeman, R. (1995) Equal educational opportunity for language minority students: From policy to practice at Oyster Bilingual School. *Issues in Applied Linguistics* 6, 39–63.

Gee, J.P. (1996) *Social Linguistics and Literacies: Ideologies in Discourses* (2nd edn). London: Taylor and Francis.

Gibbons, P. (1991) *Learning to Learn in a Second Language.* NSW: Primary English Teaching Association.

Giddens, A. (1991) *Modernity and Self-Identity: Self and Society in the Late Modern Age.* Cambridge: Polity Press.

Giles, H. and Johnson, P. (1981) The role of language in ethnic group formation. In J.C. Turner and H. Giles (eds) *Intergroup Behaviour* (pp. 199–243). Oxford: Basil Blackwell.

Giroux, H. (1990) *Curriculum Discourse and Postmodernist Critical Practice.* Geelong: Deakin University Press.

Giroux, H. (1992) Resisting difference: Cultural studies and the discourse of critical pedagogy. In L. Grossberg, C. Nelson and P. Treichler (eds) *Cultural Studies* (pp. 199–212). New York: Routledge.

Glesne, C. and Peshkin, A. (1992) *Becoming Qualitative Researchers: An Introduction.* New York: Longman.

Goldstein, T. (1997) Bilingual life in a multilingual high school classroom: Teaching and learning in Cantonese and English. *Canadian Modern Language Review* 53, 115–124.

Goldstein, T. (2003) *Teaching and Learning in a Multilingual School: Choices, Risks and Dilemmas.* Mahwah, NJ: Lawrence Erlbaum.

Grundy, S. (1994) Being and becoming an Australian: Classroom discourse and the construction of identity. *Discourse* 15, 16–31.

Gubrium, J. and Holstein, J. (1997) *The New Language of Qualitative Method.* New York: Oxford.

Guiora, A., Brannon, R. and Dull, C. (1972) Empathy and second language learning. *Language Learning* 22, 111–130.

Gumperz, J. (1996) The linguistic and cultural relativity of conversational inference. In J. Gumperz and S. Levinson (eds) *Rethinking Linguistic Relativity* (pp. 374–406). Cambridge: Cambridge University Press.

Gumperz, J. and Hymes, D. (1986) *Directions in Sociolinguistics* (2nd edn). Oxford: Basil Blackwell.

Hall, S. (1996) Introduction: Who needs identity? In S. Hall and P. du Gay (eds) *Questions of Cultural Identity* (pp. 1–17). London: Sage.

Hall, S. and du Gay, P. (eds) (1996) *Questions of Cultural Identity.* London: Sage.

Hammersley, M. (1992) *What's Wrong With Ethnography? Methodological Explorations.* London: Routledge.

Heller, M. (1987) The role of language in the formation of ethnic identity. In J. Phinney and M. Rotheram (eds) *Children's Ethnic Socialization* (pp. 180–200). Newbury Park, CA: Sage.

Heller, M. (1994) *Crosswords: Language, Education and Ethnicity in French Ontario.* Berlin and New York: Mouton de Gruyter.

Hornberger, N. (1995) Ethnography in linguistic perspective: Understanding school processes. *Language and Education* 9, 233–248.

Hughes, R. (1997, May 24-5) The cult of identity. *The Weekend Australian* (p. 3).

Hutchby, I. and Wooffitt, R. (1998) *Principles, Practices and Applications.* Malden, MA: Polity Press.

Hymes, D. (1996) *Ethnography, Linguistics, Narrative Inequality: Toward an Understanding of Voice.* London: Taylor and Francis.

Jenkins, R. (1992) *Pierre Bourdieu.* London: Routledge.

Johnson-Powell, G. (1996) Alice's little sister: The self concealed behind the self. In B. Thompson and S. Tyagi (eds) *Names We Call Home: Autobiography on Racial Identity* (pp. 53–61). New York: Routledge.

Kalantzis, M. (1997) The mainstream, wedge politics and the revival of xenophobia: What future for multicultural education? *TESOL in Context* 7, 5–12.

Kalantzis, M. *et al.* (1990) *Cultures of Schooling.* London: Falmer Press.

Kaspar, G. (1997) 'A' stands for acquisition: A response to Firth and Wagner. *The Modern Language Journal* 81, 307–312.

Kelly Hall, J. (1995) (Re)creating our world with words: A sociohistorical perspective of face-to-face interaction. *Applied Linguistics* 16, 206–232.

komninos (1991) *Komninos.* St Lucia: University of Queensland Press.

Krashen, S. (1978) The monitor model for second-language acquisition. In R.C. Gingras (ed.) *Second Language Acquisition and Foreign Language Teaching* (pp. 1–26). Arlington, VA: Center for Applied Linguistics.

Krashen, S. (1981) *Second Language Acquisition and Second Language Learning.* Oxford: Pergamon.

Labov, W. (1972) *Language in the Inner City.* Philadelphia: University of Pennsylvania Press.

Lantolf, J. (ed.) (2000) *Sociocultural Theory and Second Language Learning.* Oxford: Oxford University Press.

Le Page, R. and Tabouret-Keller, A. (1985) *Acts of Identity: Creole-based Approaches to Language and Ethnicity.* Cambridge, MA: Cambridge University Press.

Létourneau, J. (1997) The current great narrative of Québecois identity. In V.Y. Mudimbe (ed.) *Nations, Identities, Cultures* (pp. 59–74). Durham and London: Duke University Press.

Leung, C., Harris, R. and Rampton, B. (1997) The idealised native speaker, reified ethnicities, and classroom realities. *TESOL Quarterly* 31, 543–560.

Lightbown, P.M. and Spada, N. (1999) *How Languages are Learned.* Oxford: Oxford University Press.

Lippi-Green, R. (1997) *English With an Accent: Language, Ideology and Discrimination in the United States.* London: Routledge.

Lo Bianco, J. (1987) *National Policy on Languages.* Canberra: Australian Government Publishing Service.

Lo Bianco, J. (1997) English and pluralistic policies: The case of Australia. In W. Eggington and H. Wren (eds) *Language Policy: Dominant English, Pluralist Challenges* (pp. 107–120). Canberra: John Benjamins B.V. and Language Australia Ltd.

Lo Bianco, J. (1998) Literacy, citizenship and multiculturalism. *TESOL in Context* 8, 3–6.

Lo Bianco, J. (1998a, 30 March) Looking back to the future: The ESL agenda in Australia. Lecture to the Queensland TESOL Association, Brisbane.

Lo Bianco, J. (2002) Keynote address at Australian Council of TESOL Association National Conference, Adelaide.

Luke, A. (1992) The body literate: Discourse and inscription in early literacy training. *Linguistics and Education* 4, 107–129.

Luke, A. (1995–6) Text and discourse in education: An introduction to critical discourse analysis. In M. Apple (ed.) *Review of Research in Education 21* (pp. 3–48). Washington: American Educational Research Association.

Luke, A. (1998) Critical discourse analysis. In L. Saha (ed.) *International Encyclopedia of the Sociology of Education* (pp. 50–57). New York: Elsevier Science.

Luke, A., McHoul, A. and Mey, J. (1990) On the limits of language planning: Class, state and power. In R. Baldauf Jr and A. Luke (eds) *Language Planning and Education in Australasia and the South Pacific* (pp. 25–44). Clevedon: Multilingual Matters.

Luke, C. and Luke, A. (1998) Interethnic families: Difference within difference. *Ethnic and Racial Studies* 21, 728–753.

May, S. (2001) *Language and Minority Rights: Ethnicity, Nationalism and the Politics of Language*. Harlow, UK: Longman.

McKay, P. (1995) Developing ESL profiency descriptions for the school context: The NLLIA bandscales. In G. Brindley (ed.) *Language Assessment in Action*. Sydney: NCELTR.

McKay, P. (1999) *The Literacy Benchmarks and ESL*. ACTA Background Papers No. 2.

McKay, S.L. and Wong, S.C. (1996) Multiple discourses, multiple identities: Investment and agency in second language learning among Chinese adolescent immigrant students. *Harvard Educational Review* 3, 577–608.

McLaren, P. (1994) *Life in Schools*. New York: Longman.

McLeod, J. and Yates, L. (1997) Can we find out about girls and boys today – or must we settle for just talking about ourselves? Dilemmas of a feminist, qualitative, longitudinal research project. *Australian Educational Researcher* 24, 21–42.

McNamara, T. (1997) Theorizing social identity. *TESOL Quarterly* 31, 561–567.

McRobbie, A. (1996) Different youthful subjectivities. In I. Chambers and L. Curti (eds) *The Post-Colonial Question: Common Skies, Divided Horizons* (pp. 30–46). London: Routledge.

Merriam, S. (1998) *Case Study Research in Education*. San Francisco: Jossey-Bass.

Mey, J. (1985) *Whose Language? A Study in Linguistic Pragmatics*. Amsterdam/ Philadelphia: John Benjamins.

Miller, J. (1997) Reframing methodology in second language research: From language to discourse. *Australian Educational Researcher* 24, 43–56.

Miller, J. (1999) Becoming audible: Social identity and second language use. *Journal of Intercultural Studies* 20, 149–165.

Miller, J. (2000) Language use, identity and social interaction: Migrant students in Australia. *Research on Language and Social Interaction* 33, 69–11.

Miller, J. (in press) Identity and language use: The politics of speaking in schools. In A. Pavlenko and A. Blackledge (eds) *Negotiation of Identity in Multilingual Contexts*. Clevedon: Multilingual Matters.

Moerman, M. (1993) Ariadne's thread and Indra's net: Reflections on ethnography, ethnicity, identity, culture and interaction. *Research on Language and Social Interaction* 26, 85–98.

Moerman, M. (1996) The field of analysing foreign language conversations. *Journal of Pragmatics* 26, 147–158.

Morley, D. and Chen, K. (eds) (1996) *Stuart Hall: Critical Dialogues in Cultural Studies*. London: Routledge.

Nash, R. (1990) Bourdieu on education and social and cultural reproduction. *British Journal of Sociology of Education* 11, 431–447.

Nation, P. (1998) Vocabulary learning from input. In *Challenge in Change*, Occasional Papers from the 5th Biennial QATESOL Conference, Brisbane.

Nelson, C., Treichler, P. and Grossberg, L. (1992) Cultural studies: An introduction. In L. Grossberg, C. Nelson and P. Treichler (eds) *Cultural Studies* (pp. 1–16). New York: Routledge.

Norton Peirce, B. (1995) Social identity, investment, and language learning. *TESOL Quarterly* 29, 9–32.

Norton, B. (1997) Language, identity and the ownership of English. *TESOL Quarterly* 31, 409–429.

Norton, B. (2000) *Identity and Language Learning: Gender, Ethnicity and Educational Change*. Harlow: Longman/Pearson Education.

Norton, B. and Toohey, K. (2001) Changing perspectives on good language learners. *TESOL Quarterly* 35, 307–322.

Nunan, D. (1995) Closing the gap between learning and instruction. *TESOL Quarterly* 29, 133–158.

O'Malley, J.M. and Chamot, A.U. (1990) *Learning Strategies in Second Language Acquisition*. Cambridge: Cambridge University Press.

Ozolins, U. (1993) *The Politics of Language in Australia*. Cambridge: Cambridge University Press.

Partington, G. and McCudden, V. (1992) *Ethnicity and Education*. Wentworth Falls, NSW: Social Science Press.

Pavlenko, A. and Lantolf, J. (2000) Second language learning as participation and the (re)construction of selves. In J. Lantolf (ed.) *Sociocultural Theory and Second Language Learning* (pp. 155–177). Oxford: Oxford University Press.

Pavlenko A. and Blackledge, A. (eds) (in press) *Negotiation of Identities in Multilingual Contexts*. Clevedon: Multilingual Matters.

Pennycook, A. (2001) *Critical Applied Linguistics: A Critical Introduction*. New Jersey: Lawrence Erlbaum.

Psathas, G. (1995) *Conversation Analysis: The Study of Talk in Interaction*. Thousand Oaks, CA: Sage.

Rampton, B. (1987) Stylistic variability and not speaking 'normal' English. In R. Ellis (ed.) *Second Language Acquisition in Context* (pp. 47–58). Oxford: Pergamon.

Rampton, B. (1995) *Crossings*. London: Longman.

Riggins, S. (1997) The rhetoric of othering. In S. Riggins (ed.) *The Language and Politics of Exclusion: Others in Discourse* (pp. 1–30). Thousand Oaks, CA: Sage.

Ryan, J. (1997) Student communities in a culturally diverse school setting: Identity, representation and association. *Discourse: Studies in the Cultural Politics of Education* 18, 37–53.

Savignon, S. (1991) Communicative language teaching: State of the art. *TESOL Quarterly* 25, 261–277.

Schiffrin, D. (1996) Narrative as self-portrait: Sociolinguistic constructions of identity. *Language in Society* 25, 167–203.

Schumann, J. (1986) Research on the acculturation model for second language acquisition. *Journal of Multilingual and Multicultural Development* 7, 379–92.

Seidman, I. (1991) *Interviewing as Qualitative Research: A Guide for Researchers in Education and the Social Sciences.* New York: Teachers College Press.

Sharkey, J. and Layzer, C. (2000) Whose definition of success? Identifying factors that affect English language learners' access to academic success and resources. *TESOL Quarterly* 34, 352–368.

Shaw Findlay, M. (1995) Who has the right answer? Differential cultural emphasis in question/answer structures and the case of Hmong students at a Northern Californian high school. *Issues in Applied Linguistics* 6, 23–38.

Silverman, D. (1997) Introducing qualitative research. In D. Silverman (ed.) *Qualitative Method and Research: Theory, Method and Practice* (pp. 1–7). London: Sage.

Spolsky, B. (1989) *Conditions for Second Language Learning.* Oxford: Oxford University Press.

Spolsky, B. (1998) *Sociolinguistics.* Oxford: Oxford University Press.

Tabouret-Keller, A. (1997) Language and identity. In F. Coulmas (ed.) *The Handbook of Sociolinguistics* (pp. 315–326) Oxford: Blackwell.

Tajfel, H. (1981) *Human Groups and Social Categories.* Cambridge: Cambridge University Press

Theoroux, P. (1996) *The Pillars of Hercules.* London: Penguin.

Thesen, L. (1997) Voices, discourse, and transition: In search of new categories in EAP. *TESOL Quarterly* 31, 487–512.

Thompson, J. (ed.) (1991) Introduction to *Pierre Bourdieu, Language and Symbolic Power* (pp. 1–31). Oxford: Polity Press.

Ting-Toomey, S. (1999) *Communicating across Cultures.* New York: Guilford Press.

Toohey, K. (2000) *Learning English at School: Identity, Social Relations and Classroom Practice.* Clevedon: Multilingual Matters.

Trueba, H. (1989) *Raising Silent Voices: Educating the Linguistic Minorities for the 21st Century.* New York: Newbury House Publishers.

Tsui. A. (1996) Reticence and anxiety in second language learning. In K. Bailey and D. Nunan (eds) *Voices From the Language Classroom* (pp. 145–167). Cambridge: Cambridge University Press.

Tyagi, S. (1996) Writing in search of a home: Geography, culture and language in the creation of racial identity. In B. Thompson and S. Tyagi (eds) *Names We Call Home: Autobiography on Racial Identity* (pp. 53–61). New York: Routledge.

van Dijk, T. (1996) Discourse, access and power. In C. Caldas-Coulthard and M. Coulthard (eds) *Texts and Practices: Readings in Critical Discourse Analysis* (pp. 84–106). London: Routledge.

van Dijk, T. (ed.) (1997a) *Discourse as Social Interaction.* London: Sage.

van Dijk, T. (1997b) Political discourse and racism: Describing others in western parliaments. In S. Riggins (ed.) *The Language and Politics of Exclusion: Others in Discourse* (pp. 31–64). Thousand Oaks, CA: Sage.

van Dijk, T., Ting-Toomey, S., Smitherman, G. and Troutman, D. (1997) Discourse, ethnicity, culture and racism. In T. van Dijk (ed.) *Discourse as Social Interaction.* London: Sage.

van Lier, L. (1988) *The Classroom and the Language Learner.* London: Longman.

Van Maanen, J. (1998) *Tales of the Field: On Writing Ethnography.* Chicago: University of Chicago Press.

Weedon, C. (1987) *Feminist Practice and Postructuralist Theory*. Oxford: Basil Blackwell.

Welch, A. (1996) *Australian Education: Reform or Crisis?* Sydney: Allen and Unwin.

Wexler, P. (1992) *Becoming Somebody: Toward a Social Psychology of School*. London: Falmer Press.

Williams, G. (1992) *Sociolinguistics: A Sociological Critique*. London: Routledge.

Wong Fillmore, L. (1998, January) At the crossroads: Can bilingual education survive California politics? Paper presented at OISE Seminar, Toronto.

Wyn, J. and White, R. (1997) *Rethinking Youth*. London: Sage.

Index

Authors

Subjects